THE NEW CANON

The New Canon

AN ANTHOLOGY OF CANADIAN POETRY

EDITED BY

Carmine Starnino

SIGNAL EDITIONS IS AN IMPRINT OF VÉHICULE PRESS

Published with the generous assistance of The Canada Council for the Arts, the
Book Publishing Industry Development Program of the Department of Canadian
Heritage. and the Société de développement des entreprises culturelles du Québec
(SODEC).

Signal Editions editor: Carmine Starnino
Cover design: David Drummond
Special assistance: Vicki Marcok and Stephanie MacLean
Typeset in Minion by Simon Garamond
Printed by Marquis Book Printing Inc.

LIBRARY AND ARCHIVES CANADA CATALOGUING IN PUBLICATION DATA

The new canon : an anthology of canadian poetry
/ edited by Carmine Starnino

Includes index.
ISBN 1-55065-208-7

1. Canadian poetry (English)–20th century.
2. Canadian poetry (English)–21st century.
I. Starnino, Carmine
PS8293.1.N49 2005   C811'.5408   C2005-904604-X

Published by Véhicule Press, Montréal, Québec, Canada
www.vehiculepress.com

Distribution in Canada by LitDistCo Distribution
Distributed in the U.S. by Independent Publishers Group

Printed and bound in Canada.

Contents

Introduction

I.

ANTHOLOGIES HAVE IT HARD. Exclusive and entombing, they trap forever what is perishable. Today we don't so much read A.J.M. Smith's monumental 1960 *Oxford Book of Canadian Poetry* as indulge in a kind of Ozymandian browse, appreciating Smith's confirmed intuitions (Leonard Cohen!) and whetting our morbid thrill for all those vanishings (Myra von Riedemann?). Anthologies like *The New Canon*—anthologies that try to be what art critic Jed Pearl calls "oxygenators of the new"—have it hardest. Consensus or definitiveness isn't their goal. They are, instead, exercises in tastemaking, one editor's impatient stab at anticipating and shaping tomorrow's sorting-out. No class of anthology is more pathologically optimistic. And none, for that matter, has proven more slapdash, exclusive, narrow-minded, and divisive. As it happens, we have a vigorous tradition of such books in this country. The gatecrashing can be traced back to 1936 with *New Provinces* and F.R. Scott's preface that pushed the anthology's "new techniques" and "new direction." *New Provinces'* impact was profound, both for the window it threw open on certain careers (it introduced Pratt, Scott, Klein, and Smith) and for the way its success created the trend of relentless novelty-mongering. From *New Provinces'* earliest replicas—*Unit of Five* (1943), *New Wave Canada* (1966), *Soundings* (1970), and *Storm Warning* (1971)—to its most recent kin—*The New Canadian Poets* (1985), and *Poets 88* (1988), *Breathing Fire* (1996), and *The Last Word* (1999)—nearly all reiterate, in their introductions or publicity material, a version of Scott's sales pitch. If this brand of anthologizing remains seductive it's because it talks big and takes a bold lease on posterity. It forecasts "major" names and defers its conjectures to a future of its own contriving. In a sense, it works to conjure the very weather it endeavors to predict. After all, which editor doesn't dream of his choices assuming, by dint of time, a kind of common-sense? Which editor doesn't envisage his enthusiasms, one day, becoming the taken-for-granted? But, as with any sort of soothsaying, the rate of error is very high; making this genre, in its continued appearance, more dogged than distinguished.

The New Canon is a bit different. More summation than augury, the anthology publishes the work of fifty Canadian poets born between 1955 and 1975. While it's not unreasonable to think the next significant careers may emerge from this group, my real goal at bringing these poets together—be they thunder-stealing new arrivals, the recently risen through the ranks, or long-time mainstays of the scene—is to endorse an alternative present. In short, it is to take the last two decades of poetic activity and recast them into a radically different picture of ourselves. A 1975 cut-off year was imposed to strengthen the perception of *The New Canon* as a kind of premeditated census-taking; an attempt, using a very selective focus, to improve the visibility of a rarely perceived creative force. My crusading title, with its somewhat imperialistic definitive article, is therefore intended to be understood in three ways. First, it conveys the generational un-precedentedness of what my survey seems to have revealed. A sense of drastic distance, of getting away from the known, was one of the pleasures of editing this anthology; I hope some of that surprise has been preserved for the reader. Next, the adjective is meant to activate the meaning of canon as "tenet" or "rule". That is, I regard this book as the most concrete evidence yet of a new principle at work in our poetry—or better yet, an old principle now resurfacing. More on that shortly, but for now let's just say *The New Canon* gathers together, within its limits of inclusion, the most aurally ambitious, lexically alert, and formally intelligent poems I could find. I have no intention, however, of making watershed a body of work whose value is very much still up for dispute. Therefore, and thirdly, this book is a bid for a new kind of canon, one which the Irish critic Edna Longley has called "a properly opinionated canon." That is, a canon not handed down from above, but offered up from within the fray. Canon-making, in other words, as part of a living debate—an activity of responses and reactions. So be warned: this is not a pluralistic, broadly-based, non-partisan anthology. *The New Canon* is a justification of prejudice, an attempt to isolate a tendency in Canadian poetry and make a boast for it.

Anthologies essentially argue with each other, and mine is no different. Synchronizing itself with the birth year of the youngest poet (Erin Mouré) in *New Canadian Poets*, *The New Canon* picks up where Dennis Lee's 1985 anthology leaves off and carries the stocktaking into the early years of the twenty-first century. Resemblances pretty much stop there. To compare my book to its predecessor would expose a fundamental shift, not just in the nature of the selection-making but in the very function of the endeavor itself. By the mid-80s Canadian poetry seemed to have passed completely beyond the era of lively debate initiated during the fractious 1940s and 1950s (best characterized by John Sutherland's powerfully revisionist anthology *Other Canadians*). Indeed, one of the most remarkable facts about the poetry of the eighties is how little dispute it engendered, how sweeping and consensus-driven its assessments were, and how rarely anyone stepped forward with a genuine eccentricity of outlook. "Eclectic" was, assuredly, a popular word at the time. It provided *The New Canadian Poets* with its central plot, its ensemble cast of colourful character actors (like Dale Zieroth, Tom Wayman and Susan Musgrave) as well as its script. "Eclecticism," Lee wrote, "calls for an editorial policy as well; mine has been to follow the grain of the period and be equally eclectic." But eclecticism, for Lee, was nothing more than a term of anxious piety. It was an idea that disabled judgment and discrimination. Eclecticism simply meant that he was careful about what other poets might think. It meant he was concerned about doing the right thing, that he respected the "grain of the period" at the expense of the *poetry* of the period. And indeed the longwinded categorizing that takes up so much of Lee's introduction—during which he marks off every "school of content" he can find (Prairie documentary, feminist, immigrant, daily work, etc)—tells us much about the anthology's too-accommodating spirit. Lee's failure to connect those recitatives to a larger and more serrated argument, his unwillingness to test his readers with a more thoroughgoing divergence of taste, gives *The New Canadian Poets* its air of comfort, complacency and soft-mindedness.

Putting the best possible face on it, one can say that it was a *decent* book, a book held together by the courtesy of its diversity. And some of Lee's choices (Peter Van Toorn, Robyn Sarah, David Solway, A.F. Moritz) still wear very well. But if *The New Canadian Poets* was seen as definitive and defining, it's because it drew itself firmly into the emerging mainstream. Lee's loyalty to a perceived "scene," and his need to advocate it as a place held together by professional unanimity, conditioned the anthology into self-censorship; and it's this very sense of contented deference that has passed, uncorrected, into our present circumstances. I'm aware, therefore, that while I conceive *The New Canon* as a correction, it is directed at an audience unaware of any error. Yet I've always believed that the power of an effective anthology—Al Alvarez's *New Poetry* is an example—depends on the extent to which it depicts truths we did not necessarily anticipate. We need not agree with them, or be pleased about them, but we cannot ignore them. This anthology, then, isn't about test-driving the reputations of fifty Canadian poets. It's about what happens the next time we, as poets, sit down to write a poem. What conventions will we agree to respect and what will we allow ourselves to wincingly push past? Verse that looks experimental has assumed a competitive edge in recent years, but we are still uninspired by any vision of the good poem, are still indifferent about the particular qualities that give poems their special authority. Sound poetic practice is seen as too fussbudget to take seriously, reviews are little more than blurb-writing exercises, and almost no one can explain any principle behind why we do what we do. Maybe it's no longer possible to limn such a vision. It's certainly easier to sing the old refrains, to commend our poetry's "extraordinary variegation" or approvingly point out how it has "grown in variety." *The New Canon* suggests otherwise. It suggests that we need new ideas, yes, but we also need sane ideas, *durable* ideas—ideas that will challenge Canadian poets to remember that there is more to poetry than being a poet, that the most vital and unpredictable part of our business is actually the creation of art.

This anthology is a running start upon such a vision. It proposes that we are at the opening stages of particularly interesting historical moment: the construction, live and in real time, of a distinct generation of Canadian poets. Many names in this selection may no doubt be unfamiliar. Earlier anthologies—*Poets 88, Breathing Fire, New Canadian Poetry* and *Open Field*—have already sifted out several of them; critical acclaim and prizes have brought visibility to others. Only four have not, as yet, published any books. Their appearance in *The New Canon* is meant to provide the opportunity to rethink these figures as part of a representative group, one with its own methods, textures, and signature accomplishments. This is not to suggest the collection is definitive. There are poets of excellence— poets in intuitive accord with this shift in the wind—who should have found themselves in this snapshot. Two in particular, Zachariah Wells and Mark Callanan, fell outside the frame (born, respectively, in 1976 and 1979). And if one moved the viewfinder five years to the left, we would find, among others, Robert Moore, Brian Bartlett, Ross Leckie, Lynn Davies, and Mary Dalton. Notable poets who did meet the criteria for inclusion and are not represented are many. It's all too easy to quibble about who's in and who's out—and I expect reviewers will find it difficult to resist. But I'd like to say, for the record, that this anthology marks a lost opportunity to widen the awareness of a number of talents: Adam Levin, Lyle Neff, and Matt Rader came to my attention too late to be considered when the selection absolutely needed to be locked down. Among the excluded are Chris Jennings, Shane Rhodes, Diana Fitzgerald Bryden, Adam Getty, Tammy Armstrong, Paul Vermeersch, Mike Barnes, Russell Thornton, Ken Howe, Christine Weisenthal, Adam Dickinson, Lisa Robertson. There's no question this *salon des refusés* would itself comprise a fine and valuable anthology. In the end, even fifty poets drawn from twenty presses barely addresses the dilemma of how to properly attend to the astonishing volume of first-rate work available. One would be wise to be humble, like the Irish fisherman observing quietly that the sea was so wide and his boat so small.

But while I admit to the presence of arbitrariness, I won't apologize for it. Anthologies are no less catch-as-catch-can as any act of criticism—they are, to quote the editors of *The Morrow Anthology of Younger American Poets*, "one moment's judgment and an arranged opinion." Readers who have kept up with

George Elliott Clarke and Stephanie Bolster obviously don't need my book to be introduced to their writings. But I hope this selection will parade any such long-standing loves in a changed setting—the same changed setting that might also give short shrift to other long-standing loves. Puzzlement, for instance, might greet my decision to lead with Mark Abley rather than, say, Jan Zwicky or Ann Michaels. I don't intend to suggest that Abley stands at the threshold of this period or that he steers its practice and taste. I simply want the unexpectedness of his name to brake sharply on our tendency to put money on the same sure bets. This period is richer and more substantial than has generally been accepted, and Abley is a deserving part of it. That's not to say I didn't have healthy doubts every step of the way. After reading nearly 400 books—I compiled a shortlist, re-cast it after revisiting the poems, reconsidered my reassessments, doubted once-firm choices, grew bored with early favourites, urged myself to love different things—I'm surprised by some of my decisions, and am reminded of Randall Jarrell who urged critics to "admire writers whom his readers will snicker at him for admiring, and dislike writers whom it will place him among barbarians to dislike." It would be daft to expect you to love all these poems, or for me to endorse these poets as the only ones deserving your notice. Anthologists suffer lapses; there's no sense denying it. That said, the strengths on display—clear individuality, authority and linguistic initiative—survive any sin of omission. Whatever hairs you may want to split over this book's general policy, its introduction, or its editor, nothing will excuse your failure to give these 330 pages of poetry their full due. Anthologies cannot be all things to all people, but they can never give up on the first principle of their existence: to find good poems. And these poems are *very* good.

Which, for me, is where things get interesting. Because while the excellence of these poets deserves to be noted, the particularities of that excellence raise exciting questions about where the Canadian poem is headed. And in classifying what our poetry is fast becoming, the surest guide is what it has *been*—or what it has largely failed to be. If marriage with the tradition is the basis of every poet's creative equilibrium, then Canadian poetry follows a very unmistakable arc: courtship, honeymoon, vigorous cohabitation, then growing disaffection and estrangement, separate beds, and then separate rooms. The specifics are obviously far more vexing and complicated than a metaphor like that can admit—it didn't help to have Canadian poets and critics cite the "colonial oppression" of such nuptials—but suffice it to say that after a long line of poets working arrestingly and brilliantly in poetic form (E.J. Pratt, A.G. Bailey, Charles Bruce, John Glassco, Margaret Avison, P.K. Page, A.M. Klein, George Johnston), the sixties and seventies witnessed the rise of poets who at no time in their careers laboured with prosody. Full rhyme, half rhyme, internal rhyme, metre, syntax, as well as the sonnet, the villanelle, syllabics, alliteration—all these devices and forms went underground. This was not entirely true, of course, as the English tradition continued to provide an alternative, and in some cases an adversarial recourse, for poets like David Solway and Peter Van Toorn. But the day (a day now many decades old) belonged to the plain-style, to near-epistolary emotional forthrightness breathing in excited sync with the line-break (though with no real grasp of why the line-break needed to exist in the first place). Hair-raising examples can still be found in *The New Canadian Poets*, with poets like Monty Reid writing in what sounds like Basic English, without texture or verbal relish, as if they were channeling Berlitz. One can hardly overstate how aesthetically destitute this writing was—this loosely organized, free-verse, DIY period poem. Or how it dominated practically unchallenged. Steven Heighton provides an excellent thumbnail sketch of our drift towards poetic slovenliness in his essay "The Electrocution of the World."

> During the six years I spent reading manuscripts for *Quarry* Magazine I saw several literary fashions rise and fall and various issues vise-grip the public imagination then slacken their hold, but underlying these theme-oriented trends was a general "evolution" towards sectional fragmentation, increasing brevity, increasing simplicity and sameness of vocabulary, punctuation, and syntax, and a growing absence of concrete sensuous detail—a drift into the dry and lifeless spheres of the abstract.

All impulses, Yeats argued, exhaust themselves and give way to counter-impulses. One doesn't want to be rash in reading the signs, but I think it's safe to say the vocal verve has begun to hurry back, that freshets of extravagance are reviving much of what had been torpid. History, in fact, has never traveled in Canadian poetry as fast as it has during the last decade. In a country where time seemed to have stopped with TISH, we have, effectively, restarted the clock. When I began writing poetry in the early 1990s, names like Ralph Gustafson and George Johnston were hardly more than rumours, times-of-yore examples of something called "formal poetry." Richard Outram, Christopher Wiseman, and Eric Ormsby were treated as establishment off-cuts, poets who had lost their way. A young poet writing today, however, inhabits a very different context, one that includes David Manicom's *A Sense of Season*, Steven Heighton's *Stalin's Carnival*, Bruce Taylor's *Cold Rubber Feet*, Diana Brebner's *Radiant Life Forms*, Richard Sanger's *The Shadow Cabinet*, Jeffery Donaldson's *Once Out of Nature*, David O'Meara's *Storm Still*, Eric Miller's *Song of a Vulgar Starling*, Barbara Nickel's, *The Gladys Elegies*, Ken Babstock's *Mean*, Karen Solie's *Short Haul Engine*, Elise Partridge's *Fielder's Choice*, Joe Denham's *Flux*, and Geoffrey Cook's *Postscript*. With these debuts churning up contemporary circumstances, a freer formal energy is entering our poetry. Lines are again heating up with verbs and adjectives, phrase-making has rediscovered its poise, syntax its fluidity and flow. "Man is only half himself," wrote Emerson, "the other half is his expression." Likewise, these poets seem to insist that *what* they say be judged by *how* they say it—that devices like tone, vocabulary, and metaphorical aptitude are essential in establishing a poem's theme and subject. In brief, poets who write word-clusters like "Absolute sun / condescends to wear fog's qualification" or "the cardinals' big whistle out of old realms of cedar" or "trawlers chugged in, holds flipping with silver" are asking that their work be admired not only for the seriousness of its content, but for the flair and precision of its structure and diction.

In other words, the very music of those lines—how "condescend" creates the perfect consonantal enclosure to hear the echo of "sun" in "qualification"; or how the kinetic vividness of "flipping" wins the image its brevity—becomes an expression of resistance and retrenchment. They are big whistles out of old realms. Most unfashionably, the poets in this anthology treat poetry in the highest terms. Whether philosophical, speculative or allusive, they clearly regard it as a major form for the examination of ideas, but consider it first and foremost a *form*. And because they are always prepared to grant form its own free pleasures, their studied husbanding of poetic effect often disappears into the truth-seeking exertions of fresh thought. More than thinking enacted, these poems are about thinking *in action*. Insights are tested by the technical difficulty of their expression. Cadences bloom with intellectual scruple. Wit lives in the tiny shifts in tone, the simultaneous and careful meshing of structures. This self-confidence also means many of these poets have become masters at the long shot. They like playing with worst-case prosodic scenarios and turning lyric liabilities into assets. If Canadian poetry has been largely a list of prohibitions, then these poets are fervent with proposals. They want their poems to do more, not less. Extremists of a kind, they indulge in all sorts of tricks of voice. It's precisely that stylistic greed on which this anthology is premised. Of course, not every poet in this anthology innovates using the same means, but every poet demonstrates the eagerness to bend and modify the existing means to his needs. These poets—these *neologists*, as I like to call them—are lovers of vernacular, diction-dowsers, with a feel for unusual words and intricate arrangements. In fact I'd go so far as to say that if Stephen Henighan is right to argue in his book *When Words Deny the World* that Canadian fiction during the 90s gave up the healthy eccentricities of its "marginality" for linguistically flattened-out global fame, then I suggest Canadian poetry took up the cause. This anthology assumes that some of the most uncompromising, jubilant, restless and maverick writing can be found in our poems.

To ask these poets to march under the same aesthetic banner would be to oversimplify their poetry and overstretch my case. After all, I chose only what I liked; a principle of selection that gauged a poem's pleasure-giving quotient, not its suitability for school or movement. But there *are* qualities they share. Their imaginations are, on the whole, less contemplative, less single-focus, less mawkish than the previous generation. I think of Tonja Gunvaldsen Klaassen's urgent-feeling coinages (the "birch bitings and burnt flutter" of an evening in the country, her view of scribbles as the "longhand drift / of morning's matter-of-fact kind of muddle") or the coltish quality of Anita Lahey's rhythms ("How ordinary, quick, this staining of the pail, / this weighing of bodies, scalping of scales."). You will find fewer moments of firm-jawed earnestness, or heavy-stepping whimsy. These poets like the kick of surprise, they like the pounced-on spontaneity of *le mot juste*. The vespers-hush of so much of our nature poetry is given a body blow by Babstock whose imagery runs from spirited to gale-force ("The small hinged cap atop a burping exhaust pipe / flapped in slow panic like the mother killdeer who'd taken a clip"). And instead of the usual submitting-to-cliché simplicity we have Adam Sol's narrators rapping out their lyrical, gleeful, peppery opinions ("It was a festival of denials: there was the No, / and the Nono, and the Please no.") These poets have created—according to my ear—a new topography of eloquence. They've not only trained their eye to accurately register the texture of things but have also kept an ear cocked to catch, in their stanzas, a more aggressive musicality, a more active cadence. A larger vocabulary distinguishes them as well. They are far more aware of the words they use: their historical associations, social habits, syntactic traditions. Moreover, the line—as a traditional tool, not a free-verse trend—is a far more adaptable thing for them. They can, like Mark Sinnett, stretch it out into something colloquially open, sprawled and pell-mell; or like Brebner tighten it to fit their scrupulous phrasing; or slow it down, as Donaldson does, to create a deep-timbred, sonorous descriptiveness.

Aside from offering readers new fields of competence, these poets talk about their work in very different ways. When asked to describe his style, Babstock answered, "I have a hard time allowing a line to drift towards prose. Or to speak in a toned down, conversational voice. I'm more drawn toward compression and the kind of clanging of consonants and vowels that I fell in love with from reading poets that I like." Cook has discussed the "dynamic relation" between metre and syntax, and how he likes poems that "exploit the drama of syntax, particularly as that energy is caught up in stanzaic and metrical structures." Compare this to Crozier's statement that "poetry is an intimacy that connects. It should move us to a heightened state of awareness and at the same time remind us of our shared humanity." Or Zwicky's definition of poetry as "the imprint of the unsayable on what is said—and there is an enormous range in the ways the unsayable manifests itself." There's no right or wrong here, except that phrases like "intimacy that connects" and "the unsayable" seem to indicate imaginations that feel deeply uncomfortable with poems as anything more than vehicles for themes. Anyone who reads poems for their "heightened state of awareness" or ghostly "imprints" risks betraying a blindness to what makes poems beautiful, or even in what makes them poems. It's astonishing, in fact, how little of the considerable technical creativity that goes into writing a good poem is perceived and appreciated in this country. Poets deserve a criticism—and a canon—that can recognize *why* their product is poetry. And what counts isn't the dramatization of some "shared humanity" but the creation of a voice so linguistically striking that whatever is made "sayable" takes on life—not merely from its inherent biographical or cultural interest, but from its being expressed in a wholly idiosyncratic form. So while standards are being pushed upwards and ambition is finding its head, *The New Canon* intends to follow through on what Canadian poetry anthologies often promise but fail to provide—it intends to honour the aesthetic success that poets prize more than anything: the living utterance, the perfected expression of a sensibility in language.

While these poets display a higher standard of craftsmanship than the general run of poems produced today in Canada, craft was not the chief criterion for entry into this book. Style was. More specifically, a coherent, plausible, one-of-a-kind voiceprint. I was attracted to poetry where everyday language had been retrieved and rigourously patterned; an eccentricity rooted in the enthusiastic acknowledgment of its own word-bound life. No two of these poets sound alike because no two use the panoply of syntax, rhetoric, and cadence in quite the same manner. But if the prosodic methods in *The New Canon* are diverse, they are united in vision. Despite the different directions they face, these fifty poets serve to illustrate an alternate *modus vivendi*, a different way of going forward in language. This is not simply an accident of my arrangement. These poets are contributing to something bigger than themselves, an event that transcends the limits and operational bias of this anthology to represent a larger creative blossoming. John MacKenzie's "Thor, Shanghaied by Yahweh to Tend the World..." could even be said to provide a kind of credo for this climate. As an expression of a ludic, shape-shifting imagination, the poem represents the *The New Canon* ambition, one devoted to putting a redefining spin on every word and image. Eric Miller's "Song of the Vulgar Starling" is a similar manifesto, as is Taylor's "Social Studies." What we are seeing is a new Canadianism, one that, as Moritz writes in his introduction to *New Canadian Poetry*, "is not only a building up of the nation's voice but a breaking down of that voice, a needed destruction of whatever has been merely nostalgic or ideological." I looked for this "destruction" in the poems I choose, poems which drew on devices often recognized as traditional, but by improvisingly sidestepping convention were able to unearth an apt, unforeseen language. I wanted to avoid poems where the thinking progressed predictably in any one direction. Instead I was after big rhetoric, eccentric detail, arresting phrases. I wanted actively jarring, mood-puncturing poems, poems as aesthetic betrayal. Indeed, more than minting every phrase afresh, I wanted poems that egged themselves on, saying "If it ain't broke, break it."

Needless to say, I didn't always find *exactly* these poems. In preparing *The New Canon* I was often reminded of mediaeval alchemy's hunt for a substance that could turn base metal into gold. They provisionally called it "the philosopher's stone," and while they stumbled across all sorts of useful discoveries in their pursuit—such as Dresden porcelain and gunpowder—they never found it. Anthologizing involves the very same mix of disappointment and triumph. Notwithstanding all vows to uncompromising clear-sightedness and cold scrutiny, the process produces an approximation: a book that bears witness to the unwritten, undiscovered, but endlessly hoped-for poem. In other words, anthologies are nods toward a prosodic "philosopher's stone." The best you can hope for is bold, surprising, and practical equivalents; superior stunt-doubles, if you will. And the vigour of what I've assembled—which makes the place-oriented, image-based descriptiveness of our staid, middle-aged poetry look very tired—tells me my hope was not misplaced. Maybe it's too naive to believe this anthology can become the agent for some great transformation of sensibility, but I'd like to think that poems like Taylor's "The Slough" or Babstock's "Tractor" or Brebner's "Eleven Paintings by Mary Pratt" or Warner's "Gumshoe" or Donaldson's "Above the River" can quicken an artisanal pride still latent in our poetry. Over the last five years we have turned more than a calendrical corner, we have turned an aesthetic one as well. The perspective that comes with this change threatens to knock the popular image of 20th century Canadian poetry off its perch. *The New Canon* is a sign of this youthquake, of young poets on the move and in the mood for new poems. In many cases they are writing these poems for the same reason Bob Dylan, in the 1960s, took up songwriting: because no one else was creating the kind of songs they wanted to sing. But just as their poems make the inhibited newly visible and viable, they've also created a chance to single-handedly reclaim an entire strain of formally intelligent, sonorous poetry—reclaim it, steady it, and forward it on to the future.

Good anthologies are reckoners. They remind you that nothing is certain, that all canons are conditional, the dust of their last reconstruction still floating in the air. Anthologies do this not only by breaking new ground, but by clearing a trail backwards. Selections that dramatize an aesthetic—especially those that do so to discredit specific received assumptions—can allow overlooked achievements to shine forth more frankly and unmistakably. And in our case, it's no surprise that young poets who find refreshment in neglected, previously-shameful resources invite curiosity about the careers that once drew on those resources. "The need for a new kind of poetry in the present," to quote Seamus Heaney, "has called into being precursors out of the past." Anthologies like *The New Canon*, in other words, are valuable for the reputations they retroactively bring into focus. It should be said, of course, that precursor doesn't necessarily mean progenitor. If Richard Sanger brings to mind John Glassco, it isn't as an acolyte. One simply spots evidence of a shared sensibility. Both use fluent line-making, sparkling rhythms and well-balanced arguments as devices for getting meaning into a reader's mind and making it stick. Such hitherto-unsuspected synchronicities can help clarify taste, sharpen judgment, and guide creative activity. Indeed if I'm right in suggesting that *The New Canon* represents a poetry that Canadian readers need to take seriously—and not in coming decades, but right now— then I can't insist on a course of action more likely to clarify the virtues of this work than a thoroughgoing immersion in what preceded it. We've grown accustomed to evaluating poets in conjunction with their contemporaries, but the originality of the *The New Canon* poets emerge all the more vividly when they are placed beside the likes of Charles Bruce, George Johnston, Ralph Gustafson, John Thompson, Margaret Avison and Peter Van Toorn. By reading these pre-decessors in light of what has been assembled in *The New Canon*, hindsight forces us to retrieve a new national line. These realignments of influence make the potential for change extraordinary. And I believe that *The New Canon* can provide the present, calm-surfaced circumstances with exactly this depth-charge.

Many commentators will insist that my reading is overzealous, that it singles out, for attention, too small an aesthetic. Yet the notion of Canadian poets as what Charles Simic has called "voluptuaries of words" should not be dismissed, because the element *is* present in the poetry. We tend to ignore it, but we are wrong to ignore it. We have become set in our ways, and our expectations have thus made us deaf to competing noises. We expect a certain method, a certain effect, something to do with "simplicity" or "sincerity", and when we see it, the poem lights up. When we see its opposite, however, the words go dark and we silently exclude it. Free verse has been an essential Canadian mode, and while there's no need to deny its value it is very far from the *only* Canadian mode. W.J. Keith has argued that "the predominance of 'free verse' in twentieth-century poetry in English—both in Canada and elsewhere—has been much exaggerated." And indeed the story we tell ourselves about Canadian poetry—as the triumphal breaking loose from form into free verse—is much too simplistic. When we examine the different types of poetry that our best poets have written, we discover that it often ties us to the oldest traditions in poetry much more than one might have supposed. We believe ourselves to be a verse-culture of taciturnity, of getting-the-job-done unfussiness. But this doesn't fit the facts. It doesn't fit the facts of the poetry that runs from Pratt to Acorn, and it doesn't fit the facts of *The New Canon* poems with their textures and palpabilities, sensuousness and acoustic verve. Yet we go on repeating the same tired narrative. Confounded by the protean reach and presence of this work, critics have simply closed off those rooms to make their job less curatorially taxing. It seems apparent, however, that students and readers of Canadian poetry—here and abroad—have been left at a considerable disadvantage. Just as the best poetry can only be written when all options, free and formal, are open to the poet, an accurate account of twentieth-century Canadian poetry will be impossible without proper recognition of those, who, in Eliot's words, are interested in "making new experiments with traditional forms."

If the free-verse account of Canadian poetry feels doctrinal, it's because such lyrics were once seen as breaking free from "foreign" forms, thus permitting free-verse to be neatly folded into our catechism on nationalism. This is no longer the case. In fact what finally defines these eager experimenters—the last feature that helps complete the distance traveled from Lee's *The New Canadian Poets*—is their indifference to native chauvinism. They see themselves less as "Canadian" than as part of a total English-language culture. As such, they have no interest in revealing themselves through easy emoting, but instead put their personalities, if not their citizenship, into the sounds and verbal textures of their poetry. This means two things. It means that a line like "A brick wall is stoic toil," with its head-on briskness and the acute wit of its half-rhyme, can only have been written by David O'Meara. Next, it means that while the phrase-pitch of that line is distinctively Canadian (no reader will ever mistake O'Meara for a Scot) it also owes a powerful debt to Edward Thomas, one of the first proto-modernists to wed a subtle pensiveness to a crisp colloquiality of language. Similar inter-nationalist pedigrees can be traced for any voice in this anthology. It would, in fact, be willful to overlook the degree to which the dominant influences over these poets have come from elsewhere. These imported-from-abroad adaptations have led to departures so prodigious that reading a poem by David Manicom, for example, feels like an activity of a different kind from reading a poem by Dale Zieroth. Not just the challenges posed, but the abilities required and the rewards offered are intrinsically different too. To cherish these poems you must love qualities not often cherished in the last thirty years. *The New Canon* therefore does more than confirm the ascendancy of a gifted group of poets; it confirms what was, until recently, unthinkable: formal poetry has returned to the fore. With stanza, metre, and rhyme suddenly in saddle and war-whooping down on the empire, it may be time to declare the ruling aesthetic since the 1970s—the plain, the soft-spoken, the flatly prosy, the paraphrasingly simple, the accessibly Canadian—in its last throes.

BUT HERE's the thing. There exists a group who *already* oppose this one-party poetic—or "official verse culture" as they sometimes call it—and who voiced their dissent long before anyone else did. Charter clan members include Daphne Marlatt, Steve McCaffery, Erin Mouré, Christopher Dewdney, Fred Wah, and Roy Miki. They, and younger firebrands like Derek Beaulieu and Jay Millar, publish in magazines like *dANDelion, filling Station* and *Capilano Review*; they publish with presses like Coach House, Talonbooks, ECW and Anansi; they teach at the new flagship creative writing department set up at the University of Calgary, or at the original insurgent "hot spot" of Vancouver's Kootenay School of Writing. These poets make common cause with American avant-gardists like Charles Bernstein, Lyn Hejinian and Susan Howe, who, in turn, round out a group portrait alongside pivotal experimenters like Gertrude Stein and Ezra Pound as well as various French theorists and the L=A=N=G=U=A=G=E poetry movement of the 1970s and 80s. Affiliation is certified by use of fragmentation, layered texts, collage and the embrace of—why not say it?—nonsense. One of their more unusual enthusiasms, at least in this country, is a concrete poetry that draws on letters of the alphabet; add-ons include visuals, photographs, paint, ink, pencils, and cartoons. Unsurprisingly, they resist "traditional forms of meaning," and seek to disrupt any "ideological-aesthetic hegemonies" that bolster malignant "social encodings." They have, by now, developed a number of complex methods by which to explain what they do, making their self-created image as outsiders seem at variance with the sometimes near-fanatical academic bent of their product. But never mind. Crusaders against gendered reading and writing practices, their graduate writing programmes and workshops are often organized around issues of cultural appropriation and forms of oppression based on race, class, and sexuality. They are very organized, ecstatically like-minded, theoretically self-pleasuring, and impossible to ignore. Postmodernist. Experimental. Avant-Garde. Call it what you will, our poetry is now a zoo of rampant esotericisms.

Ironic, then, that this accelerated growth in "radical poetries" has overlapped with the mounting interest in traditional form, and has led Canadian poetry into what can only be described as a schismatic phase, with polar-end options developing in almost simultaneous reaction to each other. Opposing the speaking-in-tongues avant-garde evangelists are, we are told, the capital-F formalists (often prefixed with "neo" to convey the drasticness of their suspected conservatism). As I'm determined to demonstrate with *The New Canon*, no such formalism exists—if it ever did. What we actually have is a very loosely confederated group of poets who, like their Language peers, seek to stand outside consensus, but who, unlike them, seed their iconoclasm inside recognizable poetic modes. The intended effect, as Derek Mahon described it in an interview, is of "hissing chemicals inside the well-wrought urn; an urnful of explosives." But what is interesting is how, in their mutual detestation of the prose-domesticated mainstream, the two camps have forged an improbable alliance. This coincidence of intentions shouldn't be too much of a surprise: both camps demonstrate a boredom with conventional forms, both have thought hard about why a tradition like (say) the sonnet should persist, and both display an equal striving to leave behind anything that looks like "poetry". They differ starkly in the vocabulary they use to describe their declared intolerances (not to mention the kind of poems those vocabularies coax into life), but the so-called traditionalists offer the same basic reply to the questions that have long held the attention of the experimentalists. Can poetry function as a department of disturbances, running athwart whatever linguistic, political, or cultural securities we might hold? (Yes.) Can poetry be an irritant and a discomforter, an unflinching, erratic, searing, and eccentric force? (Absolutely.) The two factions might seem, at first, to have nothing in common except the partisan reflections they provide for each other. And indeed the dispute they represent has become a powerful cliché of literary thought. But it's worth keeping in mind that as rival responses to the dominant discourse, they are siblings, essentially born of the same poetic crisis.

And why is it worth keeping in mind? Because while both camps have begun to complicate our sense of poetry's procedures, we have yet to credit the most enriching sense of complication to the *right* poets. This two-rubric vision of Canadian poetry—traditionalists as hidebound, postmodernists as farsighted—exists because of the avant-garde's success in peddling their antagonistic, unnuanced theory of innovation. Many of us believe, for no other reason than because the avant-garde has told us, that the traditional forms are dead and that their continued use is reactionary. Such forms are alleged to evince a "dangerous nostalgia" and set the stage for a possible "new conservatism in Canadian poetry," a return to "old values" and "retrograde poetics." We've all come across this tough talk; the blogs are especially awash with it. The notion of formal poetry as a historical U-turn, or a setback, is nothing new to Canadian poetry (Bob Hilderly and Ken Norris in *Poets 88*, noticed that some poets seemed interested in "a much more formal poetry," a development they described as "most curious" and which caused them to lament the "conservation that now appears to mark our poetry.") Thankfully a number of exceptional poets such as George Johnston, Richard Outram, Michael Harris, David Solway, Christopher Wiseman and Robyn Sarah have done much to stave off biases against form. But the avant-gardists have found lots of ways to keep this controversy alive, and like most controversies—like most clichés—it's modestly useful. After all, it's true that traditional form has often appeared a bit short on nerve. And yes, there are serious pitfalls to any staunchly formalist approach. But when the avant-garde deplore the constrictiveness of traditional form, they are—as they very well know—shouting at a straw man. The complaint only makes sense if we agree to view this sort of poetry as a fixed activity with fixed rules. But as the *New Canon* poets demonstrate, a great deal of the thrill comes from bending, if not breaking, those rules. What this anthology aims to suggest, in other words, is that the avant-garde's tactic of splitting the traditional from the experimental, while polemically convenient, is bogus.

Perhaps the most obvious objection to avant-garde's disdain for traditional form's "conventionality" is this: why should traditional form make innovation impossible? After all, experimental poetry is itself full of displaced or redirected formalism. Traditional form shapes the vision even of poets who claim to disown it. Christian Bök's remarkable "Geodes," with its dense word-grids of geological sense-data, is an excellent example of a poet taking just what he needs from long-established devices in order to make a fascinating postmodern argument about language. Or are avant-gardists so naïve as to not realize that any "anarchistic critique" draws its sting from the very structural principles of the tradition it is trying to kill? "Is there really any difference," the late Michael Donaghy once argued, "between Language-poet Ron Silliman's strict adherence to a mathematical sequence and Tom Disch's use of the alphabet as a formal device?" As a matter of fact there is, and we'll get to that difference shortly. Donaghy's point, though, is firm: no form, no poem. Poetry requires patterns capable of distinguishing it from prose, and these are patterns even the avant-garde is compelled to find. The avant-garde would no doubt argue their patterns are better: epistemologically grittier, politically braver. Yet the important and overlooked truth here—one that tests the avant-garde's vaunted exceptionalism—is that the conformist aesthetic under attack is the same aesthetic *New Canon* poets endlessly tease, sidestep, and refute. Unlike the avant-garde, however, these poets don't call the results "experimental"; they call it poetry. No special activism is being publicized when Gil Adamson introduces a provocative mingle of registers into her strange parables or when Iain Higgins runs his words together to capture a speedy accent. Both write in eager avoidance of the ordinary sentence, both go to emphatic lengths to disrupt the standard literary vernacular. Yet the revisionist energy flowing through their lines refuses division into "traditional" or "experimental." To be innovative, poems need only to be accident-prone, not avant-garde. Start arranging words and strange things will happen; if you're lucky those surprises will rip into the pondered calm of tradition itself.

To argue, as I am now doing, that innovation is a fundamental principle of creativity rather than an act of theoretical intrepidness is not to deny the avant-garde its radical character, but to deny it any special role in conversations about risk-taking. "Risk" is, by now, a widespread term in contemporary poetry. No poet or critic hesitates to use it; and rightly so, because to consider poetry without taking into account the gambles it takes—with language, with ideas—is a mistake. Yet subversion is not a signature of postmodern sophistication; it is an irreducibly primary aspect of poetry. No poem has ever come alive without first behaving experimentally. We can see this impatience with convention as far back as 2000 B.C. when—before any sort of literary legacy even existed—an obscure Egyptian scribe named Khakheperresenb lashed out at the already-said: "Would I had phrases that are not known, utterances that are strange, in a new language that has not been used, free from repetition, not an utterance that has grown stale, which men of old have spoken." That sentence could easily be the mantra for any of the *New Canon* poets. As independents who keep their own council, however, they might be shocked to be characterized as belonging to a group. But that's precisely my point. Their innovations are self-directed, freestanding, beyond the need for imprimatur. If I'm hostile to the belief that innovation requires a clinching minimum of ingredients (e.g. nonlinearity, randomness, disruption) it's because the inculcation of a program of demystification is no substitute for free play. And free play, like the poetic instinct itself, is an unteachable and unlearnable enthusiasm. What German poet Gottfried Benn called "a fascinating way with words" is innate. Either you own an imagination that can't help setting the reader's expectations at a tilt (shifting stanzaic forms within a single poem, using unusual rhymes to leak illogicality into a narrative, stretching syntax to carry a sentence's complex meander), or you don't; studying Derrida won't change that. And it's this free play that accounts for the experimental thrust of the technical ideas on display in *The New Canon*, many of which have, in their own way, nurtured considerable and original poems.

But the avant-garde claims to go further than free play: it sells itself as category of futurity. We forget that the term avant-garde began as a military metaphor: it referred to the forerunners in battle who paved the way for the rest of the army. The avant-garde is thus, by definition, ahead of its time, and its current claimants repeatedly burnish this premise to create the impression that they've arrived at an advanced stage of thinking about literature. This fetish for progress—in which new forms of writing relentlessly displace older ones—has no relationship to poetry. Poetry is an incremental art: skills are added to the repertory slowly, and if useful, stay. They don't hang around until supplanted by something "better." The poets in this anthology make up new ways to love a poem; but those new ways, when studied, look a lot like the old ways. "What made poetry 2000 years ago," wrote Thomas Hardy, "makes poetry now." An insight Frost reprised and improved when he said of E.A. Robinson that he "was content with the old-fashioned way to be new." Mary Kinzie tells us in her *A Poet's Guide to Poetry* that "poetry is the product of experiments on the past, acts of recombining already invented substances in such a way that they are transformed." It is striking to consider, moreover, that the 20th century avant-garde was the most radically conservative movement on record. Poems by grand old mavericks like Pound, Eliot, and Cummings were fiercely traditional in their formal pith and bite. Stein may be the mascot of all enterprises experimental—but this wasn't her term; her formula for what she was doing was "to make a whole present of something that it has taken a great deal of time to find out." John Peale Bishop maintained all poets were both conservative and radical. He argued that drastic changes, upon closer look, are actually current flowerings of older traditions. "Tradition," Paul Valéry said, "does not consist of doing again what others have done before, but in recapturing the spirit that went into what they did—and would have done differently in a different age." In other words, while poetry develops (breaks bonds, strives for the untested) it does not evolve (grow by mechanisms of mass extinction and replacement). Pound learned his modernity, after all, from Propertius, Li Po and Cavalcanti.

Unfortunately the notion of formalism as unadventurous has had some very long innings in Canada, allowing our avant-garde communities to aggressively set the terms for any debate on innovation. The consensus has fallen as follows: formal poetry is well-wrought and pleasing but thoroughly circumscribed by its historical moment, while experimental poetry supplies what Fred Wah calls "possibilities for shifts in consciousness." It sounds reasonable enough, and to young poets with no inherited sense of poetic tradition such simple, repeatable liturgies involving "shifts in consciousness" can have a powerful effect. This makes it even more crucial that there be those of us willing to answer back. The problem, however, is that the widespread belief that experimentalists "understand" innovation can only have been made possible by the unintentional assistance of the so-called mainstream. It is *our* acceptance of formalism as a stand-pat force—and our failed attempts to unseat, within our own communities, the bias behind such a perception—that remains one of the leading obstacles for anyone who hopes to successfully reframe the discussion. We're stuck playing defense because we've allowed experimentalists to take the lead in the larger hermeneutical war. They've captured its political language, you might say. And in some cases, literally so. The avant-garde has gotten awfully good at assailing traditional form as ideologically questionable, even dangerous. Such an analogy, created by using rhetoric more appropriate to the criticism of totalitarian governments, corrupts thought. Form—be it rhymed or free—carries no specific theme or attitude. Nor is form intrinsically hierarchical, elitist or repressive. This is because form is essentially vacant—an iamb, for instance, merely defines an abstract pattern. Form therefore stays forever open to multifold meanings, to new uses and unexpected inflections. A sonnet's insurrectionist credentials depend on that openness. But what eludes us—and prevents our criticism from catching up with the avant-garde's formidable idea machine—is how these unexpected inflections, and their revolutionary potential, might be found in "conventional" poets like Bruce Taylor:

> What's under the mud that schmecks our boots?
> A raft of bedsprings lashed with roots,
> spavined lumber, cans of glue,
> electrical cables, lampreys, newts,
> and, if what the neighbours say is true,
> the ribs of a horse that once fell through
> while pursuing a dog, who's in there too:
> so all poor beasts that flit or thud
> lie down with the frogs in the lathered mud,
> who mate in the ruts where the tractor treads,
> spin their milky gelatinous threads
> of spunk and spittle and clean, green eggs
> that hatch like bean-sprouts, sprout hind legs
> and rise, scientifically, out of the ooze
> to walk upright in soft-soled shoes
> and ponder the matter of what or who's
> in the slough.

These lines are taken from "The Slough," a poem that puts many of Taylor's experimental qualities on record. First thing to notice is the vivid diction: "schmecks," "spavined." Second is how those words are fitly spoken: "*schmecks our boots*", "*spavined* lumber." Right off the bat, you know that Taylor has a real ear, not simply a literary one. Thirdly, the simple rhymes (thud/mud) are energizing. By that I mean they help give the calmly surreal images ("so all poor beasts that flit or *thud* / lie down with the frogs in the lathered *mud*") a clear tonal and rhetorical distinction. What we see here is form grappling with an unusual mind and barely able to contain the old-shaped ideas it flings at it. The result, with its schoolboy air of naive declaration and nursery-rhyme jag, is a pungent, eccentric, unstable precision. Call it slough-speak: a primer-like voice that defies decoding but trains readers into original perception. How does one describe the prosodic indiscretions of an effort like this? They flaunt no politicized lyric matrix. They enact no tension between meaning and oppression. By these standards the below-surface detonations of Taylor's auditory pyrotechnics, brilliant as they are, risk going unnoticed. It's hard to appreciate a music of subtle modulation when you believe that, to be useful, violations must first be blatant. The sonically incisive language Taylor devised for his poem requires a broader theory of innovation, something consistent with the intuitions Primo Levi drew on when he argued that rhyme inspires, rather than hinders, formal experimentation. "The restriction of rhyme," Levi asserted, "obliges the poet to resort to the unpredictable: compels him to invent, to 'find'; and to enrich his lexicon with unusual terms; bend his syntax; in short, to innovate." We need critics who not only write with wooing detail of such minute structural irregularities, but recognize those irregularities as a platform for radical achievement. This is vital because what we have no words for, we're unlikely to notice. Form's route back to relevance therefore depends, in part, on a critical vocabulary able to transmit the strange flavour of discreet stylistic defiances; a vocabulary able to help readers feel the ferocity driving the most intricate recalibrations.

Radical gambles can prosper without freakish postmodern payoff, though it should be said that radicality, as a concept, is a red herring. Poems cannot be radical or conservative; they can only be faithful to the experience they stalk and the formal means they invent to catch it. Innovation therefore starts the exact moment no ready word exists, and picks up the scent of whatever rhythm, rhyme, and metaphor will describe what resists description. And defeating the inexpressible means, of course, resisting the formulaic. It's exactly the micro-level artifice of these resistances—the verbal carefulness and the balancing of sounds that nourishes every little oral riot of eloquence—that makes a successful poem so challenging. A greater challenge, surely, than the perfect self-reflexive doubt and ideological position-taking of young poets who attend creative writing programs to study how to be avant-garde. What I mean is that Taylor's refusal to tolerate the *idée recue*—and this point can just as easily be extended to any of the poets in this anthology—issues from a place deeper than the craving for merit badges. Innovation is now so overwhelmingly a matter of creating exceptional moments that its emotional components are lost altogether. Yet poems move us by their distinctively felt statements, not their avant-garde otherness. And it is curiosity about the strength of those emotional messages—their power to startle and unsettle—that then causes us to examine the coercing oddities of the prosody. In other words, linguistic and formal surprise goes hand in hand with feeling and conviction, which is why the claim that forms grow "old" is so false. It ignores that good poets don't replicate forms; they adapt them. Thus it makes no sense to call the forms in this book—forms that have been urgently broken and remade—"given" or "received" as if the poets passively accepted them. In short, these are poets with a taste for hybridity, for nonpareil concoctions. If, compared to the avant-garde's linguistic lab-work, their impatience with convention feels deeper and more sincere, the reason is simple: their poems are an eruption of necessary speech.

Innovation, for the *New Canon* poets, is a public act. The need to coin new terms is inextricably tied to the need to communicate. The oddity of their poems emanates from human oddity—desire, grief, exultation—and not from obstructionism. Troubled and troubling, many of these poems carry within themselves trace elements of their motivating anxiety, with each nonce shape perfectly devised, in O'Meara's phrase, "to burn off / some mean undirected compulsion." The avant-garde, too, is driven by concern. Yet whatever the merits of their antifoundational goad the results tend to add up to nothing because there is nothing to keep in your head. The avant-garde cheer every collision with sense but fail to see that without an emotional center of gravity any rule-flouting— no matter how bourgeois-baiting it strives to be—floats off into hyperactive whimsy. Experimentalism is thus practiced as an easy obligation. Fragmentation, dissociation and sense-erasure may be the ideal recipe for dissolving the authorial self, but that doesn't change the fact these devices are actually the poetic equivalent of a special handshake: that is to say, they are a duty of membership, a law of the coterie. One is impressed by the avant-garde's obsessive openness to the deviant, the ill-fitting, the anti-melodic, but like all obsessions there's little sense of quality control. Avant-garde poems have nothing coherent to "say" because *not* being mainstream is mutiny enough. As long as hindrance is promoted, a poem is doing good and proper "anticathartic" work. But the instant any reaching-out is sought, the poem is denounced as part of the "Euro-American colonial axis." It's no use, in other words, squaring the intentions of these poets with their innovations. This is because no such innovations exist. All you have is an iconoclastic attitude pinch-hitting for an activity that is emotionally and creatively beyond them. What defines these poets, therefore, is an overweening awareness of their market status as rebel firebrands and a correspondingly large blind spot: the interests of the reader. As hardline proposals that can only catch the attention of staunch party supporters, the avant-garde represents nothing more than dog-whistle poetics.

The avant-garde's election pledge has been to enrich the modus operandi of contemporary writing. And they've gone to incredible lengths to establish themselves as cutting-edge, the latest thing, thrillingly zeitgeist. Of course, anyone who cares about poetry will always be interested in any movement that extends the possibilities of expression. Surrealism and Imagism are but two examples of experiments that allowed poets to think and feel in idioms of considerable strangeness and sophistication. The styles have since declined into artificial gesture and cheap exoticism, but our tradition is richer for having absorbed those discoveries. The avant-garde, however, offers poets not breakthroughs but trick-truisms. It overpromises the way sham politicians do. It promotes itself as a transgressive force but its strategies actually harm poetry's ability to unsettle and unnerve because they restrict language to a relationship with "modes of cultural consumption" rather than readers. The poetry is completely unrelated to anything outside the structures of power and authority it pretends to be in deep dialogue with. The chief danger for this sort of writing, then, is that its words are prevented from being motive-bearing agents and begin to wither from an anorexia of sensibility: language is starved of its inner life. The avant-garde's reply might be that their poets see—and in seeing, try to expose—language as a system, not as an utterance. This, no doubt, would explain why the results always look like a random trawl through an information-processing textbook. The *New Canon* poets, however, push what can actually be *said* with language. They not only see afresh, but see a reader at the other end of their words. "The meaning of a word," W.S. Graham wrote, "is never more than its position. The meaning of a poem is itself, not less a comma. But then to each man it comes into new life. It is brought to life by the reader and takes part in the reader's change." An innovation doesn't fail because its politics fail. It fails because talent fails. And what is talent for— what are innovations for—except to find new ways to synchronize the reader's experience with the poem? "The poem," Frank O'Hara wrote, "is between two persons instead of two pages."

But great experiments in form and language are, alas, no longer expected to be accessible. And as the list of outrightly unreadable poetry continues to grow, the avant-garde has officially closed its borders to everyday language. The speaking voice, busy in its little hive of egotism and accessibility, is written off as one of the tyrannies of canonical literature. We see this in Robert Grenier's infamous *crie-de-coeur* that created Language poetry in 1971—"I hate speech"—and it emerges again in McCaffery's recent calls for the "demise of the phenomenological voice." If you find nothing much the matter with those last couple of sentences then that's yet a further example of how the School of Theory has stared down our doubts. We might shake our heads at the extremity of its findings, but we psychologically cede it the victory. The avant-garde have used this silent consent to sour terms like "experiment" to better cast their little sentiments of post-structural sanity against big bad traditionalism. This is not a new problem. Back in the 1930s Robert Frost began to worry about a situation where most critics began to equate what was "new" not with poets who had "their ear on the speaking voice" but with the sort of poet who wrote so as "to force, to dislocate, if necessary, language into his meaning." I believe we're at a similar impasse now. Unlike the Kootenay trendies with their cut-and-paste obliquities, the *New Canon* poets' first loyalty is to what Wordsworth called the "language really used by men." This anthology, in fact, is chock-full of spoken shorthands, of idiolects that blend the elision of poetry with the wit of colloquial English. What else, for instance, is the endlessly extended talkativeness of poems by McGimpsey and George Murray but an act of pleasurably lingering—and thus insisting—on the presence of the human voice? Those pleasures, however, have been traduced by bardic-academic cant. We need critics who can splash cold water on those theoretically overheated terms if we ever hope to wake to the poetry in this anthology: poetry at once linguistically speculative and emotionally moving, poetry that fashions its experiments from the rib of tradition and converts those experiments into the skiddings and veerings of conversational speech.

These, as I understand them, are the implications of *The New Canon* poets. In a country where it's not quite gentlemanly to make declarations for anything more than modest excellence, I feel perfectly at ease saying that *The New Canon* represents, to my mind, the most impressive and potentially transformative group of poets since the superleague of A.M. Klein, Irving Layton, Margaret Avison and P.K. Page. None of this makes a difference, of course, unless the poems themselves can stand as the most formidable manifesto. Too many anthologists persuade by appeals, but fail to convince forensically. Indeed, this was exactly the failing I saw in Dennis Lee's anthology. So I hope that this anthology will make its points without my having to score them, and I hope this in the simple belief that excellence is a sufficient sell (if not a sufficient calling). "No one ever writes good poems to convince anyone of anything," argued Charles Bruce, "we convince by other means. We write good poems to write good poems." All anthologies believe in the freshness of their forecasts, but never foresee their dotage on a bookshelf. The battle lines I've described in this introduction are the sort that currently accompany the too-small world of Canadian poetry, and I am not so proud to ignore that nothing gathers dust faster than a literary fight. Ordinary readers, indifferent (if not blessedly immune) to this sort of schism-mongering and sectarianism, will simply find themselves faced with first-rate writing. It is easy to forget that this is one of the major reasons we read poetry, as a joy that has nothing to do with debates about poetic taste. Included in this book are the central players of a generation whose poems have already begun to add to the stock of Canadian poetry's available reality. The extent to which this introduction can be deemed special pleading is in my belief that to civilly estrange oneself from the attritional tendencies of a literary scene is to encourage a certain intellectual softening. But these poems matter not because I believe them appropriate at the present moment. They matter because, each in their own way, they keep the English language alive. We read good poems to read good poems.

Montreal, 2005.

Mark Abley

[b. 1955]

Mark Abley grew up in Saskatchewan and Alberta. He has written or edited ten books, including the non-fiction work *Spoken Here: Travels Among Threatened Languages* (2003). His poetry books include *Glasburyon* (1994) and *The Silver Palace Restaurant* (2005). Abley has received both a Rhodes Scholarship and a Guggenheim Fellowship. He lives in Montreal.

A WOODEN ALPHABET

My summer project is to learn the script
these withered twigs spell out against the air—
the ones that look so still, against the frantic
    bobbing of ash leaves above and below,
and their downward-spiralling keys, and the clouds
cruising past the shoreline like a toy flotilla
framed by an alphabet of naked, spindly,
        rickety wood.

It's not a fruit tree, so I can't believe
a gardener's clumsy grafting has to bear
the blame for this gnarled calligraphy. Stripped
    to the bone, these limbs resist the talons
of a great horned owl. I've heard it calling from
some leafy vantage when the light drew in,
as though to give the mice a final chance
        to flee for home.

Letters in the sky: the more you study them
hanging like a lost refrain above the lake,
the more convinced you grow of their lucidity;
    and the less certain it becomes
that such exact articulations are
nothing but the leftovers of lightning, mold
or leaf-devouring beetles. True, if you surveyed
        the pattern from

a wider angle, the shapes would alter,
the way a dialect mutates a vowel-sound,
yet their branching language would remain the same:
    a skeleton in search of flesh
if not a koan waiting for a student's
enlightened yell—"It spells FRUSTRATION, yes!"
And also this: the poetry of earth
      is made of death.

DOWN

These are the trees chopped down, chopped in a day.
The mahogany stretches from here to St. Eustache.
Teak sprawls even farther in the opposite direction.
Oaks are jostling ginkgos, figs rub up against maples,
date palms disturb the highways; the birchbark is white trash.
These are the trees chopped down, chopped in a day.

These are the trees chopped down, chopped in the night.
I never thought so many walnut logs could fit on the back
of a truck. Now nothing surprises me: not the littered olives,
not the stink of eucalyptus, not even the crumpled
mountains of bamboo. Something lived in a snarl of sumac.
These are the trees chopped down, chopped in the night.

These are the trees chopped down, chopped by the hour.
Tomorrow they'll emerge as plywood, pulp or fire.
A lifetime ago last week they sheltered rainbows in a canopy
or tangled against snow, subarctic bonsai:
willow, larch, arbutus, the chainsawed fruits of desire.
These are the trees chopped down, chopped by the hour.

WHITE ON WHITE

Energy is Eternal Delight, said Mr. Blake

now I face a February morning by the lake
below a gull at work in the delighted air

as the wet snow settles, flake by flake,
onto melting ridges that sketch a line of jagged
puddles in the churning, half-solid water

soon, I think, the weather will have to break
but soon means nothing to this granite wind
or the dour, unbroken mass of clouds transforming
the far shore to a moist abstraction

luckily the mirrored pier declines to fall
though its legs look akilter, a cubist slushpile,
ice and former ice in a cracked reflection

a watercolour still life that keeps on shifting
while a frozen artist tries to freeze the action

and the ghost of Mr. Blake cries satisfaction

EDGEWISE

Is it illusion that
when I was younger
my voice was far more
confident, stronger,

raring to hold a
difficult stance—
or just plain arrogant?
It had big plans

and rarely shied from
denunciation.
Now it chokes on
information.

Can its pain be trusted,
these lines included?
My voice is leached out,
clear-cut, denuded,

nutrient-starved amid
the updated noise
(but sometimes, look, I get
a word in edgewise).

Diana Brebner
[1956-2001]

Diane Brebner grew up in Frankford, Ontario and on Île Perrot, near Montreal. Her
books include *The Golden Lotus* (1993) and *Flora & Fauna* (1996). She received the Gerald
Lampert Memorial Award, the Pat Lowther Memorial Award and the Archibald Lamp-
man Award. In 1992 she won first prize in the CBC Radio Literary Awards.

FROM "ELEVEN PAINTINGS BY MARY PRATT"

for Susan

II *Salmon between Two Sinks*

Between heaven and earth, this gasping space
I leap: free, of your hands, free, even

of death's clasping. You never could hold me,
and now you know: the silver, salmon feeling

slipping between old times, and new. Now,
our life has been gutted. A knife removes

every false move, every wish for bright things
easily come by. O, I sink, deeper in history,

and into all the doctrines promising: ascent,
eternity, and the flashing joy of the obvious

pleasures. Deep in a pool of stilly light
everything comes back. Your hands cold, and

the words I mouth, mute as a fish, all speckled
in its story. Come to me. Be with me. If I leap,

one last time, let it be, into your open arms, all
gory, with birth and love, such messy, bloody glory.

III *Silver Fish on Crimson Foil*

This is the river of blood, the salmon run;
so ruthless, in their dark bed, the dusk years

bring to bear, upon anything, or all things
that we care to call dreams. You want to

believe it will be easy, clear & fluid; life
looks you straight in the eye, and you flourish.

You want to believe: if you swim like crazy
everything turns out right at the end. Now,

I ask myself: What bloody river is this? I set
my mouth (that wants to gape) stubbornly shut.

I carry on, one silver creature on the heraldic
field, companion to lions and unicorns, worthy

of shields. I carry on. Up the river I go
to my crimson foil, the river, and bed,

that I am carried on; and the blue heavens
will move, reflected in all, and the silver

fishflash of my joy will shout, and then
every good thing will be words in my mouth.

THE BLUE LIGHT OF THE NEUTRON POOL

All the generations of me go up with you,
past Petawawa and the military convoys,
past Chalk River, Deep River, Rolphton, and
the rivers of nuclear power, past the
quiet churches: Our Lady of the Snows,
St. Andrew's Among the Pines, and the spires
in Mattawa where we turn. This is when
we are most together, driving the highways

that lead to our wild places. In an old car,
loaded up with: packs, boots, a borrowed
canoe, we go up to Kioshkokwi, leaving
the city and the everglowing sky behind,
hoping to see the darkness in each other,
the black joy of an empty night, the little
cries of the hidden stars as they become
visible and beloved. When we were leaving

Cally shouted "Have a good trip" and then,
unexpectedly, "We love you." So many people
are left behind, the ones who will not,
or cannot be with us. I bring them with me
and carry their eyes, old lamps in the dark.
Who are we to travel over water to the
islands of pines and spirit? Portaging in
mystic green worlds, the red leaves warning,

the winter coming, and wading small rivers,
leading the canoe in the turbulent waters,
I remember my friends and take their peace
with me. And you, constant man, who changes
shape with the days, with the weather: raven,
brother loon, river merganser, holy fish
as you leap in the water, companion, silent
comrade; be assured, I could never leave you.

First early hours in the north of Algonquin:
we are listening to the freight trains rumbling
on to North Bay. We see the eerie glow of
settlement to the northwest. Later, the loons
will greet us in the grey morning, the clouds
on the water. Then small rain, like a blessing,
dampens the day. A moose and her calf
browse in the shallows where our next portage

begins. We can wait. The baby canters
on the surface, confident, kicking its heels
like a small horse, and the mother, benign
madonna, watches and chews. In the forest
we will encounter silence, a man and his dog,
the cathedral green of lichen, moss, and
the emptying gothic of the columnar trees.
Winds are up at the beach at Manitou Lake;

a pair of ravens stand guard at the shore.
I, who have lived as a mind, cogito's captive,
must submit: this is a world of body and
spirit. In purity, or violence, the water
receives you, and you become it. Thunderbird
roars overhead and the drumbeats of the
spirit pound, detonations in the heart.
There is no turning back from fear, or joy,

and our moment of salutation. Every green
branch and living thing springs up, every
fish becomes a silver word. On the island
of pines, unmapped on the lake, we come
home to the animate universe, the breathing
earth. I'm alone. So, how can I explain: in all
my prayers, I am with you, and you are here.
In the morning we will walk among stones

and broken shells, naked as children, in
the living water. I will think of my friends,
the lovers and the beloved, the believers
and the quiet companions. The scientist lives
for the moment of light, to have one night
when the code unravels, or to spend a life
without politics or worry, her face alive in
the blue light of the neutron pool. My friend,

the believer, asks for enlightenment;
my friend, the painter, for vison; my
friend, northern boy, for the green country
of childhood that his heart cannot forget.
As for me, Thunderbird, I ask that you take
me with you, in a boat that crosses to the
world of spirits. I want to dance at my death,
to make a little thunder the earth will hear.

PORT

Sometimes the tricks you learn as a child
are useful later on. When I was beaten
or raped I learned to move myself away
to a place without pain or degradation,

to stick it out and watch at a distance,
and never to vomit. I have been lucky
in joy, and have felt exultation. I have
been moved to tears and, nowadays,

I am hardly ever beside myself. I've
read that there is a science of pain
management. I think I could be an
expert. When the surgeon removed

my port, small metal disc implanted
just under the skin of my shoulder
to make delivery of chemotherapy less
painful (and which, by the way, was

never used by the tired nurses in a hurry
who could just stick an intravenous in
a good vein and get on with it), he was
doublebooked and did the procedure

during his lunch hour. I liked this man,
he spoke honestly and listened to me
but everyone has their bad days and
this was one. In the outpatient surgery

he began and I wondered, idly, why
I could feel so much, my shoulder
deadened with anaesthetic. We talked
and he worked and I said I could feel

his hands and the instruments as he
worked and he said: No you cannot.
Can. Cannot. Can. Mutual panic
as the pain increased and he knew

he was alone, had to proceed, could
not call for help and I said: OK, Listen up.
I have gone to the top of a mountain
where it is very cold, so cold I am

frozen and cannot feel, but I can see.
And way, way down at the bottom of
the mountain there you are, tending
a fire. I can see the red flames and

imagine the heat but here I am, up at
the peak, feeling nothing. He looked
at me strangely and was silent, worked
quickly and then left me, quite alone.

I waited a long time up on that
mountain but gradually the fire went
out, and he never did come back.
I got up, and walked home, was

a body but not wholly connected.
As the afternoon wore on, the cold
wore off. I began to shake: my
hands frozen, my teeth chattering. I

couldn't stop shaking and imagined
someone lost in a storm, perhaps
at sea, hoping like crazy to make
it to port, to the safe place that is

calm, and the first thing to do when
you arrive is to be sick to your
stomach, to know you have survived
but also to know that out there,

in the dark centre of destruction,
someone you loved, and had known
so well she might have been yourself
was lost, irretrievably, at sea.

THE PICTURES OF MY HEART

1

When you enter the research
wing there are no signs,
nothing tells you that here
your body is necessarily
an object of study. There

are no plans to weigh your
soul. No-one gives a damn
(for the purpose of clinical
trials) if you believe in
anything, or even yourself.

The drugs have a cardiotoxic
effect and machines will
measure how much you can take.
I wait while my heart fills
up with light. I imagine

angels with their research
wings, beating like test
flight pilots, crashing and
rising up, hitting walls
of despair. The walls are

mounted with hypotheses,
results, and names. There
are little brass plaques
on the doors. What would
you think about if your

heart was pumping glowing
particles? May and Mary
argue with a stubborn computer.
Karen small-talks while
Sharon Ann checks the iv.

We wait for the pictures
of my heart. They will
look like dogfighting
planes in a war. Wreckage
and bodies wash up later.

2

At the heart institute the hearts,
and their companion bodies, all
hold sway. Everyone runs when one
heart stops. Now, in the research

wing, hands are still at my side
(some of them mine) preparing for
an out-of-body experience. In the
silence of panic I become a Hindu

god, ornate and many-handed, each
hand with a life of its own. One
clambers up the air, temple monkey
in a tree. One lifts, benediction,

to your face. Some hands remain
beside themselves with imagination.
Some are imagination. One turns a
face to the light and begins to

speak sign language, the hands of
girls dancing in their jewels and
headdresses (their gold clothes
fitting like gloves.) Some hands

wave good-bye, sadly with hankies.
Some wave swords. One black hand
reaches out for the pictures of
my heart, lifts them to the blue light

and shows them to its companions.
They pass from hand to hand, like
photographs of a birthday, a baby
or a vacation. Every hand stares

in recognition. One by one, like
ribs of a Chinese fan, they fall,
folding into my arms, the pictures
splayed in a hand, like old cards.

3

Polaroid pictures of my heart
are pinned on their white
storyboard. Other pictures
of hearts are sappy valentines
compared to these pointillist
mug shots, strictures for

love's centre patiently
constructed out of dots. The
heart's a shadowed pear,
a city by satellite,
computer imaged memory,
blemished fruit, a sunspot

flare. The colour pictures
of my heart confirm
a world: bizarre, disorderly,
but calm. Terminals show
lurid blots that squirm
pink, orange, red and blue.

Each is a balm, the bright
carnal and carnival of the
expected. Now, when I send
you some message of love,
it won't be a Parzival call
to *amor*. A grailed heart's

not true enough for that.
I think I'll just call on
your hands for love. I'll
leave the masque of despair
to the heart: an old dance,
heartbreak, a suitable task.

Carla Hartsfield

[b. 1956]

Carla Hartsfield was born in Waxahachie, Texas and now lives in Toronto. A classically trained pianist, a singer-songwriter, a music teacher, and visual artist, she has published three collections of poetry: *The Invisible Moon* (1988), *Fire Never Sleeps* (1995) and *Your Last Day on Earth* (2003).

ON MOVING TO A DIFFERENT COUNTRY

I'm told there are seven winters
within each one, released like
lying breaths, reluctantly. I keep slow count
as they harden in frosted air, invent
new selves melting in rain, those black
crystals plying their dirt.

My decapitated snow man wars
with an army of twigs sealed in ice mounds
next door. Driveways blacken on command. Dim
borders of water separate houses,
yards disperse into melting counties.

From everywhere the muted
yells of neighbourhood children
escape from windows, their voices
like manhole-steam.

This is a new country with rules of its own.
I don't know how many winters are left.

A NIGHT

when starts come up
diluted; glaze the lake
from underneath, glinting
like fish.

A sultry moon
humpbacked and sour,
fills the horizon with pale light,
a wall of vapours.

I used to be wary of
approaching a scene like this, though
not anymore. I welcome anything
that reminds me of you, the broken pieces

of moon and stars walking in the dark lake;
unstable lights quavering in diverse directions like
your tongue in my mouth, that intricate melody;

even the lucid water with its
silver scales, sliding
through my fingers
much too quickly.

IF CLOUDS WORE BOUFFANT HAIRDOS

Only in Texas is the word
"backcomb" synonymous
with all that's beautiful

in older women. They cruise
the streets shellacked
as dimestore mannequins.

Their voices wail like
they truly know what wends
in the upper stratosphere.

Face paint heavy, prominent
as any chartreuse sunset,
that hair towering high
as cumulous clouds.

I'd recognize those
whining expressions anywhere, better
than if I'd sprayed myself
into the mural.

My theory about the flatlands
(with crickets locking faces
until the nightwind aches,
trailer lots and poor

farmers living in shacks
unpainted so long
the wood rots sure
as cancers on their skin)

is that those old farmers
tying these women to their arms keep
to this lie of beauty, hope. What

cloud hangs fire overhead
causes hands to come up empty.
Who needs paintings either
with women like these?

Or clouds looking like
gods embodied, carrying
streams of rainbows in their
whimsical structures. Even

poisonous liquids can look
tantalizing. I can't
take my eyes off the clouds.

And these men can't take
their eyes off the women, smelling
of beauty parlour chemicals, sour
as crops ruining in fields.

REAGOR SPRINGS, TEXAS

I've also crossed the railroad tracks,
sallied potholes, heard geese
quibbling at pond's edge. It
was so muddy when my mother

was born here they fetched
the doctor on a mule. My father dragging
his red wagon everywhere, left marks
still visible on these porchsteps.

Tonight I sleep in their room:
the one with pink curtains,
chintz wallpaper, hand-made quilts;
and dream the old dream:

that there was never anything
at the end of this road
in Reagor Springs, Texas.
No house, no railroad tracks,

no fence with broken wires,
no sound. Just the gate
with rusted cattleguard.
Before I knew it

I'd leapt across, homefree.
Not daring to look back
at the line of
dough-faced ancestors

gathering behind me with
knitting needles and plows.
This dream chases after
the moon's bald light

dividing into slivered jewels
at pond's edge. How many more
times will I cross the teeth
in the cattleguard before

it swallows an ankle or toe?
I've been lucky. *Might miss.*
Someone will have to send
for the mule.

SELVAGES

Clouds sweep, blocking
fresh heat, a low flung
autumn sun. The trail's

full of brown seed pods, their locust-
shapes popping silver hairs
like silk. They feather our necks.
I don't say I know why
you brought me here. I'm gathering
leaves now too selectively, my feet
splitting silence like axe blows.

We hold tight. Look up instead.
Spotted leaves hang precarious, thin
selvages clinging to white limbs.
Like us, they know it can't last.

Anne Simpson
[b. 1956]

Nova Scotia poet and novelist Anne Simpson's first collection of poetry, *Light Falls Through You* (2000) won the Gerald Lampert Memorial Award and the Atlantic Poetry Prize, and was a finalist for the Pat Lowther Memorial Award. Her second poetry book, *Loop* (2003), won the Griffin Prize, and was shortlisted for the Governor General's Literary Award for Poetry.

LIGHT FALLS THROUGH YOU

After many years avoiding the place, I lift the latch
(which disappears as it is touched) and find

you are young as always, while I have closed thousands
of little doors in my skin. Perhaps small words, such as love,

still exist, floating through air in the far distance. Like kites,
they come back when I pull on them, so I've lost

nothing, not even your hands, full of something discarded:
the nests of birds, complete with eggs, or feathery ostrich ferns.

But look, there is snow on the floorboards, where the wind
brings it under the door. You are in shadow and then light,

as you lean forward. Now I see wrens hiding in your hair,
field mice scampering down your leg. I pause, catching the scent

of earth, and realize your arms are moss, fingers about to blossom—
the wrong season, but never mind, your eyes are the same,

uncannily. I see everything planted in you unfurling new leaves
and flourishing. I reach out fondly, at the same moment

sunlight falls through you. After all, I should have known
you would dissolve into something clear and unresolved,

like water, and that I would put my hands deep in you
and they would come up empty, wet from the touch of my own face.

SEVEN PAINTINGS BY BRUEGHEL

The Triumph of Death

These watches. Ticking, still. Each hour is cold:
the rims surround quick voices. Shut in rooms.
Gone. *Tick.* The towers. *Tock.* Of fire. A fold
in air. We're smoke, drifting. A painted doom
where cities burn and ships go down. Death's
dark sky—a grainy docudrama. Time
swings bones on circus wheels. Listen: wind's breath,
a shriek. *Theatrum Mundi.* In their prime,
the living. Leapt. That buckling of knees.
Then gunshots: plastic bags on fences. Snapping.
Or loose. *Thank you—shop—at.* The lovers see
nothing. He plays a lute. She sings. Clapping—
machines sift through debris for the remains.
A sales receipt, a shoe. The silvery rain.

Landscape with the Parable of the Sower

A sales receipt, a shoe. The silvery rain
has many hands. A stream—Fresh Kills—elides
with river. Thick and slow. A landfill plain:
a ghost in biohazard gear. Gulls ride
the thermals, circling high as barges come,
a linking chain. Blue metropolis, far-
off glints of light. The cranes all lift and hum,
making hills of metal, bone. Crushed cars.
So garbage rises: this stench is monument.
Yet Brueghel's farmer takes the seeds, flings wide
his arm. A miracle: small event. We meant
to go, but every boat was laden. Tides
pulled home, pulled here, then left us for the birds.
We take the shape of soil, abandon words.

The Tower of Babel I

We take the shape of soil, abandon words.
The world will change without us. Did we glean
a little shine? Perhaps. These wheeling birds
drift down to earth. Crying. The air, unseen,
seeks entry without keys. All locked, shut down.
A spackled light gets through. We merely craved
a taste. *Hello, my name is* _____. A crown,
a king. One makes the other into slave.
Behind is Babel's core. Red as a heart
opened for bypass. Laid bare. Wind, idling.
It's quiet. Still. The horses, loaded carts,
are stuck. The ships, the docks. Thin bridles
of cloud. All stopped. Each thing unclocked, undone.
A man who kneels to plead his case. Warm sun.

The Tower of Babel II

That man who knelt to plead his case, that sun:
they're gone. In time, air hardens, growing dark.
The wars go on; beyond the TV, guns
talk to themselves. One, two. They whisper, bark.
Erotica. And Babel: height's desire
is weary of itself, but there's no end
to greed. A cruise, a condo. Guests for hire.
On the rug: a shirt, a shoe. Whatever bends
one body to another. We've forgotten.
Those painted clouds are knives. Slipped in walls
between the ribs. This plot device: rotten—
the thing exploded from within. Small
papers, white flakes. Last wish. Someone's cellphone.
("Are you still there? *Are you?*") A voice falls. Stone.

The Slaughter of the Innocents

"Are you still there? *Are you?*" A voice falls. Stone,
unbearable stone. It grinds. It tastes of grief.
Don't watch. Go blind. Oh Lord, those moans
will haunt us. This one. That one there. Brief
lives. Snow. And here, between the black trees, blood.
A leaping dog. A bird. Everywhere we turn
there's whiteness in the air. And memory, a flood
of killings no kindness can assuage. Urns
half-full of ashes: nothing that we knew
of those we loved. So young. Such shining hair,
those gleams recalled. A silence follows through
the rooms of when and how. Now. up the stairs
a rescuer is climbing. But he's too late.
And look what happened. This. Short straw of fate.

Hunters in the Snow

Who knows what happened? A short straw of fate,
all that. Years ago. But now we've changed;
those terrors tucked back in the heart. "Just great,
that weekend special: everything arranged."
We return; the house looks strange. Each thing
deceives. The counters, cutlery. Believe
the chairs; they guard the table in a ring.
The hunters come. They're trudging, slow. Reprieve
makes curving flight, a song in evening's sky:
pale green at dusk. Some children skate; they laugh.
and history has no place. Easy to lie
on queen-sized beds, *dream a little dream.* Half-
heard, the phantoms speak: No, you weren't there—
We turn; we sleep. But once there was a prayer.

Christic and the Adulteress

We turn; we sleep. But once there was a prayer,
a way to finger mystery. It floats,
one plastic bag, freed from the fence, that snare
with loops of wire. We translate into motes,
a glimmer in a shaft of sun. One glide,
we're gone. A painted scene: against this plea
is set a stone. An end. Each thing is tried.
A man makes notes in sand. The wind goes free.
One gust: his words are ghosts. The dust, absolved,
has vanished too. First kiss, last glance. *Tick. Tock.*
All goes to ground. We kneel down and dissolve.
Turn in. Turn out of time. Where nothing's clocked.
A touch: so light. Love's breath. Things we can't hold:
these watches. Ticking. Still. Each hour is cold.

John Barton

[b. 1957]

John Barton has published eight books, including *Designs from the Interior* (1994), *Sweet Ellipsis* (1998), and *Hypothesis* (2001). A three-time winner of the Archibald Lampman Award and a CBC Literary Award, he lives in Victoria where he edits *The Malahat Review*.

BODY BAG

The results came back
negative and already I am

beginning not to remember your name
its syllables fading from the plastic

bracelet they have yet to
cut from your wrist, the letters

broken from the outset
the impression left

by the exhausted printer
at Admissions further

blurred by nocturnal sweats.
You lie unclaimed

on a gurney pushed to one side
of the isolation ward where you

waited out your final hours
back and thighs tender

with bedsores attended to
gently, though you were barely

aware or awake, your body
stripped of everything

but a pyjama jacket
and tubes exchanging

sweet stupor for wastes.
You might have looked

through them to the ceiling
so far off, outside

the reach of whatever
vision you had, not always

apprehending cracked plaster
could not forever hold back

the clouds or their leaden descent.
The results came back negative

months ago and already I am
starting not to remember

the briefs you wore that night
only how your body cast

them off, how it welcomed me
inside you in the middle

of the few hours I knew you
how it seemed to have nothing

to protect, so in a hurry
as it rode me, so unconnected

to your brain with its clouds
so dispersed I did not see

them settle until too late
your body riding the unfocused

eye of my own storm
the condom I slipped on

belatedly a windsock
I filled full force and then

the wind dropped
and then

you told me, your bed
adrift and anchorless

in the doldrums without
compass or horizon.

The results came back negative
years ago and already

I am beginning not to remember
your hands or the way

they touched me, how they so
casually joined with mine or how

exactly
I came to be afraid.

The orange body bag I am sure
awaits each one of us is

one-size-fits-all, contains any
weather without effort, zips

open and closed over you
irreversibly from the outside.

SKY NEWS

It was a place we did not go, though
the road signs, if we let them, would have

taken us off course, crossing the plateau
between Albuquerque and Flagstaff, ceaseless

terra cotta clouds of grit almost
sweeping us from the interstate, driven

and insentient, the wind unaware
of how it shook us, of how I gripped

the wheel, the loneliness
of my concentration, as I steered

between the gusts, the mountains west
of Flagstaff impossibly celestial

snow falling when we pulled in for coffee
before pressing on, time not sacrificed

to distance, or wherever farther on
we felt we had to go, realizing

too late what we had passed by—
the crater outside town where the meteor

struck, record of one of the smaller
impacts to disturb the countenance

of the Earth, devastating
in its clarity, only a mile across

I am told, and therefore comprehensible
in this landscape, how it came

out of nowhere and did not miss
suggesting, even to the casual

eye how what we can never expect
or aim to ignore, still leaves

its mark—news
from the sky, we should have

watched for it, the whole planet watching
for it, fearful inventories kept of the near

Earth asteroids, networked
telescopes plotting their degrading

erratic orbits, hoping to deflect
disaster or welcome its approach

how it might remake us so completely
unforeseen versions of ourselves

afterward documenting the site
of the collision, the breadth

and unfated depth of its depression
bringing to light unearthly shrapnel still

able, several geologic ages later, to reveal
how it came to be here or any other

suspect signs of life it may have
brought from elsewhere, elusive

yet distracting, while in the immediate
fallout whole categories of phyla

died out, the petrified
hope, the ignored evolutionary

possibilities of leaf and wing
they left behind useless

portents, though the horseshoe
crab grappling up through the layers

sidesteps the trilobite
into what we call the present

—though you (whoever you are
and what I made you) may have

stopped listening (my obsessions
projections into your—or is it my—inner

space) the small impact we had
on each other no more

lasting than any meteor burning up
in-atmosphere, the brilliance

of our brief light
as we drove into the stars

past Flagstaff extinguished
before we had a chance

to notice, leaving no evidence
of its descent except in memory

and this too will fade—love's tiny
universal scale and the uses

to be made of it only a tracker of near
misses can ever predict fully

as I plot the hazy coordinates
of some place whose inevitability

we think this once
we bypassed.

Julie Bruck
[b. 1957]

Julie Bruck is the author of two books of poetry, *The End of Travel* (1999), and *The Woman Downstairs* (1993). Her work has appeared in such magazines as *Ms*, *Ploughshares* and *The New Yorker*. A former Montrealer, she lives in San Francisco.

THE WOMAN DOWNSTAIRS USED TO BE BEAUTIFUL

This summer she's grown huge, a ham with legs,
she lumbers below, watering the garden with a hose.
From my balcony, the evening light seems kind
to the extra flesh, soft
on her print shift, the scarf that holds back
her dark hair, and for once I want to believe
she's not unhappy, not stuffing her face
to fill the distance between her
and the unusually thin husband who travels, not hiding
in the body of the proverbial fat woman,
passed in the street without notice.
Instead, that she wants to be of consequence,
clearly visible to her small son stationed
on their balcony, that he never lose sight of such a broad floral back,
think she might leave him, vanish in the leaves below.
But the wail that comes from him's a thin, unwavering cry,
as if he never comes up for air, this wordless child's siren
of *come back, not enough, too far,* that has brought me
and, gradually, other neighbours onto our balconies
to look first on a small boy, who, thirty years from now
will turn his life over, say: *there was always*
too much of her, she swallowed me up—and then down
on a fat woman, breathlessly bending.

TIMING YOUR RUN

Philippe Laheurte (1957-1991)

The night before there was a break-in at your store.
There was an afternoon when the lock had been fixed,
and you said you'd drop an extra key at Laurent's place
after work. There was a call from your wife. All day,
you'd waited to run, but just as you went out,
it really started pouring. You were like a little boy
in the rain, Albert Mah said, and you came back drenched,
pleased with your time. There was a pair of New Balance
trainers for a customer with narrow feet, the rain
on the shoulders of the UPS man who waited
while you signed. A tuna sandwich made for you
at the dépanneur next door. Your thin fingers
on the brown paper bag. There was a blue car.
There was what you said about this run of bad luck—
robberies at the store, a fire on New Year's Day, about
training for a comeback in the fall, believing everything
could turn around. How happy the woman with long,
narrow feet was when you called to say her shoes
were in. There was your hand, hours after dark, slipping
the extra key through Laurent's mail slot, Laurent asleep.
There was a car coming. The key lay on the floor all night.
After running you'd showered in the store's tiny bathroom.
There was the bar of soap, still wet. There was a blue car
slicing a corner. There was your black car, stopped
at the light. There was Laurent, awake in the morning,
a freshly-cut key on the cool floor. There is tonight's
news footage of you winning races, explaining
the difference between two kinds of heel cups,
bending a shoe as you speak. There was the key
you wanted Laurent to have in case something
happened. There is Laurent, half-asleep, picking it up.

WHO WE ARE NOW

The man who runs the parking lot at St. Hubert & Duluth
holds our keys in one closed hand, curses this country
with the other. *In Soviet Union, I am doctor, like Chekhov*—
his fifth identity in the last six months. *Here I clean hospital
after midnight. You must pick up keys by eleven.*

My friends plan their lives in a nearby Greek restaurant:
plans subject to jobs, lovers, children, or lack of same—
most of all, this constant gnawing at who we are,
exactly what we're supposed to be doing here.
After the meal, the wine, strong Greek coffee,
a ballpoint meanders on the paper tablecloth, variations
on the same story—each year, less embellishment.

I have seen him wave off customers he didn't like the look of:
In Greece, I am anthropologist—he barks, shaking his fist
at a blue Chevette that has backed out in search of a meter.
Quebec people are racist—*Canadians are worse. I do not think,*
he says, squinting at us, *that you are pure Canadian.*

When we finally head home in our reclaimed vehicles,
it is always early April, always snowing, always unseasonal.
We huddle in the glow of the car's dials and gauges, stare
into the red light at Cherrier like some kind of second sun,
longing for sleep, for dreams to redeem us.

I am Armenian, he states proudly, *and this place is dead.
In Moscow, my cousin has fourteen fruit stores.*
He thrusts the wrong keys at us, I point to the correct hook.
*East Europe is living. Next year, I sell antibiotics in Bucharest.
Good business*, he says, releasing our keys. *Good night.*

CAFETERIA

Some beauty will be born of this,
said my friend's blind mother
across the hospital cafeteria table
hours after the doctor said
inoperable and closed her daughter up.
All morning we'd drifted in and out
of the flower-sweetened room,
watching the morphine drip, taking
Kate's hand, holding her gaze.

I don't know about beauty, I said
and got up to order our lunch
from two woman who'd been a comfort all week,
their small Scottish kindnesses a balm.
We ate our egg salads on whole wheat
as though we'd never tasted real food—
the creamy sweetness of the filling, surprise
bite of green onion—and drank Diet Cokes
until we'd washed our mouths clean.

I loved everything about our lunch—
the newsprint placemats with their oily spots,
crumbs on the unbreakable plates,
and especially the metal napkin dispenser
recently replenished by someone's deft hand
with what the Scottish women would call
serviettes, *Help yourself, dearie*, in that burr.
I loved the hospital employees on break,
smoking outside the window, jousting
and flirting with their serviceable bodies.

I loved Edgar Jones, the deaf man
interviewed on the radio last night—
a music archivist who says it doesn't
matter if he can't hear anymore: he still
feels the way he did when he first heard Sibelius,
It's in my heart, you understand?
I loved Kate's mother's lined, outdoor face,
the loose wisps of white hair

framing her fine bones, the lively, blue,
unseeing eyes. I loved the shed paper
skin of the plastic straws, the way
the straws rose slowly in the Coke cans
and we pushed them back down to drink.

I loved the terra cotta walls around us,
freshly painted by people who'd done
their job adequately; loved the moment
someone decided to place the poster
of a whitewashed Greek village *there*,
and not an inch higher or lower.
I wanted to eat all my meals at the hospital
cafeteria, each bite a tiny explosion.
I don't know about beauty, I said.

SEX NEXT DOOR

It's rare, slow as a creaking of oars,
and she is so frail and short of breath
on the street, the stairs—tiny, Lilliputian,
one wonders how they do it.
So, wakened by the shiftings of their bed nudging
our shared wall as a boat rubs its pilings,
I want it to continue, before her awful
hollow coughing fit begins. And when
they have to stop (always), until it passes, let
us praise that resumed rhythm, no more than a twitch
really, of our common floorboards. And how
he's waited for her before pushing off
in their rusted vessel, bailing when they have to,
but moving out anyway, across the black water.

Elise Partridge

[b. 1958]

Elise Partridge's poems have appeared in *Canadian Literature, Poetry* (Chicago), *Books in Canada, Slate, The Southern Review, Poetry Ireland Review, The Fiddlehead* and elsewhere. *Fielder's Choice* (2002), her debut poetry collection, was shortlisted for the Gerald Lampert Memorial Award. She lives in Vancouver.

PLAGUE

Heal-all, angelica, alum-root,
yarrow, sweet Annie, valerian shoots—
swinging under foxgloves' lavender bells
a secret to make a sick heart well—
at that eastern farm we waded flowers
and herbs renowned for their healing powers.
Black-eyed Susans in orange beds,
yellow primroses nodded their heads
as I followed the signs into the wood.
It was plicking, dim, laundry-room humid;
mosquitoes like dust-motes blown into flight
almost haphazardly settled to bite.
Two pinks caught my eye. Bending down,
I saw a caterpillar going to town
on a faltering stem; its body was slung
underneath, like a sloth's; the feet clung;
the head chewed. Four were making a meal
beneath a spray of Solomon's-seal
whose white drops kept quivering. Paired prongs,
their six front legs worked like icemen's tongs,
curving to stab. The rear-guard pylons,
gray, flat-soled, ten dutiful cousins,
helped shiver along the elegant back,
red and blue pustules edged with black.
Veering into a sunny aisle
—magenta bee-balm, white chamomile—
I saw dozens more, tan heads like helmets
bobbing over the lambs-ears' velvet.
*These maidenhair ferns were brewed for tea
to soothe a sore throat, cure pleurisy—*

their two-inch, humping, whiskered lines
were even strewn on the naturalists' signs.
They sprawled under the spindly buds
of red-root, used to strengthen the blood;
a jewelweed's freckled orange scoops
hung over gnawed leaves; a spicebush drooped;
this wake-robin looked pocked, that ginger torn,
violets' poulticing sprouts had been shorn,
betonys' too—I could find no leaf
that hadn't already come to grief.
Running down the path, now I could see
they were pasted to the bole of every tree;
the plicking I'd thought was rain in my ears
sounded like snips of miniature shears—
their migrant, hungry, adhering strips
made, as I stood there, sawtoothed rips
in thousands more seedlings. Soon
they'd each find a twig and start to spin;
one moon-rise not too far from this,
fresh from a cracking chrysalis,
their tawny, fluttering selves would come
tilting to this wild geranium,
alight on finer, fewer legs
and discharge arsenals of eggs.

A VALEDICTION

Thump on the roof.
The owl again?
Rising short shrieks—
mouse? rat?
I counted ten.

Terrified yelps
squeezed by a talon.
To have that be
your final say!
And your last vision

looming feathers,
diving beak.
Clutched, wriggling,
squeaking—
speak!

What was he crying—
"Mother, help me"?
"Have mercy on me,
Eli, Eli"?
"I am not ready"?

Neck snapped, dangling;
a moment: taken.
Hamlet wouldn't
kill Claudius, so.
Too small a ration.

Foraging, scrabbling,
snatched; plea.
Hunching wings,
wad of bones
spat under a tree.

RUIN

Boulevards with planted medians,
hotels like perfume boxes
strewn around the landscape,
a pink mall looming by a lagoon—

the tourists set out for jungle
on a new road
laid like electrical tape
through the trees.

Cola trucks veered past,
their bottles jumping.
Chickens turning circles
in muddy yards,

cul-de-sac,
lake,
white pigs snuffling
in the dirt—

the group bought tickets
at a shed
shading packets of film
on a styrofoam cooler.

Birdsong tinging,
bright beads of water—
they plunged under
branches swagged

with Spanish moss—
ancient rains
that had caught and frayed —
posed by a stela,

fumbled deeper—
"There!" "I saw it first!"
Two hundred feet high,
white stone sown with green.

They clambered up.
From the pyramid's top
all they could see
was slash-horizon,

green pelt bunching
on the land's back.
The guidebook said
towns thousands of years old

lay clenched underneath.
—Down again, at the cola stand:
a sad-eyed monkey
scampered the length

of his twine leash,
dropped to his haunches.
Long, elegant fingers,
a baby's nails—

someone offered a sip
from her bottle of water.
He tilted it, took a swig.
Her piece of egg he threw in the dirt.

On their way back
they snapped a jaguar
crouching to keep its balance
in the bed of a pickup.

BUYING THE FARM

Crossing over—
will we be standing at a dory's prow,
clouds cooperating grandly in the background,
profiles like captains charting the Passage,
new moon, ice floes, capes?

Pass away
like an unlucky dynasty
or a craze for snuff bottles,
our lives no thicker than a snowflake?

A little folding of the hands to sleep—
straw hat tipped over my nose,
I'm dozing to the lilac's inquisitive wrens;
you, your spade still beside you,
sprawl, just starting to snore.

It's curtains for us,
clasping hands behind the dusty, still-swaying swag—
at last these doublets can come off,
the swipes of rouge and sideburns, then we'll stroll
to greet the flashing city with our true faces.

Let's *sleep with the fish,*
—yellow tangs flocking like suns,
eels with Sid Caesar eyes
easing into a Romanesque coral-arch.

It's the end of the line,
the train nudges its way to the platform's edge,
we're the only two in the graffiti-swirled car
softshoeing down the gum-gobbed aisle.

And yes, let's *buy the farm*—
the loft's tucked full of hay,
the combines are waiting,
here is your morning basket of fresh eggs.

THE BOOK OF STEVE

1

Scene from a romance: rambling through the wood,
suddenly I stumble across a giant.
"Are you a creature of good?" You nod.
Together we adventure to the next scene.

2

The kitten that followed you home one day—
how did it scent your benevolence?
Tentative shadow glimpsed through the screen,
shyly at dusk it would slip from the curb,
ears radaring forward when it caught your tone,
nuzzling your gentling fingertips.

Fifteen years later, each time I appear
you set down bowl after bowl for me.

3

What would I find, touring your sweet head?
Nooks packed with facts, quartz-glitters of wit,
green terraces orderly thoughts plash down;
knowledges bundled, a forklift memory
to scoop them out. Scenes with cousins; alcoves
cluttered with dumptrucks, bubblegum cards,
pâpier-maché models—Saturn, Mars, Earth—
plastic weaponry, a catcher's thumped glove.
Quiet zones like pools we found up the mountain,
truths as plain as a prairie sky.

4

I moved west to join you with what I could lug
in one stuffed suitcase. Coyotes yowled
from salmonberry clumps, minor alps loomed
at our street's end. Rain pattering on grape,
twinflower, bedstraw, bird's-foot trefoil—
every moment sponsored new blossoms.
Marsh wren swaying in a barely-tethered nest
on our cattail stalk, I clung, bowed, sang.

5

Minarets shimmying in mauve pools . . .
Jahan, you have nothing on my edifice,
this perfect dwelling I've designed for Steve.
The former tenant, a book-collector,
left basement troves we're still discovering—
eighteen-clause titles, rococo colophons.
Our chimney bricks are precisely aligned
so winds play themes from Mozart concerti.
Self-cleaning gutters, lawnmowing sheep. . . .
Miraculous for a temperate climate,
our back yard sports a banana tree;
you pluck your snack each night from its fronds.
Birds of paradise nest in our eaves.

6

Driving cross-country, in the prairie center,
I leapt out to capture a sunset blaze
and snapped you instead, poised at the wheel.
How many crumpled maps have I squinted at
on long peregrinations north, south, east?
Let me accompany you everyplace—
glance in your rear-view, you'll catch me winking,
flip down the sunshield, I'll slip to your wrist;
tune the radio above the stations
past static-crackle, then hear me hum.

7

Pink "Stargazers," white lilies you planted
that spring brocaded the garage's hem;
dabbing in each with affectionate thumbs,
you coaxed up seedlings an eyelash wide.
And that dahlia that tried so hard to live!
Translucent fist-bud almost pulsing,
it looked like it would burst, aching green.
The light-ration dwindled, but it stretched, leaned, craned
till even the sturdy chestnut-trees flared.
Hoping for petals till the very last,
swivelling, basking under your smile,
if I had to go, I would yearn toward you.

8

Travel memories: thatch, oriels—
we would have been peasants in the Old World,
you monitoring a herd of deer
in a sullen drizzle; evenings I'd have shone
the master's salt cellars, scraped blobs of wax
from a turret sconce. But together we'd have crept
along draughty halls under long-nosed portraits
when the lord was riding, to his library:
mysteries of minuscule; parchment grails.
In the Brueghel painting of the villagefest,
everyone's armwrestling, leapfrogging, whacking a ball;
we hunch on stumps teaching ourselves to read.

9

Exchanging jokes no one can overhear—
me trailing robes, you flourishing a hat—
we embrace in the parchment initial's ring.
Or, crimson birds with implausible tails,
we go on calling across the margins
over Gothic letters of a *demande d'amour:*
"Who was the most free?" Arveragus
or Dorigen? You're first—no, you are, dear . . .
we tumble in a lattice of forget-me-nots.

10

Our particular parliament of fowls:
each year, southering from Siberia,
squawking the whole three thousand miles,
the snow geese glide to Vancouver marsh.
What are they doing so far from home,
skidding amid these alien pumpkins?
Basking in the shallows, they gab and gab,
weary, weary—yet they mate for life.
—No hemlock owls bearing swooping doom,
but paired bald eagles in pine candelabra:
I want that for us, leisure, long views,
sharing through decades one dauntless raft.
—The yellow-headed blackbird, once-a-life vision:
gold vouchsafed on a rusting sedge.

11

Whenever you look up, there I shall be—
and whenever I look up, there will be you
said Gabriel Oak to Miss Everdene,
the wild girl who didn't have the wisdom
to curl with her shepherd by the inglenook.
He sought her when she was lost and silly,
not for a pen but to set her free.

—I stumble in, shaky on my legs,
I nestle in the crook of your arms.

12

And I have found Demetrius like a jewel,
Mine own, and not mine own. Yes, you are both,
rare nugget blazing in the general slab,
coveted, safe in my pouch of a heart;
fortuitous prize whose shine I want to share
with others who admire its brilliance too.
Untarnished, rustproof, through fire and ice
your adamant lasts. Glinting on my finger
I wear a hint of you, etched "Courage, Truth, Love."

13

Our idea of paradise: a night at Stuart's—
café of wobbling tables, coffeemaker lamps,
choice of paperbacks comfortably slumped,
students gnawing pens on scraped velvet chairs.
The nearby pawnshop is stacked with striped frisbees,
tie-dyes are fluttering by the Seed 'N Feed.
Chocolate cake, two forks; folksinger twanging—
here I can almost pretend we're twenty,
we've just escaped home, we've got enough verve
to light city blocks. All these years with you!
A sense of infinite possibility
flares before me as you touch my hand.

14

Let's age together like old-growth trees,
our knobby elbows sueded with moss,
draped over each other in a tipsy embrace
like a couple after their thousandth waltz.
Woodpecker pendants, mushroom-studded ankles,
we'll toast each year with another ring,
welcome hawks like finials to our balding heights.

When the end comes, shall we crash to earth
as comic and good-natured about it
as the bridal couple in the video
toppling as they tango the town-hall floor?
Thudding to the ferns, we'll sleep like spoons again,
looped with huckleberry, frogs booming at our feet,
nurse-logs to saplings bowering a new age.

Noah Leznoff
[b. 1959]

Noah Leznoff was born in Montreal. His work appears in the collection *Mad Angels and Amphetamines* (1994) which received Honourable Mention in the first annual Bronwen Wallace Memorial Award. His most recent book is *Outside Magic* (2003). He lives in Markham, Ontario.

SLEEPING IN THE GRASS

Kiss me Laura, but not on the mouth
your flowering hickey, my nipple

an upturned face in the circle
with no centre; astride the permian

moss, mouldering stump, blue blossoms
observe our bed; midges loiter

in this open-mouthed rale.
O dream-heart, fiddler crab, you

artless giving in, giving out!
Leave us now with leaf-stem,

bone braided in our thinning hair.
A damselfly, I swear it, left

her string of jelly under
my tongue, beside the pebble

a jackdaw brought, plucked
from the salmon-eyed rill.

AN ODD INVISIBILITY, THIS

On the staff corkboard someone'd tacked
    a personals ad: *Kittens Need a Home*
    (large felt heading, soft-lit

polaroid of kitten in classic mid-back-roll,
   paws frozen in classic mid-swipe at classic
cat toy—a belled cloth mouse)
   and under this:
   I'm thoroughly irresistible
   must spoil me with love

and so on

Phyllis and them—I knew it—
   small, fist-faced termagants or,
con/versely, women of unfathomable
seismic passion;
   they sit at any rate
smoking at the math table
   with Claire Winston, who
first class each term counts
leather jackets in the back row
and numbers their days,
actually says squinting:...*and period three—*
   six leather jackets! I give them a week.
   Kids call her "The Terminator";
the math dysfunctional
   especially males, something like
   hate her
but I'll grant this:
each Halloween she does it up full
   tilt as a witch.

But watch them go ape-shit at
   Christmas!
these women with extra-big
December issues of *Cat Fancier*
   or catalogues of cat stuff
ailurophile paraphernalia,
ribbons, strange largesse,
photo album exchanges of plum-sized
hearts—their own framed in
   endearing or dignified poses
   some on pedestals,
long-stemmed bouquets

or murky blue depths-of-field
in the background
—professional portrait photography
is what I'm saying.

   Kittens need a home.
 Okay, it's a humanizing thing.
   But how could I not scrawl
between photocopies of Stilt Jack
and Layton
glancing over my shoulder
—each flash a detonation—

   faking the high road or struck
impatient with human misery: *How about*

a canvas bag and a lake?

PUSHING IN THE GROCERY LINE

and it's all fine, a tight thursday, till the sudden
opening of a new register—that, and our standing
elbow-to-elbow from the free lane, me and the black-
draped crow, end-of-the-week hag whose brain's
some feral abacus clicking:
   the number of carts in each line
   the number of items per basket
   the relative efficiency of sandy or k.c.
or jean. *can i help the next in line, please?*
yeah, and I'm out first with a head-fake
or maybe she is
   anyway, it's started: our steps
quicken like those skittering xylophonic
birds', sandpipers; open coats, carts
rattling, a bit of the hip as we log-jam
cater-corner at the chocolate and tabloid rack.
   and here's adept thickness! her flummery
jaw set fierce, eyes stone cold
to my gritted nods and smiles,

my begged sardonic pardon and inching
basket of steel—but she's nudging
too! staring clear through me
staring through and leaning hard
so that but for the force of her in my wrists
and forearms I know what it means
to be invisible.
    do you laugh or swat her,
take by the throat or in your arms?
I'm seeing turn-of-the-century furrows, ox cart
tracks thick in the mud, potatoes,
a sandy-haired farm boy crazy
with wonder for the strength of her kiss
—that boy running home, swinging his arms
wide at the scend of an open blue hill
trying to fly because of her.
have I kissed the crone, her tongue
like moss? *Baba-Yaga!!*
here's yelling, confusion, people:
    and outside a rush-hour horn blast
and the sudden-cold darkness coming fast

BLUE JETS

> She takes blessedly
> Giving with full hands.
>   –Milton Acorn

    Thirteen, bored and giddy
with our maleness
we'd sit around some
summer evenings, cock our asses
in the air, brace back our
    thighs with our forearms,
    strike the match
    hold it there, and let fly
the incendiary fart: Ka-
    boom!

boys boys boys

86

hilarity, the brute puissance,
Apollo 11-ish,
of the blue spurt shooting
from our very own holes
flaring along the perineum
(the blunt sandpaper landing-strip
that begins under the testicles
and terminates darkly at the anus,
that place)—

the flame riding the mid-seam
of our jeans, sputtering beads
if the flatus dribbled,
the burnt-fingered diminuendo
of the dud—*who knows what lurks?*
or fanning shockingly out
if rich and deeply baffled
the trapped blast, supernova,
combusting in the grotto then spreading
like wings from our thighs
like violets
so we'd have to beat
it back: stop drop and roll.

Later, I'd grin learning
the blue jet was very like
what Hamlet meant
by *hoist by their own petard*—it would
all come back to me

but for now, for then: for the girls
who over the span of summers
let us kiss and feel them
in the incest of cottage
rotations, neat eclipses of
the X-ed calendar, another August's
early darkening,

it confirmed us: *demented
immature* and *gross*

just what we needed from them
—antidote to the top-forty love songs
they sang soulfully as dumkas,
arms liked, weaving with flashlights
down gravel roads
as we, twenty paces back,
   practiced walking and pissing
at the same time

COOPERMAN'S FISH: HABITAT

for the kids, of course, one fantail each:
   a standard gold, and a rock-mottled
black, foil, and amber
number—though within a week the girls
ignore them, till, months later,

   some other passing rush
of promises, and then you've four,
   an aquarium, spouting filter pump, coloured
pebbles, de-chlorinator—though you've
fended off the castle, plastic

kelp, background wallpaper of Hawaiian
sunset, and (i guess for thrash-punk
   fishkeepers) day-glo skull with eye-holes
big enough to swim through; no, half-sensible
you, it's a backyard rock, a conch

from the Cape as cover—and you're set,
   rigged for life, they're yours. to cart
the whole contraption come vacation
to the neighbours; though after time
it's not the fish

you look for, but, lying on the couch
the house asleep, dim light on a poem
or two—that steady purl: in the dead
precious silence after day, a resident gurgle

Iain Higgins

[1959]

Iain Higgins' newest book is *Then Again* (2005). His translations of contemporary Polish poetry have been published in numerous magazines in Canada, the UK, Ireland, and the United States, including *Descant*, *London Magazine*, *Metre* and *Chicago Review*.

FROM "THEN AGAIN (SOMETHING OF A LIFE)"

65/66

Unexamined lives were not for the living, which meant school.
Ink pink you stink, but they were neither Native nor Doukhobor, he & his
    brother, so fitting in was practically easy.
Use your fists like this, his father explained, & the lesson worked, mostly.
Conjuring up the smokes was easy after you'd gathered enough empties—*A
    packet of Player's for my mother, please* & Howie just handed them
    over—the trick was getting rid of the invisible smell.
A new bike remade the horizon he was learning by heart, but the first horse
    he rode had its own domain, & threw him.
The trolley-bus took them to Dr Chow's.
Mummy, look at the garbagemen! he said, seeing the staff in their medical
    whites.
Onward Christian soldiers marching as to war was sometimes a lullaby
    against the dark, the puzzled clock.
Birthday cards came from overseas addressed to young 'Master' so-&-so, &
    could lead to surprises—*The Big Rock Candy Mountain*, for instance,
    his first 78.
DP, wop, kike, dago, jap, chink—mystery words that emerged in the
    suburban woodwork, but got forbidden at home, unheard now for how
    long?
The engine on the family car had to be cranked first, yet this was already

67/68

You could see the prison farm from across Deer Lake, wondering why that
    was punishment.
Bugs, a can of water, & some drano.

There you were, then, half nonsense, half flesh, holding your own amongst
     gods & cold warriors.
He hung a peace sign in his window, hoping the hippies would notice as
     they drove past the house towards SFU.
The bush gave way to a golf course, & suddenly there were ponds to swim
     in, swiped balls for resale at the clubhouse.
The zoo, though, is gone now, out of phase with the pace clock, the polar
     bear alone having lived to see my older son as it saw me.
Sometimes they threw rocks at the passing trains, but even now I can't say
     what we were up to.
I remember biking home.
Slaphappy might be the word for it, but who really knows.
Too much Hallowe'en candy, the doctor said, *the pain will pass*, & it did, but
not till the incision healed—& by then I'd forgotten to ask what my
     appendix was for.
Someone in Capetown just got a new heart, they told him, someone else's,
& this was also a wonder.
It was just one of those *look-ma-no-hands* sort of things, a little exuberance
     after a long day at the golf course, except that he had nothing on but his
     bathing suit.
Skinned & still bleeding, his brother half-blind from another fall, they
     wheeled their bent bikes to the door.

70/71

Your ass from a hole in the ground, etc.
He could be an enthusiast, & this didn't always sit well.
TV was suddenly memorable now that they'd reached the War Measures
     Act.
The plane was designed to circle you like a gas-powered satellite on a string,
     but he flew it at first like an earth-eating meteor.
Bullied sometimes, you had to learn to defend yourself, & that might
     explain something now—mightn't it?
Then there was that achy edginess that flowered in him that still does.
The trail was crisscrossed with cedar roots & deadfalls, but we never went
     without our bikes.
The bush was its own world, & perfect when the salmonberries were ripe.
No place comes to mind without its lived-in time, known through leaf, say,
     or sky, or the clothes he had to wear.

You make your own luck, they said, but he might have been busy with scale
    models.
A three-hulled ark was taking shape in the garage, his father's work—
    trucked one night to a tidal river, then eased to the sea as if for solace.
The language of sheets & stays & *hard a-lee.*
Chopsticks were simpler than a knife & fork, & so that much harder to use.
Best always to tell the truth, though words could fail him.

72/73

A spurt of boys from the schoolbus home, their halting dance of punch &
    counterpunch for some imagined Judy, & saltsweet blood streaming
    from his nose.
Their flesh was grass sown in the same season, but some now were ripening
    faster, thickening out.
Shorter, softer, he considered the solace of a second wind.
By bike still, but more & more often by thumb (the odd crazy, sure, but also
    local dads, good sams, & once only: rhapsody in a candy-red corvette).
Solitude was a choice companion.
He'd begun to read the paper, wandering in its easy weave of death, advice,
    & advertising.
You could know the tides without the tidetable, though.
Learning to skate might also be a metaphor.
What he never really saw or didn't know to notice (list incomplete): the
    Semiahmoo Reserve (contemporary) by the train tracks, the
    petroglyphs (also contemporary, but differently) downline by the other
    beach.
A quick study, yes, but a slow learner.
Social studies not history, & nothing at all of there where you were, the
    tracks, errors, accidents that emerged as this here now.
Ritual objects were always a concern: a lacrosse ball, for instance, a goalie's
    mask, or, from a distance, another, her.
The plums were sweet, yellow like the gorged wasps, & he loved the spirea
    so much he got to cut it down, seed the lawn.
He woke to find his side wet—no Eve though.
Several dads lived next door, later a gent who gardened in cardigan & tie,
    took tea in the shade.

73/74

Crab, cod, oysters, mussels, clams, then a bouillabaise, all in a day's work
    amongst islands, sails furled, the sun slow to go.
The clock no matter what, but you could always forget to wind your watch.
And what if he had paid more attention?
All five feet of him shooting hoops with the Duke brothers down the road, a
    baker's dozen between them.
But you had to have the right touch, no?
Much time was mostly spent in school, & I can remember the daydreams.
She was still a foot taller, yes.
The Loneliness of the Long Distance Runner was something to read, but he
    preferred his own running, his own second wind—as if running harder
    might make you grow.
Orange August moon rising full again beyond Baker, the dormant cone
    barely steamplumed sometimes, & tangerine now in the just-gone
    daylight.
All night in the barn, catching, cleaning, then a quick turn on the boss's
    motorcycle at dawn, a broken arm.
A pillow on a boy's lap was recommended before necking, one mother said.
But having a pillow was not the same as having a chance, was it?
Men have died from time to time, oh yes, *& worms have eaten 'em, but not
    for love.*
What's-his-name was stoned again, bumper-skiing in a rare snow, cracked
    his head hard—that desk stayed empty.
The deer too were on their way out.
No wonder he preferred tending goal.

Laura Lush

[b. 1959]

Laura Lush's first book, *Hometown,* was a finalist for the 1992 Governor General's Literary Award for Poetry. She has since published two more books of poems, *Fault Line* (1997) and *The First Day of Winter* (2002) as well as a short story collection, *Going to the Zoo* (2002). She taught English in Japan for five years and is now living in Toronto.

WITNESS

My father at 61
clings to this farm
like blood to an accident.
How for thirteen years he's tried
to make it work.
I watch his geese bobbing behind him,
the water balloons of their bodies
splashing forward, their necks
loose white springs.
Watch him chase his heifers
across the fields, his legs
graceful as a hockey player's.
And I watch him drive the tractor back
to the barn at night, hunched over,
the porch blossoming with moths.
But mostly I watch him watch
other farmers falling.
Their big hands
fold over their faces while
the earth tightens.

CHOICES

She tells me of the day she met him
in the vets' hospital, leaning over his bed
listening to his lungs' clog.
The mustard gas from Vimy, a hot yellow muffler.
He saw the white sleeve of her uniform,
her hands holding the sharp silk pick

before it slid like ice beneath his skin.
Three days later he asked her to marry him.
She'd said no to Eddie Barrett, his calm June voice.
Chose this one instead, in spite of the coughing,
whiskey on his tongue.
Years like that, until
those breath-shreds finally stopped.

SUMO WRESTLERS

When we saw the *sumo* wrestlers
in Shinjuku station we felt
two mountains had been dug up
and pushed over just for us.
The way they'd pace across
the floor, hair smooth
as black bones.
every one in a while they'd
bend their large knees
so we could hear the flesh
settle over them, the way
the buried must hear the avalanche.

THE ACCIDENT

Out of the pool she dragged him,
his three-year-old body—swollen milkpod,
lips like tiny purple erasers.
"It was an accident," she said.
Faces floated up at her from the crowd
serene as ink. Forgiveness seemed to want
to be everywhere, the sun a benevolent yellow.
Except for him, his five o'clock car
rolling up the driveway, accusations
snapping in his head like guitar strings.
She could only offer him her open arms,
the distance of grief stretching between them.

DECIPHERING THE SEA

Today something under a wave split
my foot open, drew the blood
like a long thinning breath.
I'd gone to the beach to watch
the water leisurely unbraid the tide—
the private strands, the whispering
threads bright as sunweed.
Under the sunlight, fresh and luminous
all the lies glowing each other to death.

THE CROSSING GUARD

So often!
That man in the great yellow slicker
standing like a mustard pack against
a chest of snow, in rubber boots
like old ox tongues,
would hold out his hand weather-gnarled—
rain rotted, ice crunched, fog rumpled
down to knuckle-chew.
That pucker of a face
dogged and cap covered, nodding us on
to cross over
dirt, gravel, mud—those snapshot puddles
catching the stretch of our fresh legs.

Susan Gillis
[b. 1959]

Susan Gillis' first book, *Swimming Among the Ruins* (2000) was shortlisted for the Pat Lowther Memorial Award and the ReLit Award. Her second book, *Volta*, won the 2003 QWF A.M. Klein Prize for Poetry. She lives in Montreal where she teaches English.

BACKYARD LIGHT

We're in the backyard again. This time
we have brought out the gas lantern and lit candles
around our talk. Scott tells of the field behind

a house he stayed in in France, the day he was walking
and missed a step, stumbled over what turned out to be
a Stone Age axe head. For a moment a candle flickered

and dark gathered around the back of my hand
as I cupped the flame. Someone returned from inside,
letting the screen door wheeze. The breeze went down,

and with it the dark, winging the yards, and stars appeared
as small fires across a plain, then flipped
back into place as stars. Our talk

turned to family and how we fly—and how a kid
can't—and somebody's heard—d'you think there'll be—
or will it turn—If hell is repetition....

When we finally fell silent the bats radared out
exactly as if they'd been waiting. Across the yards,
faint sounds of people arguing,

making supper, making love, music,
children playing, and animals.
Did you keep it, I asked him

and he opened the gas, just a notch,
and said yes,
of course.

EAGLE BRIDGE

You would like this mill brook.
It shivers. It rushes down its bed
as though rushing from cold.

Its bed is full of rocks
that scratch and break it.

Its bed curves up the banks
so you can see how curved the earth is
and water's curvaceous course on it.

It is a noisy lover.

On the bottom a bottle, a blue milk carton
and a scrap of foil, appearing to ripple—
the brook's smiling trick.

Skinpricks of mist and the scale of trees,
wet cedar the whole of June.
And the slugs, when they stretch?
Glorious.

A fine rain began as I crossed
and green moss sprang underfoot
just so, and boughs held forth rainwater
with your scent. I had to stop.
Had to rest my forehead against a white birch.

Having been invited in.

Having thought so little of it.

SUMMER HOLIDAY

I'd heard chanterelles could be found
near the creekbed on the opposite shore
after a rain so when the air cleared
and the lake was calm we paddled out,

me in the stern for a change, steering.
We crossed under a high circling osprey,
slid up to the bank through reeds
and lily pads; Marilyn stepped out,

hauled the canoe onto sand
bruising the wild mint that spread
in all directions, fur-leaved, stems
nearly purple with vigour. On the lake

the sun had been warm; here
redwood and Douglas fir rose a cool
fifty feet before branching. We started in
through the shade, picking our way

between mud-bound roots toward
the sound of the creek, the ground
sucking at our weight. Marilyn
walked ahead, til the mud

took my foot. Swallowed
my leg up to the knee, pitching me forward,
hands scrabbling at roots,
and I shouted, and Marilyn turned,

but the shout continued on past both Marilyn
and the creek, visible now through the trees,
to a pile of white bones, big ones,
a large animal picked clean,

their light clarifying the murk the way
creekwater sharpens the sound of mud,
the way osprey dive after rain.
Pulling out was a rehearsal for death—

Marilyn offered her arms,
        I held on, we
                pulled. We did,

though she may have forgotten that now.
As I have forgotten
whose arm, mine or hers, sank back
to retrieve my sandal, my

physical memory—strength
of a superhero wresting the hapless
from certain doom—may be invention.
We washed in the creek,

then we examined the bones. Took three
back: a single vertebra
and two longish paddles
with spatulate ends; held them up

to our necks and ears as though
decking ourselves out for a trip to town
and someone took a picture.
Marilyn kept two; the third

stayed on the porch and became
the spine of a wasp's nest.
We did find the chanterelles,
picked some for supper, cooked them

with garlic and mint. I would like sometime
to have another look at those bones.
When I gave her the picture the winter I left,
Marilyn held it by a corner and said "Oh"

and gave a short laugh.
There's nothing mysterious after all;
mud fills a space between roots,
a cow wanders out from the farm over the hill.

SLEEP WALKING

Twigs and scraps of yellow leaf in the eaves.
Outside the window stretching away rooftops and windows.
When the temperature reaches a certain degree.
The dun pigeon ruffles its breast.
I read aloud the blind sheep from *One Fish Two Fish*.
Marching "from there to here, from here to there."
Sam sleeps. I tuck the blanket over his shoulders.

The path is a transverse angle that crosses so.
As I move downward the hill to the left rises.
To the right rooftops and windows fall away glittering.
Through them far below the silver river.
When the air reaches a certain temperature.
Clouds ruffle in from the east dun-grey and bulging.
I pull the jacket over my shoulders.

Jeffery Donaldson
[b. 1960]

Jeffery Donaldson teaches poetry in the English department at McMaster University.
He has published two books of poetry, *Once Out of Nature* (1991) and *Waterglass* (1999).
He lives on the Niagara Escarpment near Grimsby with his wife and two children.

RENTED SPACE

Casual snow shortages at first,
cutbacks and inconspicuous
diminishments, the field stretching
to make ends meet: uncoverings.
Then, nothing left but a matted
quilt of old grass, re-stitched in parts
with needlings of a thready brook
that just catch the disentangled
seamings cornerwise; and closer
to where we stand, a stooped maple
set to one side like the bulbless

antique base of a standing lamp,
long since missing its shade.
But for the light that goes quietly
straightening about in the first
hours, there is no movement
in the place: a stillness, a clearing
of unseasonable weather.
A vacancy! Autumn's the first
to drop everything, but can't
unload its rose mahoganies,
and who will lift down summer's green
chandeliers in a tinkling wind?
In light of such unforthcoming
appearances, in come leafbuds strung
on their branches like a festive
string of unblinking fairy lights,
an impossible looking weed,
and five or six flustered tulips
aiming frantically to pitch
themselves into a shifting wind,
making the best of things. For spring,
the question is one of being
in the right place at the right time.

WIND

Forty paces from the house I live in,
across the street, beside the stone wall
of mottled grey boulders cobbled into place,
the men appear once more, the ones who come

without a word or sign to stand beside
the tall, medieval, wooden catapult
wheeled on stone wheels down the street in the dark
from across the bare outlands, stopping there

opposite my house, beside the stone wall,
and together load awkward, unwieldy
sandbags that are the size of dead bodies
onto the catapult and launch them one

after another against the house front,
and sometimes one of them will come straight up
to the house and bang on the window panes
with his bare fist and then go back to his place,

and when I have just about had enough
they will suddenly stop, break up, and go,
and just leave the sandbags and the catapult
where they lie, if you can believe it.

BEARINGS

Four chubby angels, like grown cherubim,
blow at their simple trumpets from the four
corners of the page, a yellowing cloth

aged some few hundred years, wrinkled and stained.
Such outsize messengers are the only
recognizable human furniture

to be found on this chart of otherwise
distant islands, faintly green blocks of land
sketched within the margins of drawn water,

numbers of ink-spill settlements upstream,
and more than enough sea to get there by,
from where we begin. And still farther north,

regions of the unobserved, with the odd
guessed-at frontier ventured: the conveniently
unknown used for titles and legends.

It isn't anywhere that we know of
by heart, a landscape only dimly
reminiscent of where people might once

have got to, or neared, circling and recircling
till the track they followed forward was their own.
How they must have looked then by the green place,

beyond themselves, entrusting their giddy
presence to the bearings they jotted down,
recounting details that returned to them

of the ways taken, wanting as they did
to come back. Hard to believe, as it is,
that anyone then or even later

could have used this page, water stiffened,
to get anywhere, least of all that broad
unfinished landscape we navigate towards,

being, as we are, unable to point out,
put a finger on, the small print that legend
has it marks our settling forth: *you are here.*

SPENDING PART OF THE WINTER

On a bunch of cold Sundays
in March you brought flowers,
always early at breakfast,
adding them each one by one

to a vase of fresh water
on a table near the door.
They came alone—each one
wilting before the second

coming–stemmed the bouquet
I imagined we were
gathering there, and rose
clear as the empty vase.

ABOVE THE RIVER

for John Reibetanz

The paperweight was like a crystal ball,
or half of one. At bottom its round sphere
was flat, shelved high on the kitchen wall.

The concave glass and water clear as air,
if nothing I could read a future by,
cast light on the small elfin theatre

that glowed within the bowl, of earth and sky,
a pastoral stage of maple tree and field,
threaded by a small brook, and a grain-high

stone wall that climbs to where any child
that looked in would see an empty cottage
on a hill, its lightless windows, wood piled

by the door, smokeless chimney, tiny hedge.
Every last detail, icons on the walk
of some impenetrable pilgrimage.

As though a day might bring me there and back.
Not far from here, a valley of idle
pastures grazes the long walls of loose rock,

and the road that parts it in the middle
bends away from itself, like a stick
in water, and then straightens and sidles

through a stand of elms to a thicket
of primrose on a hill, and disappears.
A soft muck in the fields, and a small lake

always come of the rain that falls and clears,
falls and clears endlessly, gorging the streams
and running like silk over the filled cisterns.

One stream comes through under the stand of elms,
turns there and passes beyond the primrose
bushes, where it rises, overwhelms

the stone footings of a small bridge, flows
under, back out, and keeps to the field's edge.
A voice of looped water-rubble echoes

its giggles under the arch of the bridge,
then turns suddenly quiet in the daylight.
Often enough, there was a dark green sedge

on the bank, meadow grass, a featherweight
of broom and milkwort. I would look to find
them most times knocking around in the bright

fall airs, or chittering about the wind,
but with the endless rains the water's brim
crested the ledge, and lurched at the streamlined

bank so high the flora bowed to the swim
and lope of it and went under. Grasses
wavered in the silent aquarium.

The sinews, tendons and slippery laces
were nudged and suppled by the lavish flow,
and watercouch lolled in the oasis.

A sleepy action, a buoyant heft of slow-
motion undulance in the drowned flowers
drew you in, and its eddy dizzied you.

On the surface, above the dim parlours
of underwater flumes and myriad ways,
the skylights stirred, diaphanous colour

of fleece, or a lusterless silver gauze
that was frayed out like flag-shreds rustled
in the wind, and blinded you in a maze

of flippant writhings. It was all restless
shimmer and mirage, a tomfoolery
of angled cloud-lights on the brim, useless

in all until you looked within, through tea-
coloured water to the luminous glade
where the soporific green rocked dreamily,

where emerald torches and a phosphor-jade,
the tapered ambers of a chandelier
burned in the foliage, glimmered and swayed,

and worked like a charm. That moment you peer
deep into the paperweight's crystal dome,
the underwater globe of house and tree

are depths in which you breathe—the shaken home
long stilled—a clear floating of tinsel snow
that descends out of nowhere like a dream.

And from his kitchen chair, a watchful boy
looks up to it, sees what might someday pass
for true: his twilight's egg-shell afterglow

of blue, his picture of imagined peace
in fluid airs that magnify and cleanse
the small firmament in the waterglass.

So the greens there under the crescent lens
of the water wavered and broke through. The trees
and scrub in the open field, an ambiance

of flowers in the summer-evening breeze,
the stone wall on the hill, the cold, slow
bend of the river itself, all of these

were seen for what they are, imagine how
high above, in a vanishing jet stream,
sky-lit reflections looked through until now.

Gold flux, lapis crest, the earth's limbic brim
of unclouded currents over a bent
world, blue and green, flowed over them.

I never went back to see the stream abate,
or the bank-grass bleaching and going dry,
but thought later of the paperweight,

and its field and tree, where no small boy
under unlooked-for, over-arching blues,
heads back up the winding brook with an eye

for the tiny hill-top and the house.

Bruce Taylor
[b. 1960]

Bruce Taylor is twice-winner of the A.M. Klein Award for Poetry—for *Cold Rubber Feet*
(1989) and *Facts* (1998). *Prism International* awarded him their first Earle Birney Prize
for Poetry. He was born in Vancouver and presently lives in Wakefield, Quebec.

SOCIAL STUDIES

"This is your history," said the teacher of it.
And it was. So, now, is she,
passing around her portrait of a Cree
Indian in a top hat. Any child could see
how meticulously bad that drawing was:
a face like a heraldic shield,
with stuck-on eyes and cheeks of pencil fuzz;
a mouth of line, and, dangling beneath,
a canted Celtic alphabet of teeth.
In hands like dinner forks it seemed to hold
a strip of parchment, sumptuously scrolled;
and this, Miss Ward revealed to us, revealed,
in Bible Gothic, signed with an x and sealed,
how Indians had given up the deeds
to our dominion, in return for beads.

Beside the blackboard, maps were tacked
which showed the world cut up like orange rind,
sliced and sectioned, air-brushed, dotted lined
and crammed with calculations to distract
one's young, impressionable mind
from the corrupt, the riotously inexact
contours of unornamented fact.
For there on the grid, like a spilled drink:
the land of Canada, vast and milkshake pink,
pocked with lakes spattered with islands that had lakes,
a pattern of mistakes within mistakes,
profusely annotated with the names of towns:
Manigotagan, Flin Flon, Churchill Downs,
stuck like mayflies in a web of red
roads and rails, unravelling like thread
among the moraines and glacier melts,
dust bowls, tree lines, lichen belts,
along the flumes and gravel beds
where European traders packed their pelts
across our atlas, laying traps
to capture beavers when there were no maps.

Our history—I'll be honest—is at most
a theory which the facts do not confute.
Some people came from somewhere to a coast
as ragged as the salt line on a boot,
and pitched their cabins in the wilderness,
and did the things that somehow led to this.

The country I live in is a patch of thorns
below a culvert in a sunken plot
where burly geese with necks like flugelhorns
intimidate the pigeons and are shot
by a district sales manager named Russ.
And that's it. Our lives, our landscape, us.
But near the train yard, where I catch my bus,
a late October frost has clenched the ground,
the football field is hard as frozen meat,
enormous gulls are swaggering around
with snowflakes on their orange rubber feet.
They cruise through stubble with their beaks ajar
shrieking that what they are they are they are.

WHAT THE MAGDALEN ISLANDS ARE LIKE

You come in through a rip in the fog
and touch down without radar
on House Harbour Island, if the pilot can find it,
a remnant of scuffed linoleum in the sullen
gulf. The airport sits at sea
level in the beach stubble like a sandpiper's
nest and the sea lies at eye
level like an optical illusion
as you walk downstairs out of the airplane
into the air.

The wind is unbelievable.
It roars in off the gulf,
slapping the waves like a speedboat.
It lashes your face with your own hoodstrings
and strikes panic into your plastic bags.
It evaporates the bare rock
and makes off with the topsoil. It hoots
like a bandit in the church tower,
molesting the bells, and comes at you from all
sides, smudging the islands
into the ocean and ruffling the actual map
on which they sit, flat as coffee stains, wasting
away.

The Magdalens, you realize,
are dissolving. The neat little houses are temporary.
Pitched on cinderblocks in the dunegrass
and painted like boats, they don't seem built
so much as cast
like dice and the people don't seem so much born here
as blown ashore.
They catch fish but eat canned
soup and make love
over sea caves and salt tunnels, feeling the gulf
rumble in its excavations, feeling the dry land
rolling back into the water like a whale's hump.

You pile your bags under an oilcloth
and drive out on the only road as far as it goes
to a prong of the coastline where it butts the wind.
You go walking in a borrowed raincoat
over the rocks.
You stand on the cliff wall like a bared root, your nude
cheeks scrubbed red. Around you the dwarf trees
stick out like skinned elbows, clenching rations of soil.
Below you the surf is smeared red where the red cliff
seeps and bleeds into the ocean. The gulls
make doll noises, nesting on waves.
The pack ice
pitches and tilts over a surge
of sticks and debris
and right where the gulf crawls up on the shore,
heaving and retching,
a dead cormorant flies
face down in the water.

The Magdalen Islands are like
that.

DOODLE

I have doodled a fantastic picture,
definitely worth keeping.
But what does it mean?
It shows a man in black pajamas sleeping
in a black gelatinous machine.
He is a lunatic, I think.
He dreams of piloting a submarine
in latitudes of permanent black ink
through oceans of condensed malarkey,
spirals, hieroglyphics, grids,
corkscrews, checkerboards and pyramids.
But he is not himself at all.
His mind feels funny being fondled by
that Muse of Incoherence who reclines
above him on a cloud of wavy lines,
jumbling the objects in his sky.

Chinese letters and occult designs.
What could any of it signify?
That ink is shallow, and yet deep.
That meanings mate and multiply,
tousling the air above our sleep.
That q resembles p, as x does y.

Or something else. But what? The truth
is tortuous, you'd be surprised.
This drowsy harlequin materialized
while I was on the telephone arranging
for a cheque I'd written not to bounce.
I had some funds transferred between accounts,
and as my ghostly treasures were exchanging
values in the hidden vaults
of the magnetic storage-chambers where
the ciphers of my hedonism waltz,
this thing began appearing in a corner
of a page of my agenda and
inexorably snuck across the paper,
self-engendered, eerily unplanned,
like Escher's famous drawing of a hand
that draws a hand that draws another hand.

It happens quietly, without commotion.
Your mind is elsewhere. Something interferes
with empty paper and a thing appears:
a madman on a jewelled ocean.
And that is what my poem wants as well,
to make things happen, but without exertion—
baffling arabesques unfurled
like faxes from the underworld
in one authoritative motion.

It needs the fluency and expertise
of the ingenious, brainless world,
which doodles on itself incessantly,
scribbling meanders on the parched plateaus,
Moroccan carpets on a reptile's back,
black veins in the pliations of a rose,
medieval riddles in a woodworm's track.

The world is lavish, never at a loss.
It puts a caterpillar in a ball of string,
then dresses it in oriental cloth—
batik for the monarch's wing,
paisley for the moth.

It does all that without a plan,
lacquering the beetle's shell,
kinking the horns of the gazelle,
composing tracts of timeless nonsense
in the cursive of the runner bean.
Does anyone who sits beneath a willow
know what its gesticulations mean?
The speechless bulk of the created world
is made entirely out of marginalia,
weird caprices that assail
the central tissues. Oh, to fill the pale
middle of my life with frail
finials and diaphanous rosettes
and have a heart as pink and ruffled
and confused as an azalea!

THE SLOUGH

> Are the entrails clear, immaculate cabbage?
> —Theodore Roethke, "Unfold! Unfold!"

What's under the pudding skin, down in the slough
where the weed-pods root whose heads poke through
to goggle and bob in their seedy hats,
pithless and punch-drunk, chewed by gnats,
knocked flat by a damp, disagreeable breeze,
gusts of bad weather, abrupt as a sneeze
and stilt-birds sunk to their bamboo knees
in whatever is under the slough?

What's under the mud that schmecks our boots?
A raft of bedsprings lashed with roots,
spavined lumber, cans of glue,

electrical cables, lampreys, newts,
and, if what the neighbours say is true,
the ribs of a horse that once fell through
while pursuing a dog, who's in there too:
so all poor beasts that flit or thud
lie down with the frogs in the lathered mud,
who mate in the ruts where the tractor treads,
spin their milky, gelatinous threads
of spunk and spittle and clean, green eggs
that hatch like bean-sprouts, sprout hind legs
and rise, scientifically, out of the ooze
to walk upright in soft-soled shoes
and ponder the matter of what or who's
in the slough.

Off in the aftermath, what's up there?
A million metric tons of air.
Peacocks in the weeping figs
amble through a land of twigs
and flocks of phosphorescent, screaming
crook-nosed parrots copulate
upside down inside the gleaming
spirals of an iron gate.
Plying the trackless, gassy skies,
the wild cranes have crazy eyes
and jagged claws and skinny necks.
The natural world is quite complex.
Praising nature, one suspects
the Lombardy poplars pitch and sway
because these trees are having sex
with other trees three miles away.
Help me Ted, my days are dense
with moments that do not make sense!
Where is the love that spins the gears,
that honks the goose and flaps the crane
and cranks the sun and other stars
across the crinkled diaphane?
Where is the foot that pumps the treadle?
Whose the hand that tracks the moth?
Who scales the wooden frame of evening
tacking bolts of yellow cloth?

Who ignores this? When is ever?
Why am I stupid? What is true?
None of that transmutes to answers
anywhere next to, beneath, or on top of,
over or under the slough.

LOVELY

The past is lovely, it lasts forever.
Somewhere, I'm still
lying under the lawn sprinkler
with no coppertone on,
the grass cool and elastic under my back,
a black spaniel nuzzling my feet.
The cars are old-fashioned and optimistic,
the people who drive them
have fallen in love with the future.
They can't know that when they get here
they will love the past more,
that the present will look like
a stupendous machine
for forcing things to stop existing.
Well, to live for the moment
is best, but the moments, the little
jiffies, they are startled
to be here, like
the high-shouldered cuprous beetles
that live beneath patio stones,
if you're curious you lift one up
and let it run down your arm.
The other ones scoot for cover,
struggling down into the leaf mulch,
kicking frantically.

David Manicom
[b. 1960]

David Manicom is the author of seven books, including four collections of poetry. *The Burning Eaves,* was short-listed for the 2004 Governor General's Literary Award. His first novel, *The School at Chartres* was published in 2005. A Canadian foreign-service officer, he has served in Moscow, Islamabad, and Beijing. He lives in Gatineau, Quebec.

THE BURNING EAVES

Fire to the level of my eyes, into the trees
Whose leaves now merge their colours with the birds;
Angle of sun beneath our porch's eaves
To catch at last this kitchen-window sink.

I pull white plates from grey beneath the foam
Like shells emerging from our portioned sea.
Rinsed, they shine. Brief in the rack, then swaddled
In the tea towel, in your hands. Scrub and dip and pass

As the louvered pattern of the shutters' shadow
Bands your wrists with their late summer source.
All grief is captured by the acts of love,
In how we work to hand things back and forth.

SEPTEMBER GALE WITH HIGH THEORY

Windy all day and now through a restless night
The gusts bodychecking the century timbers.

Early leavetaking of leaves in the year of storm,
All summer expected highs surpassed, the norms belied—

Though forecasters continue to rely on their weather
Systems, a scholasticism of thunder and sun,

While the telescopes study at a great remove
The history of the periodic table.

September still. Yet curled leaves the colour of old maps
Already fill each gap of hedge, heap under cedars

Or catch, tattering in chain-link.
But no season so unseasonal as to make us shrink

From the laws of nature, from the nature of having laws—
The physicists unwrap flaw after flaw, yet all fall

I've read in vain for the claim there are no laws at all.
Amid coat-rack trees after a day of gales

A singular maple is still crayola crimson
In the abandoned lot across the corner,

Flaring above a brake of lilac's barren ribs.
Hung in the pure air between

A squirrel pauses like a kink in the telephone line,
The wind whines through the wires, reaps the trees,

Two oak leaves settle on the porch like copper gloves.
All circles prove ellipses, the long slopes of gravity

Disappear into each singularity
(That empty shell without a shell),

Into the purer art of gauge bosons and charms;
An alarm of red-shifts, new measurements required—

And the hesitancy of the particles
That never exist in one particular place

Is my longing to unlace this thought without motion.
In the end, the beginning, the great inflation

Everywhere found in the wind of the same place—
Before the bang, in theory, mere fold of empty space

Not even hovering, not even silent, not even
"the field dancing out of the braking cosmic vacuum."

A November storm rocks our old house in September,
Creaks the walls like bedsprings under love.

Awake in the meantime, ears strained, a single word
Speaks flat and disembodied down the hall—

Leaf of small moan from my child dreaming,
The seam of a seam, a palm that opens and turns.

READING ANGLO-SAXON WHEN SPRING COMES EARLY

Aquiver after the downward plunge, firelit silver—
A dagger in a table top, rude trestle, mead—

The feasters sheered into vision from their venison
And victory songs by the sight of one slight sparrow

Passing from snowing darkness through their narrow hall
And into the night again. A life.

One winter evening, pinioned on the bus from work,
I wrote: *So arrival of each hoped-for future*

Means a hoped-for future lost—

Closing the phrase behind me as an awkward wing,
The lurching muteness, the bus like the apostrophe

Before possession, that still walk home.
The Outaouais
                    turns its slow, northern curve around the town

Into a dipping gallop through the gull-thick narrows
At Deschênes, and away, its speed below the yards

—Its silver plunge and sinuosity—clearing
The gaze for elevation, away in every aspect

From the gravelly streets and the plump knuckling
Of the branches when spring comes before its time

With the cardinals' big whistle out of the old realms of cedar
Through each warmer dawn, and a row of daffodils

All facing one way beneath our windowsill
With ruched collar-frills, as yellow as if our youngest child

Had filled them in with crayon. To lift the angle
Of the wing. Up the street where a chorale of tulips

Surrounds a garden's centrepiece of stone
I find my Flora and Antaeus selves, can't stop

Forever living in more than one myth, with doubling
Arrivals into loss.... Whereas the tulips

Delayed by the special beauty of delay (to lift)
Are not quite open until, at least, tomorrow—

Grooved, upheld, waxy, pursed: two prayerful hands,
So that along the swelling pods a blush of red, of white:

The seam
Of the cardinal, the sparrow, of the long, long horizon.

ANCHOR POST

I drove from downtown for one last traipse
down a sidewalk sunk into lawn, its line
of cement islands, back a chicory-blue lane
to turn on a hill and watch the barns stand,

abandoned ships. August twitch-grass rasping
at my thighs, steady *sip sip* of crickets.
The fence posts were leaning. Keeping them straight
had helped keep father standing, balanced

against need, thwarting the earth from tugging
their wood back into humus, the mossed lawns
from creeping over the nicks of his spade,
the hedgerows from colonizing fields.

Even one corner-post, waist thick but gnawed
near soil, had begun to pitch down its head.
(Half a day we'd have spent sinking that shaft
of white, shaven trunk into a four foot hole,

tamping the loose dirt with an iron pole,
bracing this anchor on its slender neighbour
with looped wire racheted to a tight steel braid
by the shovel's work-polished handle.)

Now the grey wood is rivered by wind,
the grain engraved, and knots where branches
once veered toward light have fallen away
until the dried post is filling with eyes.

Its rotting top has sunk into a nest
for finches and a portal for rain,
so decay can attack as it attacks
these counties, from inside out, eating toward skin.

There is no taut fence for it to anchor now;
the loss of what it once held up helps pull
it down. Only a few strings rusted to black
cling between the titled posts beneath the grass,

slack and gripless under whispering grass
until, perhaps, near the end of October
when the anchor is gone and the other posts
have been hauled and split and stacked in cords,

an employee of the corporate farm
that will buy and manage this stead, this small
nest-egg of acres, might feel a snag
in his six-furrow plough when levelling the land

into one, long, uninterrupted field,
and climb down to untangle the sock
from a bit of black web.
I could see father, holding the U-shaped

staples in his teeth as his smooth hammer
clipped the strands snug.... I clamped both hands
to the sunken top for leverage and jumped up
to give my weight. Stubborn fibres creaked

and split as I hugged and wrestled it flat.
It lay, thick as a barrel. I sat, then lashed
with my fist, skinning one knuckle red,
cursed its ridiculous, graceless shape,

pounded dull thuds on its passive, weathered shell.
He'd balanced so long, on the thin borders
between drench and drought, harvest and bankruptcy,
working repairs in the narrow regions of air

next to the spinning knives of machinery,
taking the edges into his creasing life.
He'd balanced so long. How he's fallen over
and these fences are following him down.

LOVE ALIGHT

Red-winged blackbird settles on brittle brown cattail
—too heavy for the perch, hawk in a sapling—
sways left and right dappling red across dull April marsh,
the fen-edge of fields harrowed, seeded, still dirt and naked
as the weather. Slaked of flight, sways, a slow metronome
stroking a portrait, a child's song, in the clear medium
of rhythm, tippling through an airy precise inscription
of the relations between the weight of a reed-riding bird
and the flightpath of a bird, and this spindle of earth
and its length, the give of its shaft, the dearth or depth
of root, the breadth of swing, its degrees of unbalancing.
Picture this: a bird tocks, beak parted and neck thrust

to whistle out to the stands of willow, until, just
 as its rocking chair dies to a stop, just as all
leanings are sketched off hand into air with the sway stalled
and almost pinned by the full stop that approaches at last,
just in the tremble—the bird is gone, a gust of wings,
cattail lingering blunt as a stump, plain as amputation,
blackbird red-winged and hectoring away, the ammunition
of the marksman, ambushing calm into motion, the sway
that undergoes us. Watch sometime: it's the way of birds
and true love: forces almost stayed, swamp still, and the bird
gone off, disturbing some other axel of the heart.

George Elliott Clarke
[b. 1960]

George Elliott Clarke is a seventh-generation African-Canadian. He has published poetry
and fiction. His dramatic works include two verse-dramas, *Whylah Falls: The Play* and
Beatrice Chancy. He has written two opera libretti, *Beatrice Chancy* and *Québécité*. In
2001 he won the Governor General's Literary Award for Poetry for *Execution Poems*. He
is the E.J. Pratt Professor of Canadian Literature at the University of Toronto. His novel,
George and Rue, was published in 2005.

LOOK HOMEWARD, EXILE

I can still see that soil crimsoned by butchered
Hog and imbrued with rye, lye, and homely
Spirituals everybody must know,
Still dream of folks who broke or cracked like shale:
Pushkin, who twisted his hands in boxing,
Marrocco, who ran girls like dogs and got stabbed,
Lavinia, her teeth decayed to black stumps,
Her lovemaking still in demand, spitting
Black phlegm—her pension after twenty towns,
And Toof, suckled on anger than no Baptist
Church could contain, who let wrinkled Eely
Seed her moist womb when she was just thirteen.
    And the tyrant sun that reared from barbed-wire
Spewed flame that charred the idiot crops

To Depression, and hurt my granddaddy
To bottle after bottle of sweet death,
His dreams beaten to one, tremendous pulp,
Until his heart seized, choked; his love gave out.
    But Beauty survived, secreted
In freight trains snorting in their pens, in babes
Whose faces were coal-black mirrors, in strange
Strummers who plucked Ghanaian banjos, hummed
Blind blues—precise, ornate, rich needlepoint,
In sermons scorched with sulphur and brimstone,
And in my love's dark, orient skin that smelled
Like orange peels and tasted like rum, good God!
    I remember my Creator in the old ways:
I sit in taverns and stare at my fists;
I knead earth into bread, spell water into wine.
Still, nothing warms my wintery exile—neither
Prayers nor fine love, neither votes nor hard drink:
For nothing heals those saints felled in green beds,
Whose loves are smashed by just one word or glance
Or pain—a screw jammed in thick, straining wood.

KING BEE BLUES

I'm an ol' king bee, honey,
Buzzin' from flower to flower.
I'm an ol' king bee, sweets,
Hummin' from flower to flower.
Women got good pollen;
I get some every hour.

There's Lily in the valley
And sweet honeysuckle Rose too;
There's Lily in the valley
And sweet honeysuckle Rose too.
And there's pretty black-eyed Susan,
Perfect as the night is blue.

You don't have to trust
A single, black word I say.

You don't have to trust
A single, black word I say.
But don't be surprised
If I sting your flower today.

MONOLOGUE FOR SELAH BRINGING SPRING TO WHYLAH FALLs

I cry, in the vernacular, this plain manifesto,
No matter how many fishmen offer you their laps,
Or how contrary you are in the morning,
Or how your hair gleams like dark lightning,
Or how many lies the encyclopedia preserves,
Because, Selah, I won't play them parlour-seducer games—
Card tricks of chat, sleight-of-hand caresses—
Or stick my head in books. I love your raspy,
Backwoods accent, your laughter like ice breaking up!
I'd burn dictionaries to love you even once!
Selah, I tell myself I come to Whylah Falls
To spy the river crocheted with apple blossoms,
To touch you whose hair fans in mystery,
Whose smile is Cheshire and shadow and bliss,
Whose scent is brown bread, molasses, and milk,
Whose love is Coca-Cola and rose petals
In a ship's cabin soaked in saltwater.
But my lies lie. My colleged speech ripens before you,
Becomes Negro-natural, those green, soiled words
Whose roots mingle with turnip, carrot, and squash,
Keeping philology fresh and tasty.
You slouch and sigh that sassy, love speech,
And aroused, very aroused, I exalt
Your decisive eyes, your definitive lips,
Your thighs that'd be emboldened by childbirth,
For when you move, every line of poetry quakes,
And I inhale your perfume—ground roses,
Distilled petals, praise your blue skirt bright
Against your bare, black legs! *You won't wear stockings!*
I'm scripting this lyric because I'm too shy
To blurt my passion for you, Selah!
My history is white wine from a charred log,
A white horse galloping in a meadow,

A dozen chicks quitting an egg carton tomb,
But also selfish, suicidal love.
I don't want that!
    Selah, I want to lie beside you
And hear you whisper this poem and giggle.
Selah, I thought this poem was finished!
Selah, I am bust upside the head with love!

BLUE ELEGIES: I. V

    October, Gothic October: no lovers loiter, lounge,
in Annapolis Royal's "Historic Gardens."
    Naturally: Love poems wither in our bleak, stony,
frigid, hostile, brutal Canuck anthologies.
    Maybe all hardy Canadian poetry erupts lavishly
from some solitary, sullen naturalist's notebook.
    See! A last bee, still stockpiling pollen, hums hotly
against this Octobral creep of cold. Octopoid
    networks and wires of downed branches and briars
and twigs, prickling and muddling and needling, obscure
    a scrappy bit of light, famished, gorging on a slice
of brown-black, brackish, leaf-plastered,
    subsidiary pond, wafting orange-green-brown lily pads
and a certain tangy tart stink—
    maybe of algae and oak leaves, decaying,
and the *bizz* of wispy, final, waifish insects.
    Everything here is allegory for allegations.
Look! The dyked marsh is sucking, slurping, the Fundy—
    the tall, hay-like grass, hay-smelling, springs
out of rank black mud, crabby, with fronds and fringes of muck,
    then sodden, mud-coralled water giving back
a sky of grey-and-white-peppered clouds, blue shards also,
    conjoining dark evergreen spikes,
grey, ghostly, scrawny things, or gold or gold-orange sprays
    and tufts the colour of a blonde *fillette.*
Nearby accumulates a pungent cascade of leaves,
    then the thick, gigantic stalks of marsh grass,
with sunlight baying in—nostalgic, regretful, imploring—
    like the speaker in a John Thompson *ghazal,*

with the last maniacal mosquitoes, whining, *comme des pleûtres*,
    and strafing still-fragrant, still-bloody roses,
near where the train tracks are *Kaput*, all torn up now,
    these roses glistening and perfuming dogmatically
while the eye hooks on notorious, flagrant, orange-red trees
    and bowers of vines, other overhanging things,
darkening, just as the sun darkens while first launching light
    against the dykes, the marsh, in dying brilliance
equivalent to what Carman paints in "Low Tide at Grand Pré."
    Dismissive of our idiot anxieties and ironies,
stately lances the august, sepulchral, elegiac light.

Richard Sanger
[b. 1960]

Richard Sanger has published two collections, *Shadow Cabinet* (1996) and *Calling Home* (2002); his poems have also appeared in such publications as the *Times Literary Supplement* and the *London Review of Books*. His plays, which include *Not Spain* and *Two Words for Snow*, have been finalists for the Chalmers Prize, the Dora Awards and the Governor General's Literary Awards.

TRAVELS WITH MY AUNT

When I first saw my mother's brother's new wife,
What I saw were two shopping bags,
Laden with food, which her arms cradled around.
She was coming up the path to the big house.

All summer long, I spent the afternoons
Reading G. A. Henty adventures for boys in the bungalow.
When we had lunch on the veranda, her bikini top
Dipped down like the sunglasses along her nose.

I was just learning to put two and two together.
She wouldn't talk to me or my brothers.
I would lie on my belly, dig my hips into the mattress
And, more likely than not, be crossing the Khyber Pass

Or holding a fort set on some promontory.
She was doing her best to remain collected, and calm,
Under the surveillance of the assembled relatives.
Her lips winced at the taste of our coffee.

The plot leaped forward: I was drifting headlong
Down a river, towards the Whirlpool of No Return.
After her swims, she lay sunbathing on the dock
And a drop of water glistened in her belly-button.

We came to a clearing. The Hun had retreated
To a temple full of incense and treasures.
An attack would be lunacy but we had no choice—
There was an English life at stake. I discarded the map

And, by examining the underside of a leaf,
Plotted the best approach. Through the window, I saw her
Meting out a laundry line of underclothes and linen.
The bungalow smelled of yellow pages and cedar.

A woodpecker tack-tack-tacked against a hollow tree.
A spider crawled up the screen. I got the message:
They had taken the General's daughter captive
And I, I was the man to free her.

RACCOON

A racket out the back door and who to blame?
Who but you, oh permanent grudge-holder,
Hunkering back for more of the same
With that permanent hunch and chip on your shoulder?
In the bug-filled evening, I stand and watch
As two dark humps go nose-first through the garbage
Like a pair of over-lunched bureaucrats
Picking their vicarious way through my files,
Picking through them till out it all spills—
The little shopliftings and indiscretions,
The unrecycled jars and unreconstructed thrills,
The filthy thoughts, the girls, I squeezed and dumped
And that unnumbered account in Switzerland…

What business of yours is it? I almost ask,
Forgetting for once the little I've learnt:
That you are me as much as I am you.
What I mean is, when mighty Gitchi Manitou
Or whoever ruled these woods and prairies
And Good and Bad sprung as randomly as berries
From the Pre-Cambrian rock, it was you alone
Who'd rubbed your nose in original sin:
You knew you were guilty from day one
And went waddling through the woods with that secret
Eating away at your guts... Oh, you may claim
You were just a beast, pure and simple,
Going proudly about your business
Like everyone else, nothing more, nothing less;
A bit decrepit maybe, but with a conscience
That was lily-white, or perhaps none at all,
As you pilfered robin's eggs in perfect innocence
Or raided the stores squirrels hid in trunks.
Yes, dear, we all had our better days... Once.
Go ahead, show us your baby pictures,
If you want, roll over and do cute tricks
For the ladies. It won't work for me—
I know all the awful things you've done
And weigh each one in my hand like a stone
—the kind of stone I'd like to brain you with—
As you malinger in the bush. Take this. And this.

LATE IN THE WEST

Speak, speak, speak. Carthage has been deleted
And on the branches, in their serried ranks,
Like diplomats clutching their valises,
The songbirds, my love, await their next posting.
I unroll an old floor plan, ponder thermal baths,
Patios, wine cellars, the whole gone gamut,
Fording mud-stopped aqueducts on my way over
For the late show at the amphitheatre.
I, who in the tarmac schoolyard fought
and in toga and laurels crossed the floor,
Now watch night nestle in the grooves
Of the fluted columns left half-assembled,

Or half-fallen down, now hear the din
Of cock-fights and combat stain the air.
Flecks of dried blood speckle the limestone
—terracotta red on the ochre surface—
And ahead the air-brushed horizon
Announces its enormous epiphanies,
doing the colours: orange, salmon pink, plum…
By all means, decline the invitation,
Pretend that life goes on, things aren't so bad,
Say you find such florid statements strange.
Familiar, though, this intrepid brood
Setting off to breast the winds and draw the curtains,
Little troublemakers, pedantic twitters,
Stringing their requiems across the western sky.

WISH

Let the afternoon sink
Slowly though, oh slowly, please,
Like Venice in the mud.
I see my schoolboy knees
Plunged in black rubber boots:
The columns, you would think—

No, let the columns sink
And the Empire's arches fall.
On an island of pines
And pink granite, just north
Of Pointe-au-Baril
And down from Manitoulin,

On the back verandah
Of an old log cabin,
Facing west, over Lake Huron,
I want to lie on the mattress
I lie on, drink white wine,
And read, and be, Lord Byron;

To lie there and swat flies
As some pliant young thing
Dances in with a tray

And a letter for me
(The Countess sends her love)
And the hum in my ears

Grows louder and louder:
Is it rush-hour Toronto,
The Turks storming Lepanto
Or the winged god that stung
This ruddy swollen sky?
I slap my shoulder. Blood.

Now let the fever rise
As the sun sinks, let it
Climb through the pink granite,
The pines, the violet sky.
Bring me a pen and paper.
Today I'm thirty-six.

MADONNA OF THE NEW WORLD

God the Father has skipped town
And left them homeless and frozen,
Two figures caught in the family snap,
Immigrants to a cold zone.
They could be waiting on the doorstep,
Passports in hand, him in swaddling clothes.

She'll never really learn English.
He'll go to school and work on Sunday
And the background will darken with varnish,
The shadows growing in Tuscany
As the sun coasts above the yard in which
He hurls a lunch-hour snow-ball.

But the target here is him, his face turned
To face us, vacant as a goldfish.
Beware, though, that arm raised to prime
Her breast, the fingers
That can't quite grasp the point
Of such bounty, such emptiness.

Walid Bitar

[b. 1961]

Walid Bitar was born in Beirut. He immigrated to Canada in 1969. He has taught English, most recently at Lebanese American University. His poetry collections are *Maps with Moving Parts* (1988), *2 Guys on Holy Land* (1993), and *Bastardi Puri* (2005)

SPORTS

My brand of surveillance, no need for gadgets—
spoils are divided between eyes and ears.
It's true I miss the latest in lasers.
But I have no trouble making out hatchets.

I work in privacy, and for that reason
they stuck a camera up my neighbour's asshole.
All day he's bent over mooning my soul.
'Beyond one's means,' they call his visions.

The tribes I'm dealing with don't prize language.
They sip away at it like grape juice.
The boys don't give it time to age.
No taste buds ... they even gnaw roots.

As for the main course, that's human flesh.
Where are the gods, the sacrifice theories?
No home base—the East is the West.
One day it's slaughter, the next touchy-feely

speeches about peace, bread and land.
What the words mean isn't part of the package,
like seven nights advertised in Baghdad.
The days are spent back home on the ranch.

One day I gave this bandwagon the finger
(unconsciously)—now I'm on some list.
They mispronounce me. I've become 'bitter'.
Some of the hangers-on even lisp,

which doesn't make them any less vicious.
Quite the contrary: they have more to prove,
insist I pose as tequila (I'm cactus).
Gentlemen, if you feel pricks in your stool,

they're not mine. They're from citizens
you recently paged to rat on the guests.
Every envious doormat a witness ...
Can hyperactive ones become hit men?

What for an encore in the next world?
No time and space there, lucre or turds—
just memory ... and what to do with it?
Eternity, after all, has some standards.

PASHA

One moment words are refugees from Troy,
the next Greeks desperate to reclaim Helen.
They have no loyalty—boy toys may stick
to their native tongues, but then comes heaven
where language, that Falstaff, can't follow its Hals.

No dictionary taught me how to rule my lands.
I threw the Hippocratic oath into evidence,
so the child would have to drown or swim,
and doctor wave after wave of testimony
to convince our jury the sea was insane.

This worked. Encouraged, I turned on mountains,
claimed they were a frozen music
the soaring temperatures left unexplained.
So I imposed an atonal rule,
martial hits mostly, because in the past
silence had ignored my romantic overtures.

Syllables that survived I divided and ruled
until not one sound had a reputation,

good or bad. Created equal,
they returned to the democratic womb.

I was no Ottoman; this brand of politics
stripped me of laws, courtiers and subjects.
On the other hand, spies sent from Vienna
were no more dangerous than pastry chefs.
There was nothing for them to discover;
they invented new flakes, new jams ...

I sampled these, and sometimes enjoyed them.
One day I may immigrate to the West;
that way I can take part in its conquest
of what I used to be, perhaps still am.
A worst-case scenario: I'll become self-possessed.

THE FOURTH PERSON

I've been narrating our life in the fourth person,
a thug who slit the other three's throats,
obsessed with liquidating their points of view,
and promoting nobody's in particular.

It was right to turn our selves into equal signs,
and chase the two sides of equations away.
We contradicted numerical laws to test
air raid sirens in an age before planes.

I hope when what we say steps out of our mouths
for a smoke, it denies it was ever inside,
pretends not to recognize us, then gives itself
and the frescoes on our palates away. After all,

you never know when you'll need to peel
the statuesque off your skin, and stripped as Galatea
slash the Pygmalion who says life is beautiful,
teach him the homely truth of murder—if it lies,

he can wake his wounds, and serve them up
a breakfast of alabaster quince, and on the side:
scalloped doubting Thomas that I am.

THE ISLAND PORCILE

The trick is to sleep without telling the eyes
which are mindless, and so easily fooled.
The objective world is programmed to prey
on narcissists willing to stare into its pools,

and what it discovers are false witnesses.
It doesn't let on; we don't care to know.
This unsigned contract is our instinct for business;
each wave conforms, except for the foam.

Those of us stationed here have been travelling.
The island addresses are largely squandered.
If they'd been money, we'd be gambling.
Every morning, we have nothing to launder.

One day we might ask: are we eternal?
We seem so makeshift, checking our watches,
these china shops we wear though we're bulls,
or hope we are. Maybe we're leeches—

how unbecoming that would be!
To think each of us, a self-styled explorer,
is high on the blood of a real odyssey's
heroine, sucking away at her pores,

and hallucinating like that Chinese general
who ran out of weapons, sent out a ship
to be rained on by the enemy's arrows,
replenishing his arsenal for the next trip.

Could this have happened, or was it a dream
of a drunken sailor whose idea of menace
was to invent things better than feats?
When he's a pigsty, a man hops his fence.

OPEN SESAME

Some shelter in madness; most rent it out
and live, off the proceeds, a balanced life,
giving and taking, but you are too proud
to line pockets of your house to house fights.

Yet I believe that they can be used,
manipulated even, and why not by us?
Don't sell your soul; just let points of view,
yours and mine, be iron and rust.

I'm here to teach you how to decay.
Custom demands that you slowly descend
from the ancient thresholds of pain
to relationships we can find you out in.

We need you to experience the banality
that's second nature to your fellow men.
Solitude has made you uppity.
We want you to mingle so we can be pals,

and find ourselves experimenting in labs,
heating fugues to an inaudible voice,
whipping one another till we're ready to rat—
confess, I mean—the day we were born.

I've read the manuals: humiliation,
the victim's cicerone, opens up
a forty thieves' cave actually hidden
in Ali Baba's soul—special eye drops

allow the free world to peer into his secrets,
favourite foods and taste in music,
his God fetish, medical diagnosis
that calls epilepsy drug-induced fits.

The pleasure, nay joy, of destroying a man
senile storytellers treat gingerly—
in truth, the torturer is a fan
drilled into the ceiling of morality

which, as we know, is a bare whitewashed room
without the windows for natural air.
Electric light bulbs mean there's no gloom.
If you're beautiful, you won't be scared,

stripped of fig leaves, back in paradise,
each inmate a new Adam or Eve.
As for the ones who come packed in ice,
they're neo-Neanderthals, different species.

How they got here nobody knows,
but nothing inhuman is foreign to us.
We even have museum pieces on loan;
the heads we can't shrink are these marble busts.

Richard Greene
[b. 1961]

Richard Greene was born in St. John's, Newfoundland. He has written two books of poetry, *Republic of Solitude* (1994) and *Crossing the Straits* (2004). He is currently writing a biography of Edith Sitwell and editing the letters of Graham Greene. He teaches Creative Writing and British Literature at the University of Toronto.

WINDOW

A window gathered light from the sky
and argued for life in a bad time,
as amid gesticulating boughs
of a stripped maple, its crooked fingers
raised in bitter emphasis,
an unseen orator spoke in mime.
The wind exhaled October like a threat
and stirred the leaves to riot
that merely loitered in their discontent.
The house itself leaked spirit
through the roof and walls,
received the cold airs passively,
those deputations bearing

seasonal warrants of arrest,
but the heart,
not ready to renounce its true estate,
saw the sky framed like a constitution
where the window gathered light.

AT THE COLLEGE

Serpentine, the path unwinds its innocence
from building to building in flickering shade
where my students feed lazy raccoons muffins

and glazed doughnuts, as if to domesticate
the last wild things on this suburban campus,
though nothing can make the few deer unafraid

of engines, words, footfalls, the human rumpus,
or subdue the fox's wily nonchalance
and teach him not to kill anything helpless.

Here, among these fierce and sentimental students,
I stand on the edge of a world not my own,
snatching small goods from the large irrelevance

of what we do, making the old sorrows known
to children bearing their first calamities,
teaching solitudes to the newly alone,

explaining writers' exile to refugees
and notions of intrinsic worth to half-fledged
bankers, already driving smart Mercedes.

Yet they live by their hope, curiously pledged
to some afterness that will reward and bless
them for gifts that nature leaves unacknowledged

or earnest labours I grade at B or less;
they know some need of love that poets speak to,
and few can absent their hearts from every class,

however many dronings they may sleep through;
they will mark a perfect image or a phrase
and hear it years from now, wilder then and new.

WHALER

Great-grandfather,
       whaler out of Nantucket,
the harder sort
       who threw the harpoon,
       drew warm blood,
made huge death on the open sea.

Came home one year
       to find his land fenced
for ecclesiastical uses,
       tore it all down,
told the priest to go to hell,
       and would do his own praying
            after that.

Sailed till his knees went stiff
       with beri-beri
on a ship stuck
       in Antarctic ice.

My father worshipped him,
       remembered his deft hands
that could "put an arsehole in a crackie"
       with a hammer and a handsaw.

       The old man signalled
his affections:
       crafty hard of hearing,
heard the boy's words,
       even took his daughter's orders
           when she called him "Sir!"

Grew old jigging cod
        on the southern shore,
then fell from a roof
        and lingered days to tell
                his last stories,
empty his mouth of good oaths.

What I have of him
        is my father's reverence for
his silence,
        a sense that pain will kill you
if you speak of it.

CROSSING THE STRAITS

The sea is moving under our passage,
an old year out and a new year in
between Port aux Basques and North Sydney.
The ship rolls in the first breaths of a gale;
it has been so long, ten or twelve years,
since I last sailed, I do not trust my legs
or stomach to hold against the weather,
so lie still as a narrow berth allows,
reminding myself that disaster
is a kind of lottery, and to sink
as hard as winning millions on dry land,
and that sailors, having made profession
of storms, know their work and die old.
In an hour, anxiety drowns in sleep;
the mind, as ever, opposes passage,
and I dream of my flat in Toronto,
its wooden deck stretching across the roof,
a ship remote from this night's turning.
At six I wake and walk through lounges
where some have sat up all night playing cards
or talking, their New Year's revels queasy
and circumspect where the ship's movement
began the hangovers before the drinks.
More have slept in the rows of Lazy-boys
before an almost bloodshot T.V. screen,

its hoarse voice still croaking festively
about the crowds that gathered in Times Square.
The gales have subsided and the sea is calm
less than an hour out of North Sydney;
a heavy breakfast later, I walk along
a deck where snow-crusted lifeboats are hung.
I imagine that in summer this is
the ship's best place, but the air is frigid
this morning, and Newfoundlanders crossing
the Straits see water enough in warmer times
to forego the prospect now, but this moment
of pent chances, between home and home,
is not mine alone, and for most who travel
there is some tear in memory between
the longed for and the given, what they left
and what they are. Nova Scotia looms,
and the purser summons drivers to cars
in the ship's belly, where tractor-trailers
are already roaring for landfall.

Steven Heighton
[b. 1961]

Steven Heighton's newest poetry book is *The Address Book* (2005). *Stalin's Carnival* (1989) received the Gerald Lampert Memorial Award and *The Ecstasy of Skeptics* (1994) was a Governor General's Literary Award finalist. He also received the Petra Kenney Award and the National Magazine Awards gold medal for poetry. He has published four works of fiction, including the novel *Afterlands* (2005).

ADDRESS BOOK

Bad luck, it's said, to enter your own name
and numbers in the new address book.
All the same, as you slowly comb
through the old one for things to pick

out and transfer, you are tempted to coin
yourself a sparkling new address,
new name, befitting the freshness of this clean-
slating, this brisk kiss

so long to the heart-renders—every friend
you buried or let drift, those Home for the Aged
maiden relations, who never raged
against the dying of anything, and in the end

just died. An end to the casualties pressed
randomly between pages—smudged, scribbled chits
with lost names, business cards with their faded
bold-fronts of confidence, solvency. The palimpsest

time made of each page; the hypocrite it made
of you. Annie, whom you tried two years to love
because she was straight-hearted, lively, and in love
with you (but no strong-arming your cells and blood);

Mad Carl, who typed poet-to-poet squibs in the pseudo-
hickish, hectoring style of Pound, all sermonfire
and block caps, as AINT FIBRE ENOUGH HERE, BOYO,
BACK TO THE OLE FLAX FIELD . . . this *re* a score

of your nature poems. When he finally vanished
into the far east, you didn't mind the silence.
Still, this guilt, as if it weighs in the balance,
every choice—as if each time your pen banished

a name it must be sensed somewhere, a ballpoint stab, hex-
needle to the heart, the treacherous
innocent *no* of Peter, every X
on the page a turncoat kiss. . . .

Bad luck, it's said, to enter your own name in the new
book—as if, years on, in the next culling,
an executor will be leafing through and calling
or sending word to every name but you.

CONSTELLATIONS

After bedtime the child climbed on her dresser
and peeled phosphorescent stars off the sloped
gable-wall, dimming the night vault of her ceiling
like a haze or the interfering glow
of a great city, small hands anticipating
eons as they raided the playful patterns
her father had mapped for her—black holes now
where the raised thumb-stubs and ears of the Bat
had been, the feet of the Turtle, wakeful
eyes of the Mourning Dove. She stuck those paper
stars on herself. One on each foot, the backs
of her hands, navel, tip of nose and so on,
then turned on the lamp by her bed and stood close
like a child chilled after a winter bath
pressed up to an air duct or a radiator
until those paper stars absorbed more light
than they could hold. Then turned off the lamp,
walked out into the dark hallway and called.

Her father came up. He heard her breathing
as he clomped upstairs preoccupied, wrenched
out of a rented film just now taking grip
on him and the child's mother, his day-end
bottle of beer set carefully on the stairs,
marking the trail back down into that evening
adult world—he could hear her breathing (or
really, more an anxious, breathy giggle) but
couldn't see her, then in the hallway stopped,
mind spinning to sort the apparition
of fireflies hovering ahead, till he sensed
his daughter and heard in her breathing
the pent, grave concentration of her pose,
mapped onto the star-chart of the darkness,
arms stretched high, head back, one foot slightly raised—
the Dancer, he supposed, and all his love
spun to centre with crushing force, to find her
momentarily fixed, as unchanging
as he and her mother must seem to her,
and the way the stars are; as if the stars are.

BLACKJACK

Hit: to take another card, and risk breaking.
Stand: to stick with what you have.

The dealer is dailiness, and the asking—
hit or stand?—comes more often than you guess.
Missed cues can fill a life. Or you signal wrong,

the house responds, no recourse. Standing with less
may be safer—you know the odds—but even then
the temptation is to hit. Sometimes loss

at long odds looks better than a sure win;
as if winning were a sure thing, ever.
In some dreams a familiar house will open

into unsuspected rooms, door after door
glides ajar, yet you hang back and consciousness
cuts in like an eviction. But what if you were

not so anxious to wake back into your less
uncharted life, and chanced those farther rooms . . .?
Caution cancels love's richer part; eros,

sequestered in home safety, always seems
to die by inches. The house wins by turning
its people into furniture. Many tombs

are made of unplayed cards. It's me I'm warning
here. Hit when the asking happens. The house
may have its system, but you're not through learning.

THE MACHINE GUNNER

I saw them. They came like ghosts out of ground-
mist, moving
over ruined earth in waves, running

no, walking, shoulder to shoulder
like a belt of bullets or like
men: tinned meat lined on a conveyor belt as the sun

exploded in thin shafts on metal
buckles, bayonets, the nodding
spires of helmets. I heard faint battle cries

and whistles, piercing through the shriek
of fire and iron falling, the slurred
cadence of big guns. As they funnelled

like a file of mourners into gaps
in the barbed wire I made quick
calculations and slipped the safety catch.

But held my fire. Alongside me
the boys in the trenches worried them with
rifles, pistols, hand grenades

but they came on, larger now, their faces
almost resolving out of hazed hot
distance, their ranks at close quarters amazing

with dumb courage, numb step, a sound of drugged
choking in gas and green mud, steaming—
Who were these men. I saw them penitent

sagging to knees. I saw their dishevelled
dying. And when finally they broke
into a run it came to me

what they had always been, how I'd always
really, seen them: boys
rushing toward us with arms

outstretched, hands clenched as if in urgent prayer,
sudden welcome or a reunion
quite unexpected. Yes. And more than this

like children, chased by something behind the lines
and hurrying to us
for rescue—

I spat and swung the gun around. Fired,
felt the metal pulse
and laid them three deep in the wire.

HIGH JUMP

Four strides the legs compass, close,
burst gravity's shell and vault

as sunrise at the pole bends
back, sickles the sun-

sleek arc of dolphin, diver, gull,
his skull at noon and hovering. There

the body contends with higher things—
sharp light, thinning air; the eclipse

and setting of records; a fixed
orbit he believes he frames. At his height

he wavers, reels like a lover and prays
his lunging survives him

in a perfect act; feels time
tug at his second hand

as the earth draws breath, pole
and body into ground. Hear it:

a hissing of wind in the high
arena, and his spikes

rattle, raised like knuckles at the sky.

Gil Adamson

[b. 1961]

Gil Adamson has published two poetry collections, *Primitive* (1991) and *Ashland* (2003), and a book of short stories, *Help Me, Jacques Cousteau* (1995). Her work has appeared in several anthologies.

MESSAGE

We hoped the disease would ignore us.
All men think they will avoid
the rocks, the boil of the waterfall.
They dream of floating in easy circles at the end,
their smiling faces upturned.

We drink in the empty tavern
or out in the rain, pissing demurely in corners,
weeping on the steps of the church.
The sight of us makes God laugh.

We lose parts of our bodies:
noses, tongues, throats.
The prostitutes wince and turn away,
tighten their belts.

A rain falls constantly,
our shoulders and thighs slippery,
a green slurry growing on our coat collars.
Sometimes we cannot wrestle our boots off
to see what has happened to our feet.

Finally, our strength becomes thin and muffled,
a circus departing town.
We sit sometimes in empty yards,
on warped fences,
watching birds fuss over tiny things.
We put guns to each others' heads,
click down on nothing,
and even this seems like a sign,
a message too simple to be ignored.

THE APPRENTICE

I was a hungry infant carried in a soldier's pocket.
He used to stroke my little head for luck.

In the city, we saw a wagonload of cheese.
All the people stood silent as it passed,
because it was for the royal family
and it was poisoned.
The soldier's rough thumb
squeezed my ear so hard that day
that I cackled like the trees do back home,
before winter catches them.

After that, we killed many people
and the taverns shut down until we were caught.
My protector was hanged
and I wept, swinging in the hammock
of his stiff fingers.
An old hen called up to me, seeming
to make polite apologies,
but really just to see me up close;
the innocent foundling.
I saw the shadow of a boot pass over her,
and swing away again.

BLACK WING

We watch a bootless boy
pass the cornfield, uniform wet from the river,
hat swinging in his hand
as if still marching.
One arm gone completely
and strange internal workings splayed out to us,
intimate and suspended.

He's somebody's little baby
smoky white, staggering to the water barrel,
bent over to kiss the dust with a swoon.

Some woman runs forward
too late to catch him.

We look away from his open mouth,
look instead at the corn, the crows
floating above the river in their private worries.
Tonight, when we turn in,
the candle will sputter and blow.
Pinched out easily, all flame
gives way to this wide black wing.

UNPLEASANT COINCIDENCE

It's night in unpleasant coincidence.
An eclipse yet.

We leave the rain-soaked horses in the hotel bar
which has no roof, no walls, no bar.

Women are everywhere in lighted tents,
their heads making fists of shadow.
But because I am dressed like a man,
I must stand out here and wallow in my success.

The galaxies spin overhead, getting a bead on us all.
We prey for food and a terrified bird
falls into our hands. I get the feet.

"Let's go," says my chorus of lice.
"Let's get out of here."
But that's what they said last time,
and now look where we are.

REST

The crow is a creature of many mysteries.
For instance he has two hearts,
one inert inside the other.
He brings darkness with him, sure,
but also glittering things.
In the sun, he looks like a crumb
from the deepest cave, and if the clouds sink low,
his shiny black head is a star, brighter and brighter.
Sleep never comes to this creature.
He closes his disc eyes and yearns for rest.

Seasons spin in their sockets,
winter falls off its shelf with a whoop,
the mouse of the field goes home.
And yet, all down the road,
dutiful fenceposts yawn a little,
strangely restless in their shallow beds.

Eric Miller
[b. 1961]

Eric Miller is the author of *Song of the Vulgar Starling* (1999), *In the Scaffolding* (2005),
and winner of the Ralph Gustafson Poetry Prize. His work has been published in literary
magazines in Canada and the United States. He teaches in the English department at the
University of Victoria.

THE QUESTION

The angel, what I thought was an angel, hovered
over me and asked, For you what happiness?
And I heard its cries of a gull in whose sky-blank
span we lie, a bird the colour of driftwood
among peeled, bleached driftwood clouds and the foam
the waves edge up onto outcrop rock at the point
of land, foam gull-feather-coloured and carrying
fallen feathers and silent the other birds
in close to me among the salt-burned spirea,

those near birds being sparrows, a song sparrow
and a tree sparrow. I saw the dark seed
focus in the sparrows' heads and slight they moved
into and out of mean limbs of the rattled
bush saying nothing. The wind thumbed them
as if sorting the feathers of their napes and flanks.
The cries of the gull glittered and slid hard
like mica then soft as pressed skin and was the gull
angel? I said, Happy now in the boat
that has capsized in the surf the angels permeate
with their song. The waves danced the dance
of close and far and the sparrows hopped in the wind
as securely on the rock as a fly that walks the floor now a ceiling.
The bush shook in the condescension of primeval
courtesy, though its necessity was rooted spindlier
than wind and gull's music, which changed as the sparrows
changed, into my answer, the vibrating, sparkling, drab-in-glory
that was the angel's beak-blown question.

SONG OF THE VULGAR STARLING

Was werde ich durch mein Tier werden, mein Erbstück?
"What will become of me through my animal—my legacy?"
—Kafka

O, ein Engel geht vorbei!
"Oh, an angel is passing!"
—*Wings of Desire*

1

Ach, Starling, what can I sing for you you haven't sung for yourself
already? When after rainfall moss and lichen glow on the pine-bark like
chlorophyllian sunrise and the formal Robins step and stop
in their courtly lawn dance like lovers at the wedding at the end
of a comedy you stomp along with your yellow schnozz screwing
around in the mud
like a legion of littermen with their pointed sticks
stabbing at every accident that provoked kids' tears and at once
became classified as garbage.

And in the spring your grey offspring bleat with the voices of dictator
sheep in the mongrel scrub by metropolitan culverts, drowning out
the dwindling Yellow Warblers and even hysterical Redwing hens,
outnumbering the clacking Grackles; and soon your kids moult
from stocks-and-bonds grey to the greasy suit that makes their shifty
eyes impossible
to scrutinize.

2

And look, I can't even write a tight-lipped gun-wielding *Moritat* cuz
though you nest in the neon of strip-joints and pace by the leaking
losers whose life-blood is the splashy red solvent
of drugs pooling like cold coffee on asphalt
you manage a sort of gentility, oblivion, as if a crack-willow mansion
by the water-striders' limpid sunfish-swum rink were the same as a vent
above the split-seamed rubby's back
alley. No, I can't sentimentalize the calamitous after-hours
of streetcorners asserting, *Here is one bad bird who knows all the moves,*
cuz face it, you can't tell an industrial from a national
park but raise your family undeterred and incorrigible, *aequo animo*
like the Stoic philosopher, *secundum Naturam*—and that's
anywhere.

So you scud over beaverponds, flap above drums of chemical sludge,
Caelum non animum mutant reads your frayed passport,
and I can't help wondering about you, let go by white guys,
their heirloom in the air of North America, ubiquitous as highways,
with your silly tune in the skies of Miami, Moosonee, and like
the damn Europeans you're a poignant plugugly lump of *je me souviens—
hélas! Où sont les oiseaux...?* Guilty you are and guilty you'll be,
driving the autochthonous Red-headed Woodpecker from his tree,
though Hölderlin heard you as Apollo's sibilous spirits
screaming in his ears while lightning tore his eyes open,
though tubercular Sterne found you enraged, chanting
encaged *I can't get out* and
now you're universally sprung—tell me, Everybird, who
can escape your freedom?

And Pliny spoke of you, Starling, Sir *Sturnus*, without detectable distaste,
nec occultantur, "nor are they hidden" (that's for sure!) but as for me I

might say, *Fuck it*, I might say *Fuck it*,
I don't want this inheritance, no thank you, Europe flapping around like a
low-grade Fury and in the sky always squealing and jumping
into every available hole
and killing and evicting and singing miserably bad.
But I confess, O Starling, you sang to me in my cradle
(over the Song Sparrow, over the Cardinal and the Flicker)—
the first sounds I heard were surely cars and Starlings
and then the chimes from the unbelievable church, child as I am
of the guys from Europe with their guns, rum, and chains
and then their for-sale signs and the world a baking parking lot.

3

Yet in the weeping willow my friend, *Salix babylonica*, willow by which
one might well sprawl and lament, you are a figure for pure idiosyncrasy
in your twinkling green coat that takes a sheen diffidently
like the bottle glass exploded at the punks' law-breaking whoop-up
in the municipal park last night. You woozy musician
with your buttercup-yellow beak! You're a heartbroken guy
vulnerable reluctantly to the pleasure of the sun who whistles a tune
to himself and plays with fresh leaves of grass in his lips
and the chlorophyll stains the skin of his elbow and his tongue—
if he could remember the words that go with the tune
he'd understand his pain better, *vielleicht, peut-être?*

Ach, Starling, anyway Charles Darwin would say, *Well Friend wait*
long enough
and you'll become something else. There's infinite hope
for something
somewhat like us. Starling, let's remember
the Galapagos. Let's wait around, eh? Let's wait, sing and change.

SEPTEMBER IN UPLANDS PARK

What was that odour? Perhaps to call it an "odour"
is already to give it an adequate name, no more
precise name is necessary and none could
dispel the savoury precision of its

saturating vagueness. It wrapped the children
more brightly in their more vibrant clothes,
they ran on the resilient mud and stones
that seemed softened between rows
of snowberries that swelled pellets
of inexact though piercing white. Was it rosehips
that steeped the sky? Or kneeling on moss,
after the first rain for weeks? Or soaking grass that,
for all the fall of water, could not expel
grey-brown from scorched lengths? Was it relief
of ancient rock that the youth of water
stroked it? Was it the oaks, stiff
vehemence doused
with spontaneity, as an accipiter made comic
by being caught in a downpour, glaring
tuft-crazy like someone startled in bed?

All smelled good, and this smell affected
the pace, the gaze, and even the late sun
raised the inexhaustible grey of a cloud to its nose.
To the query came no answer but inhalation, for no
answer right or wrong
resolves a question. Breathing
in, breathing
out mimes the structure
of question and answer.
And is neither.

HISTORY OF PETALS

On still days pollen is diffused
and like a greater tree around the tree
there is a hazy invasion, you brim uneasily
with this fertility
as though a wrong hormone were gently injected
and you fell sick with spring.

But comes a grey day, now you sip perfume,
it seems swimming around you silvered

as a swan moves with impervious breast over a pond.
So the whole season is offered you to drink
and this generosity takes you, this excess
of which you accept a just measure.
You swim and you drink, you float and you do not dive.

And a windy day casts down the petals like the glances of elated children
whose blows against each other do not bruise, but exhilarate.

Then build the drifts of still-bright blossoms in the gutter.
If your toes brush through them there is resistance,
a soggy tugging, as when the small wave, having
risen up the beach around you
pulls back at you and the sand under your soles,
a tide followed by the hard yellow of dandelions
that stick behind in the dark fierce grass.

David McGimpsey
[b. 1962]

David McGimpsey's most recent books are the poetry collection *Hamburger Valley, California* (2002) and short story collection *Certifiable* (2004). He is the author of the critical study *Imagining Baseball: America's Pastime and Popular Culture*. A songwriter and musician, he is a member of the rock band Puggy Hammer. He teaches creative writing at Concordia University, Montreal.

KOKO

There was no doubt about my boss:
he was one of the great defectives.
He claimed our poor profits in the recession
stemmed from his "fear of circus clowns."

You have to be careful around a guy like that:
test your breath, shoelaces Oxford-style—
one winter afternoon, about a month
after the operation on my foot,

I limped aggressively into the office
and *finally* told a co-worker to shutup.
My boss overheard, grabbed me and said,
"you're not the sharpest pencil in the box, are you?"

The irony was I ended up working as a clown
in front of a flower shop right there on 6th avenue.
And the boss would walk by, smelling like *Paco Rabanne*
and I was going shutup, shutup, shutup.

THE TRIP

The trip was supposed to be simple enough:
drive Hank Williams from Knoxville TN to Canton OH,
give him time to dry out, straighten up
for a New Year's Eve concert the next night.
But I had to bring the car from Montgomery AL,
the first capital of that confederacy, 1861,
where Jim Crow ruled supreme as cotton, 1954,
& where blood was spilled not thirty years ago
for daring to cast a vote, sit anywhere on a bus.
I had to take the first cadillac cowboy's cadillac
all the way through the Smoky Mountains
& through a heavy wet snow
that grounded all the planes.

I was to take him wherever he wished.
& Ole Hank (he annoyingly referred to himself
in third person) wanted to go on
just another wild ride.
He needed some shots for the pain in his back
which was real at one time, but that day
he was riding the crest of a junkie's heat,
a hot spell that eats the user like a fever
from fix to fix until, someway, it dies down.
First business in Knoxville was to see
the doctor who would oblige Ole Hank.

Instead of starting north
we tooled around the south in the white caddy.
A dusty bottle of whisky from Fort Payne AL
was soon shattered, empty on the road. Then, then, then
we got to Chattanooga TN to see another doctor
another needle that I guess he couldn't
brave himself to spike.
Picked up some chloral hydrate tablets—
something to keep him from drinking
(you kept Hank from drinking by knocking him out).
The mountains were grey in the snow
but still missing the Christmas magic
Dolly Parton associates with the region.
Travelling through you could never tell
throughout the fields; stench
is left to fester on the battlefields;
gangrene, osteomyelitis, pyemia, peritonitis,
dysentery, typhoid, pneumonia, malaria
& of course just plain shot to death,
like Lincoln. Just passing through
you wouldn't know. God is silent that way.
Hank had a guitar back there
& now & then he'd manage a few stray strums,
or an out-of-tune chorus to "I saw the light."
The guitar was so big in his scrawny lap,
so sharp in its angles,
it looked like it might mangle him
like a big greasy machine.
I tended, even then, to be disgusted
by the extent of his illness,
his Jack Daniels emaciation,
where you could see too clearly
the bony machinations of the lower jaw,
& his teeth always exposed,
brown with tobacco tartar, his lips
deprived of any healthy puff of fat.
But it was true:
he could sing your ass off,
sing you to the very brink of the country western
understanding of the world.

He wasn't the first to burn out his or her star,
& he won't be the last. He had spina bifida
& a talent for expressing loneliness,
maybe more than anybody before.
& for the longest time those songs,
so plaintive yet so sweet, nestled
in the deepest parts of my day-to-day.
Made me afraid to reach out,
seized up my knees like an ill-advised surgery
that replaced slippery cartilage
with rusty sheet metal & pins.
"Are you OK, Mr. Williams?" I asked
& he cussed & took a slug & said
"Ole Hank's alright" & we slid along,
the cadillac smooth as a skiff in the bayou,
silent, watching the grey winter forests of Tennessee,
way into the southern ridge of the Appalachian plateau
over the muddy tributaries, catfish thick,
of the Mississippi & Ohio rivers.
Jesus was on my mind, his mercy
wouldn't bring us through the snowfall, would it?
Jesus wouldn't bring us through—
through to that place like heaven
& by dawn we were in Chattanooga & Hank
saw his man & limped into the car
with another head-full of bootsauce.
He is coming.
To Chattanooga where the rebels pitched well
but disastrously lost the battle of Chickamauga,
Yankees storming their position on Missionary Ridge,
chanting, Chickamauga! Chickamauga!
& Grant's men forced General Bragg into Georgia
Nov. 25, 1863, demoralizing the CSA,
the blood of the young in the creeks,
smell of gunpowder in the fog, a huge
American flag raised at the top of the hill.
Yessir that doctor fixed Hank up pretty good
& gave me some little white things
that would keep me wide awake well into northern OH.
By the time we got back to where we started,
behind schedule,

already intolerably weary of driving,
the car stank of malt
& Hank needed more than a day to straighten up.
More than a decade.
I saw Knoxville again,
the first time I left my wife in 1984
& it was incredible, host of the World's Fair,
& I took in the humidity like a tonic
& lay around drunk just about anywhere.
Knoxville too was occupied by Union troops
in the autumn of 1863 & they resisted
any & every attempt to oust them.
I asked Hank if he wanted to stop here,
pretend all the night was a dream
& start again fresh,
maybe drive into a snowbank for fun.
But he said no & made gestures with his hand
as if to say: not now, Ole Hank
is busy making music history.
"I will you you(sic) still & always will
but that's the poison we have to pay"
is what the wreck coughed out in the back,
his last contribution to the lyric.
Snow, let it, powerful, drop heavy.
From then on, he said, I was the boss
& let loose & drove North East
& we were pulled over by this Tennessee cop.

Who snarled at the room-sized sedan
"Hey, 'bama boy," he said, looking at my plates
"that's one lawwng car. Who's in the back?"
That's all he wanted to know.
He was only there because of the snow
to watch traffic through the Virginia/Tennessee border
where, by the way, Ulysses S. Grant,
a reported boozehound & certain military victor himself,
seized the Virginia & Tennessee rail-lines
in the first serious offensives of 1864,
more dead, of course, both sides. Afternoon.
"Hey, if that guy is Hank Williams
that guy looks dead," the cop said

& caught some thick flakes in his meaty palm
& licked them like a clumsy bear cub.
& we drove on into the thick Allegheny forest,
into those beautiful blue pines, & mudslick hollers.
Into Bluefield VA, an unremarkable town,
except Mr. Williams had a doctor there
whom he said he'd like to see,
but passing through, Hank was passed out,
the chloral nitrate, the whachamacallit I thought,
& stopped & had a sandwich by myself
dry roast beef, & a heart warming beer.

I had another & another until I was pestering
the waitress, saying, "didja know
Hank Williams is this big time Dodgers fan"
because the waitress admitted she like Brooklyn too.
"& every year he gets choked when the NY Yankees
best them in the end, those Bums." Oh, O.
Hank never saw them play with Jackie Robinson
but he heard of him hustling out in AAA
for the Montreal Royals
at gentle Delormier fields not far from the
foot of the Jacques Cartier bridge.
In the end she wasn't impressed.
She turned off the grill.
Late night, had to travel slow through the snow,
Hank looked really bad.
We would never make the New Year's show.
I didn't want to find out.
I threw some take-out in the back seat,
a white paper bag that was never opened.
I thought I heard him stir when we started out
& if he had any life then
I'm sure he was thinking about the beer I bought,
the new life inside the long white cadillac.
I think it was full of song stuff.
I guess he didn't stir, passed through Princeton WV
& we were close to the limits of Confederate excursions.
West Virginia was quickly incorporated into the Union.
I was thinking we were just nitwits travelling

but 40 miles north I realized,
it was obvious, Hank Williams was dead.
Tony Bennett's version of "Cold Cold Heart"
would no longer rouse him to violence.
I stopped in Oak Hill wv to tell somebody
that there was a dead man, cold, in my car, his car,
whatever. & they came & said I was right
Hiram Williams was dead at the age of 30.
Police headquarters, telephone calls.
Excessive eulogies flowed from then on,
from people who wouldn't shake a hand before
& who looked on while the last stage of illness set in.
"The Hillbilly Shakespeare" they said,
which is only as accurate or inaccurate
as calling the Bard the Renaissance Hank.
Schubert, it seems, is the logical parallel,
but it too doesn't matter, I'm tired
& I don't know what to say any more.
Oak Hill wv, hundreds of miles south,
(too late, anyway) form the Canton OH promised land.
Canton OH, site of the Pro Football Hall of Fame,
Mike Ditka's jersey there in a football-shaped building.
Just north of Salinville, the Northermost point
of any rebel excursion: Greycoat cavalry raiders
under General Morgan surrendered there July 26 1863.
Although, once, St. Alban's vt was raided
by about 30 Confederates from their base in Canada.

EDNA LOSES THE STORE

she had quit her job to start up the shop
dyed her hair a further shade of orange
until it had a young florescent glow

like velvet paintings of Nevada sun,
it was her turn to grow & sing bluemoon
she always worked out her problems baking

"it's unusual but it works for me"
she says with her bright Wisconsin aplomb
in her famous cheese puffs, tarts & croissants

are these ingredients: a failed marriage
a guitar playing son still on the loaf
& the many trials of the girls she cares for

'Edna's Edibles' is no old bakery
along its wall you'll find onions & caviar
behind the counter there's cornbread & brie

& it all sold like hotcakes with butter
until one evening & that song of no more
that little lapse no bigger than a fly

leaving the heat on a small pan of oil
& turning around to walk to the store
oblivious to that twist of her hand

& when she got back, with 10 lettuce head
ears still buzzing with Peekskill gossip
the firemen were scooting around, swearing

This is the biggest fire they've ever seen
Peekskill seems as small as an apple
& about as dangerous to safety

there was nothing that they could really do
pretend it's the 4th of July & watch
& Edna drops & cries from the reality

how tender that olive oil looked bottled
she yells way into the Catskill mountains
"my shop! my beautiful shop! o, o girls!"

she wishes it would smell of all the shop's food
gently roasting way into the wind
instead it pours acrid plastic smoke

black as hockey tape, searing her nostrils
with its caustic smell until she chokes hard
she knows it's all over & she coughs again

she knows her policy is outdated
& will not cover it more than a layer
of yellow paint or floral wallpaper

she felt the fire take some orange away
& her hair was emptied into the flames
everybody says "at least you're not hurt

thank god nobody was hurt or killed"
but maybe it would've been better Edna thinks
to join all the angels who've died in fires

Kevin Connolly
[b. 1962]

Kevin Connolly was founding editor of the influential 1980s literary magazine *What!*.
He has published three poetry collections: *Asphalt Cigar* (1995), nominated for the
Gerald Lampert Memorial Award; *Happyland* (2002); and *Drift* (2005).

HISTORY CHANNEL

The limo driver will be drugged *and* drunk,
the route preplanned, underpass carefully chosen,
paparazzi hired specifically for the crack-up—
no need to pull film from the cameras,
there was never any there in the first place.

The shots will come from the front. Bullets
will be planted, wound doctored, autopsies
rendered incomprehensible. The chain of
custody will be sorely compromised—
golf bag gone missing, ice cream unmelted—

gloves and thumps and barking dogs.
The area will be air-access only, photos dodgy,
microchips too small to allow detection. The artists
leave fields under cover of darkness, key
witnesses meet with freak, untimely deaths.

Go ahead, dig up the rock star, he's long gone:
the homage graffiti, tombstone testimonials,
just wasted breath. The newspapers pitch
columns against us, ants pile the lies high
and deep; bees paper their cells with

whispers, gather poison behind their knees.
In the Scottish murk, the fins of ancient beasts.
In the Mojave, clear prints of a lunar lander.
A knife on the counter, voice on the wireless,
a nurse's shoes stacked neatly on the squad car.

PORCELAIN JESUS

and little shampoo Pope,
on a pee break, silhouetted
by your standard frosted window.
His acolyte, Sir Thomas, severed head
toppled over skin cream, bath salts,
an anonymous squeeze bottle.

A trapeze of leggy ivy
brought indoors to duck the cold,
the light show behind it all
storyboarded, crept up from
adjacent basements,
sifting hedge and gavel,
the weeping roof shedding snow.

Bathroom, middle of
the night, light off—
the familiar joust
of the real and the seen
that means everything
and settles nothing at all.

DOWN TO EARTH

Read backwards what's written seems hopeful.
A bell goes and begin again—wheels rolled
over wheels, a great commotion written forward.
Memos gather (task and problem), obstacles are thrown

up, examined, then brought down through some
colossal collective effort. In the afternoon it seems
calmer. You nap in the window where the day hangs
longer, watch dry grass gasp, embers of summer.

Everything's a gesture, a treatise on going forward.
There are broad arguments, checks and measures,
events fated and events clearly accidental.
There are clouds and the breaks between them,

through which pours light and what look like birds,
or leaves, or broken branches; souls, even (the poet
in you wants to say), singed and shaken, hurled
back to hard ground, a place that knows them.

RISE AND SHINE

Whatever it is, *if* it is, it's always about
a mumble or a mutter or, very rarely,
a shout: on the stairs, among wet
branches, in the gaps between the things
amusing people say to drown us out;
all over these sheets even, in my own
undelivered whispers, which console only
me, and even then not for long.

Because truthfully, there's not much
to moan about, just the growing
preponderance of sheets, their almost
routine visits now established, their
inability to make sense of all this,
mutter cutting mutter as sky divides
branches or one follows zero, and is itself

followed by what you need to believe
might be anything—a wonder, even—
it's just that so far and seemingly by chance,
it's always, again, a one: a leaf, a table,
in a boardroom, at a window listening
for words that may not come, may never
have, and certainly not for you,
blue light waxing, stars guttering in
the brightness of that thought.

REPOSSESSION

When they board up the hobby shop
only the moon notices—and the stationary
conductor waving in a train that no longer
circles the village, but is caught forever
in a chilly tunnel two peaks
north of the cheerless alpine church.

Down front, lead children
mock-shiver in the town square,
their little schnauzers parked mid-bark,
painted hands pawing for the rigid
mothers, painted sisters gathering wool
beside the Pop Shoppe.

Behind City Hall, past tumbleweed
flosses of silica snow, little train-model
glaziers slap train-model putty on train-
model trowels next to the lifelike factory,
where tradesmen stir simulated liquid
in a building without interior walls.

Out here in the genuine moonlight,
trees are still trees, light remains light,
and a die-cast freeway ducks the question,
closes up shop, turns its chair
toward the audience and bellows out
the sorry business of these worlds.

Geoffrey Cook

[b. 1963]

Geoffrey Cook's poems have appeared widely in journals and anthologies. His book, *Postscript* (2004) was a finalist for the Gerald Lampert Memorial Award. He was born in Wolfville, Nova Scotia, and currently teaches in the English department at John Abbott College, Montreal.

MOVING IN

The first time in, we passed right through
to end up on the outside of the other side
of town. *"The fog's so thick, it's like pea soup,"*
was said. All I saw beyond the taillights
of the car before us were the tollgates
then the girders and the bridge that hung
like an island where the horizon belonged,
but now was all washed up and out and away.

For two whole days Saint John did not exist,
and each time in or out of town we missed
an exit: nothing in that place
was seen until you saw it face to face.

But then, a home's not real unless it's half
imagined. We make each move not knowing if
what's coming through the fog is threat or gift.

LORNE, NOVA SCOTIA

Millstones rest their weathered bulk
against a glazed lawn;
half-buried, they look,
with one bored eye apiece, long

past visitors to this house.
His mill collapsed
some time before he cursed
and took his final steps.

Now his body's beyond mend
in some hospital bed.
Only the belligerent
tongue of his sunken head

worries the air.
Swaddled: his sheets as still
as the huge space of winter
weighing on the mill.

The dam in a caul of ice,
shushing the fall
of water underneath;
the bull-chain pulls

apart; the headsaw's seized.
Still down on the farm,
her life seems
undone. In the barn

tools blur with rust
into thin air.
In the house
wooden furniture

shines, not with polish,
but decades of use—
the set and shift of muscles,
the body's simple truth.

Time, in winter,
passes mostly in the dark.
Her bones are curling her
into a question mark.

FISHERMAN'S SONG

Black water, black water,
trout, come out;
a poor land's alders
choke the throats

of narrow rivers
washed of doubts
by happy, silver
fishes' coats.

Here are shadows,
whispering grass,
restless shallows'
limpid splash,

and leaning meadows
to lead eyes fast
beyond the willow's
weeping face.

Goldenrod bunches
braid the sun
and unhinge hunches
weighing down

the over-anxious.
Surface sound
or light enhances
tension slung

along a shoulder.
Taut lines feel
distinctly bolder,
make us kneel

in water's colder,
faster reel.
Autumn unloads her
bloodied creel

in waves of colours
startling hills
as skies cast over
and the big winds smell

of harvest and slaughter.
Then the bells—
falling dolour,
lambent knell—

of raindrops sprinkling
the surfaces
of streams wrinkling
into spaces

like the shrinking
grins on faces
and eyes now squinting
at the traces

of dark waters,
fish and doubt.
Black water, black water,
trout, come out.

THE SEALS AT GREEN ROCK

The seals at Green Rock poppled in the spume,
like buoys, like divers, like great black thumbs

from unfathomable depths: thumbs up, thumbs down
at their own whim and rhythm; mammalian,

and, beyond the child's idea of apples in
a barrel of water at a county fair—

or that those seals were playing (which they were)—
deeply sexual in shape and motion:

buoyant as young breasts, basked and firm;
the ripe grape-nipples risen from

the darkened aureolas; curvaceous, smooth,
like the slow descent from chest to stomach

to the belly-knot and slickened omphalos...
O to stroke a seal! But just as obvious

the seals' great maleness: tubular
tons of sleek and thrusting flesh! Shafts!

Pistons! Gyrating submarines! Bullets
of barking, butting blood! Meat helmets!

O but more than mockery and the mere erotics
of the seals around Green Rock,

Green Rock itself a hunch on the horizon;
a cold, dark nudge in fog and mothy night;

a whale shouldering the swell
and shrugging off the sea-road;

a stone lapped and licked and kissed by combers,
slapped by seals, rolled on and over...

O the seals and Green Rock were far beyond
us: glottal stopping, bobbing, gone!

WATERMARKS

The sun-beat, salt-scrubbed, sooty wooden boards
that run like foolscap up the walls of homes,
taking to heart time's taste for monochromes,
are all washed out from facing up to fog;
the chalk-stained slate of their wrinkled scowl
is what remains of lifetimes staring down
the local climate and the smokestacks' smog.

Among the walls of solid, happy colours
that splash the steep hill stepping from the harbour
(as if a giant child had dropped his building blocks),
these plain-faced homes, like a shoreline's watermarks,
will bear as level-headed witness as horizons,
so long as such perspectives last.
Not that their posture's one to emulate:
they pitch and lean like old men getting slow-
ly drunk alone in Legions, like woodpiles left
as a wood's libation, breakers about to crash;
but *on the level*, having seen too much
to strike at anything you'd call a pose.

Once sailors' rooms, they seem to imitate
the ocean's frown—that grey brow creased by waves—
or ruled but empty pages in a log
that's been abandoned, scattered loose-leaf sheets
I've tried to gather in a manuscript.
With nothing else to give to make up for
so many years away, nothing to
repay a landscape for the beauty laid
across a childhood like a crazy quilt,
may my words lie down on pages as
mariners may have lain on bunkhouse beds:
exhausted and grateful.

      And if these clapboard shacks
have nothing against the seasons printing them
as fading background in a local woodcut,
let them also never mind these offset lines
so much themselves like wooden siding or
irregularly breaking rows of waves.
At best, a poem's just one more bank of pass-
ing fog for them perhaps, or a rising tide
that always falls again, so fast, so fast.

Mark Sinnett

[b. 1963]

Mark Sinnett's first volume of poems, *The Landing* (1997), won the Gerald Lampert Memorial Award. He is the author of *Bull* (1998), a collection of stories and *The Border Guards* which was shortlisted for the Arthur Ellis Crime Novel Award. *Late Adventure of the Feelings* (2002) is his second poetry collection.

STUDY OF TWO FIGURES (LOVERS), 1846

There is nothing in Millet's red chalk drawing,
its round tumbling lines, to suggest the couple
is indoors, and yet I place them, predictably,
in a room that reminds me of yours, and decide they are
like us—so often and for such long stretches
of these unforgettable and wise-seeming days
are we also undraped. Even so, I doubt there is
any sign of blue velour, or leopard prints, your
glistening black pants, in the rough shamble
of clothes beyond the frame's limit. More
possible, I guess, is a small and familiar tangle
of soft velvet gloves like those I have seen on your
kitchen counter. And that when Millet is done
they might climb again, like bright bunched-up
caterpillars, the woman's unfinished arms.
The man's head (I appreciate most especially
this detail, his desire, I'm drawn to the work
because of it) rests easily on her bare shoulder.
She sits at his feet, but as an equal; it is not
a position that should be read as difficult. Her
cheek is against his leg, her arm furthermore
drapes over it, hangs free and languorous.
I realize if the hand were drawn in fully
it would ghost Marat's death, a notion that has me
riffing away to linked but recent true poems
by a friend, as well as the lurid collage next to
your fridge. This frail chain seems, end of the day,
giveaway evidence of chaos theory, its tiger's reach
through some hundred and fifty years. But
the two figures touch me, is how this adds up, all
it means, and they do it delicately, just as you do:
back of the neck and with the tip of your tongue.

ON THE IMPOSSIBILITY OF SEEING YOU

It doesn't matter a damn how early I venture out,
or for how long I roam, haunt the sun-full and
endless-seeming streets of Toronto. I still won't
see you. Not a hope. There are plenty of shopkeepers
about, their sleeves rolled up and rolling out reluctant
striped awnings. I even see myself, ghosted, rendered
see-through, in stencilled and spotless windows packed
with Italian biscuits, or bright-eyed fish, the rude sundered
legs of spring lamb, neck-wrung grouse hung in head-down
rows like bats. A girl hoses down the sidewalk and light
arcs, separates (as we have) in the intersection's indecisive
jostling air. Yeah, there are all these signs and beauties,
reminders to get on with it, to live. And I do. But never
once in the coming weeks will you breeze my way.
And that impossibility: of your hand searching out mine
(same thing with your lips, and the frequent lazy sunrise
of your hip turning towards me—so often and fondly
recalled, and that more than once forestalled anything
might be thought of as work) makes it hard some days
to leave the house. Mostly I would rather summon acute
glimpses of you from the dark star-punctured swirl
of our winter. Moments that have been carved in with
the permanence of woodcuts and can now and again
be rekindled. Only peripherally—as if regarded on a rear-
view mirror while fresh traffic piles up more demandingly
ahead—but still. They bring you as near as anything just
down the road, any of those so-pretty stores opening up
and full of nothing I need to buy, except a little later some
paper for this poem, a couple of stamps, and a decent pen.

SEPTEMBER ONE

This morning, with some coffee, and weighed down,
half-dressed, I managed (though nearly didn't) the dozen
angled, uncut steps to the dock. I read the newspaper,
as well as some serious pages of a decent book. And
then I simply sat for a while, thought on how winter

shapes up so well for us, exciting, but also on how sad
you were yesterday. At one point your tanned shoulder,
or rather the outer defined line of it—as the day greyed
and I listened to you, or later watched you sleep—
divided you from the water in a way reminded me
of medieval bronze refusing the alchemist's mercury.
The sad you, the becalmed lake. It was nothing, really,
just a dim sense of things being in flux for you, not
having the sharp resolution your shoulder did, set against
but contained within one of the world's cream-soft
afternoons. Today, as I drifted, eight hawks assembled
overhead and appeared to divide the land between them
before winging apart. Along the same line, two herons
heckled each other all the way to an island. And then,
before I came to work, two sunfish rose to kiss the thin
divide, and eyed maybe this cabin with its funhouse
and watery walls, its moss-soft roof sliding rain clatter
onto upturned rowboat. A Gillian Welch song poured
through window screens that offered a million metal-framed
and diminutive vistas. Trouble was, none of those views
contained you, and it seemed the only important point, still
does. There was only the scream somewhere north of an
unleashed bandsaw and, closer to this temporary home, the
blind drone of a dragonfly trapped under the dock's dozen
pine ribs, those twin fish mouths rising again, towards it.

COAST

There are ways to see ahead. Or rather
futures loom as oncoming traffic might
on foggy mornings, and it doesn't take
any rare gift to discern general shapes.

The second image forming dully for me
is of boats, cloud feeding among them,
and gulls wheeling above, though that
seems something that should be edited—

the life in sea towns is settled, becalmed,
won't attach to my life, still so hectic
with rare event and circumstance.
End of summer I left James Street

and there was money's quick disappearance,
its constant wane, and I saw that coming.
Same for changing clothes in parking lots
back of the gym or coffee shop, the grey

Toyota's trunk open like a mouth.
All this is predictable, I guess, or was;
nothing in the scenes would surprise any
friends. But recognition for the writing,

and praise, the odd grant, were also possible.
And if I push a little so was a place
in the city with great windows and plaster
walls, a brace of orchids nosing upwards.

Myriad scenic adventures. But there's nothing
foreseeable about this: a desperately early
morning with fragrant blistering memories
still dancing in me of S., her undraped

stretch today for a hysterical kettle,
the neverending grand tumble of hair I know
dearly now the feel of, the considerable heat.
Her laugh and touch are a bright continuous

thread among my streaming thoughts.
There's more. Another minute and I'll ride
out to work in a chapel friends offered up
as sanctuary in the fall. And muse there

on joys available should I spirit away
with S., haunt for a bit old harbours
that resolve from childhood, wild dusty
parts of Wales. Coastline I disowned

yet see her in regardless, artfully arranged
other side of a wrought-iron table and
reading aloud from the *Observer*, or else
flipping through photos that offer us

together, or slightly apart but reaching
determinedly for each other across
a backdrop of cobalt sky, bridging all
the unimaginable spaces. And with these

roughed-in words I aim for the same
connection, and I suppose also to direct,
in some localized fashion, time's traffic,
root out obscure hidden maps that might

indicate how best to move from here
to there without drifting ever into ditches
steep-banked and veering madly off
course, or into other less engaging arms.

Patrick Warner
[b. 1963]

Patrick Warner's first collection of poems, *All Manner of Misunderstanding* (2001), was
nominated for the Atlantic Poetry Prize and for the Newfoundland and Labrador Book
Awards. His most recent book is *There, there* (2005). He lives in St. John's, Newfoundland.

GUMSHOE

Packed in pick-up trucks they arrive at dawn,
these small, overalled, dark-skinned men,
from countries south of the Rio Grande,
who tend to the trees and bushes and lawns

in this mature suburban neighbourhood
where month-by-month nothing changes
except the flags, I mean the flags that flap
from slender dowels, that are set alongside

the tasselled poles that fly Old Glory,
silk flags set to mark a holiday or season,
pumpkins, shamrocks, hearts, and bunnies
signal the year-long consumer obsession,

in this neighbourhood where nobody walks,
where in places there are no sidewalks,
where no one seems to notice what I notice
when I walk, and there's no one to ask

about these inch-square zip-lock baggies
I find every morning, dew-fogged and stuck
to the pavement—what are these exactly,
sandwich bags for wee folk, for fairies?

Such folk myths belongs to the old countries,
to the Irish pubs down by the harbour,
to Germantowns, Dutchlands, Little Italies.
New World folklore is of a different order.

Myths here are a poor man's collateral,
so new they don't seem like myths at all,
but swap stocks and bonds for gold and silver
and the city skyline for the magic kingdom,

and you'll understand why these lawns
are tended each day by Guatemalans,
Mexicans, El Salvadorians, Peruvians,
and you'll know why yesterday when I found

a sanitary napkin perched on the gutter
my first thought was of a magic slipper,
followed by thoughts of the ugly sisters,
and girls who will cut off their toes to fit in,

because that's the way it is in this place,
where the bloated frog is always the prince,
where there is blind belief in tomorrow
and in the wealth tomorrow will bring.

Today it brought a pair of black underwear,
women's black Moschino underwear,
dropped in the middle of an intersection
where I barely had time to examine them.

I thought, naturally, of Puss 'n Boots,
and maybe because I knew the ogre's fate
something a bit more sinister crept in,
and, as well, I was getting these looks

from a pair of Mexicans or Guatemalans,
both of whose faces barely topped
the four-foot hedge they were trimming,
faces right off a frieze in Tenochtitlán.

What's next, I wondered, a severed finger,
an arm, a ripped-out human heart,
a dead co-ed like Snow White on a lawn
surrounded by seven diminutive men?

Not that I'm saying it's all going to happen,
(as cases go it's not open and shut),
there are reasons the future is hidden,
but clues, too, if you know how to look.

MORMON

How will a Mormon boy get a wife, I wondered,
if he declines his mission to wander the world,
spreading the Mormon word as he goes:
no wife for a Mormon boy who refuses.

So I was kind to two young Mormon men
who came to my door last Saturday morning—
the point man in short-sleeved shirt and blue tie,
his back-up in short-sleeved shirt and blue tie—

the former displaying a pulp magazine
which featured a story on the fashion industry
and its dangers, especially to young women:
anorexia, bulimia, and low self-esteem.

I listened until—as if at some prearranged signal—
the second flipped open a leather-bound book
he had held until then with a sloth-like grip.
It was my cue to say: I am not a Christian.

This has been true of my life for so long
that to say it out loud gives only a moderate high,
which in turn brings only a moderate low.
And so I did not take it too badly on coming back in

to hear my eight-year-old daughter say,
in her deepest voice: *I am not a Christian*;
though to hear her say it brought it home in a new way,
and I thought for a moment that this is serious

and that she should take it more seriously,
so I considered putting the fear into her, telling her
that if her grandfather heard her say such a thing
he would think us condemned to eternal damnation.

Instead, I sat back down on the couch beside her
where it so happened there was scheduled
an end-of-season *Fashion File*—the year's best show,
the year's best designer, the year's best newcomer.

And watching, I reserved my loudest cheers
for headdresses of ostrich and emu feathers,
for models with bleached invisible eyebrows,
for models with slack, stew-bone thighs.

While she preferred the more womanly models—
though she did not care for naked breasts—
and reserved her loudest cheers for young Marc Jacobs
and for the ready-to-wear from Donna Karan.

What a world this is for a Mormon boy, I thought,
who declines his mission to wander the world,
spreading the Mormon word as he goes:
what a world for a Mormon boy who refuses.

THE BACON COMPANY OF IRELAND

Ramps, double-decked trucks, stink, lights,
shouts, kicks, electric prods, coconuts,
the workmen's high calypso as pigs run,
speed croquet over piss-shellacked,
shit-plastered floors, gully and drain scored.

Inside, no messing in mess, the point
driven home, mallet or stun gun sets
each one staggering, a modern dance
to the skull's high pitch—don't we know
that they are as intelligent as us?

Orchestral machinery kicks in. The
conveyor belt's dangling clefs, a score
into which their hoofs are hooked.
Hoisted, they perform one leg
inverted ballet that turns to opera
that turns again into modern dance
(the classical forms will not contain)
as they flex, wriggle, twist, gyrate
all the way to the conductor,
whose shiny baton slashes.

Plashing then like sustained applause
each is conveyed to the fiery furnace
(think Shadrach, Meshach, and Abednego
without a collective agreement)
to have golden bristles singed away.

Think of mother starting up a fry,
while at the same time trying to style her hair,
while trying to get the kids out of bed—
now see the children, passing slit-eyed
along the hallway, their lips curled in a smile,
their bodies limp as if they are still
in the deepest sleep, untroubled by
the shrieks that come from far away
(and that have always lived in dreams),
as they pass one-by-one into a room
of stainless steel and shining white tile.

HIKE

Water Street West

Water Street West: gauntlet of drunks
sinking fangs into Lysol cans.
Hooray for all the young people!
Pigeons tending to opalescent plumage,
bathing in gasoline-streaked pools.
The dry-dock and the Waterford River filled
with big skillet trout, tampons,
faeces, and bottle-nosed condoms.
Southside Rd., near Buckley's house,
let the climb begin. Now.
High-top soles draw in a million bits
of cartographic data. Lactic acid monks
inscribe filigreed contours
on bulging calves, thighs.

Back of the Brow

On this occipital bun, rock shrugs off
fibrous peat and rock-splitting roots.
The hot pine funk knocked down by sea breeze.
Freshwater Bay, aquamarine where
bleached white plastic bottle buoys
mark out lobster pots. From here
the rock breakwater's a necklace of spawn
holding back black lake water.
The rest's an easy walk. Oh sure.
A slippered slope of pine, with hand holds.
Chest-high ferns where live fellatio bears.
I peel a sprig of dog rose, walk
the undermined cliff path, watch
the swaying yellow snakes of
rope beneath the sparkle.

Freshwater Bay

After coming all that way, I'm mugged
by thugs: a band of lupins. Stunned,
I stagger off, a bee with pollen-heavy legs,
come back again, lean in closer,
on hearing from their puckered lips,
Come hither hiker, lean in closer,
admire us, imagine a bouquet.
Taken, I wrestle with a bunch of stalks.
The lance point flowers stir, whiplash.
One blinds me with its perfumed tip,
one neatly tops my cigarette.
A fire starts in yellow growth;
I stamp it out.

Dusk, Near the Cape Spear Road

722-2222. I call up Jiffy on the cell.
Yis, I knows where it is. I wait. A plastic bag
bulges, snaps in the breeze,
snagged on a punk-topped spruce.
Look back. A furled stand of parasols
around the rusted, shot-pocked shell
of a car, the ground around it
littered with shards of amber.
Stop to wonder how it got there,
fifty yards in from the road
down a two-abreast trail.
Look back. Run a sunburned arm
over soft, salt-sore lips, taste
flowers, pine, this place.

WATCHING THE OCEAN

You arrived that night in a shimmering slate-blue suit,
a linen rayon weave that still smelled of the factory,
and that, depending on how and where it rumpled,
showed a silver-whitish, semen, salt-lick sheen.

And all who dropped your name in conversation
as if they knew you, were suddenly quiet about it;
they could only watch how you moved from room
to room, restless in yourself but still at ease,

watch and wonder how—even as you grazed the buffet
for sea-salt chips and a foaming glass of 7UP—
you commanded such attention, reverence:
all felt in the presence of someone magnanimous.

But better from afar, you left each one you met
feeling smaller, undermined, like a bureaucrat
before sublimity, like a connoisseur of porn
reviewing videotapes of his daughter's delivery.

And even those who subscribed to the ideal,
who wished to be scoured of conceits, scattered
like crab claws, like lost bleach-bottle buoys
and massive main timbers on an isolated beach

found that they did not care for the experience.
Hence their tales of other nights and other parties,
of gale-force winds that blew without warning,
of houses left with not a stick unbroken.

Tim Bowling

[b. 1964]

The author of six books of poetry, Tim Bowling was shortlisted for the Governor General's Literary Award for *The Witness Ghost* (2003) and *The Memory Orchard* (2004). His novel, *The Paperboy's Winter* (2003), was shortlisted for the One Book, One Vancouver Award. He lives in Gibsons, B.C.

THE LAST SOCKEYE

for my brother

Always I think of the last sockeye,
the one in late October: blind,
blood-red, half-rotted, so far
from the creeks of spawning,
it just lay beside our net
in the silt-grey water—confused
or resting, we couldn't say—
then with one weak push
gilled itself
so we had to roll it in.
The last of its kind for the season;
most had died, or spawned and died,
at least a month before:
though barely caught, I could not gaff it:
we stood in the chill north wind, bemused,
as though we'd been given an early Christmas gift,
red-wrapped and taken
from below the mountains' undecorated evergreens;
we stared at the rotted eyes
and scales like bloodied coin,
a glove of chain-mail
after a Crusades slaughter
the living hand still inside.

Three separate instincts
and a whole long winter to forget
your drinking and failed marriage
my loneliness and too often
days of great despair

over things I cannot change
and always the gap between us
as wide as the gap
between the sockeye and its goal;
three separate instincts
with nothing to win
three separate species:
I don't remember what we said
or even if we spoke at all
but the salmon, at least,
knew what it wanted,
so I gave it back to the river,
blind, rotted, and doomed,
I gave it back

while we stood in the stern like the last men
and watched the bloody hand of the year wave goodbye

LOVE POEM, MY BACK TO THE FRASER

Whale jaw, jack spring spine, rock cod gill,
scallop under the skin of my hand; these
are the bones I'm burying now. Tomcat skull,
sparrow wing, spaniel paw, full moon behind
my bluest gaze; I'm planting them all.
No animal returns to gnaw its gnawed limb
left in a trap; I've thirty years to dig
the deep six for, and hard shoulderblades
to gunnysack. Darling, carry the spade
for me, chant my years without you down;
I want the sunlight on a new foundation,
my old bricks in the wormsweet ground.
Cattle hock, heron claw, muskrat rib,
mast I hang my breathing from; I'll part
the grass and roll the die; I'll build
new castanets: here's a fresh gentility:
as the hummingbird twines its tiny nest
of spiderweb and moss, so I build
my hope and sleep from the marrow
of your kiss.

GREAT BLUE HERON

Prehistory stands in the saltmarsh
on stem-thin legs sinewy
as a sailor's twisted hemp
and cries once, brief and hoarse,
the bugle blast of a tubercular angel
heralding another apocalypse

then lifts into the ashen sky
ponderously
and skims the tufted cattails
along the muddied riverbank,
large eyes still reflecting
an earth before time,
blinking away with jaded calm
armies heaped below China's Great Wall,
the first stigmata cooled on the cross,
the basketed pallor of French aristocracy,
all the race's casual carnage
running dark and constant beneath
the beating of awkward wings

now flies through a light drizzle,
an umbrella with a broken spine
swept against the darkening sky,
a failed sketch for Kitty Hawk
slowly erased from the page

and reappears at dawn
alone as always, perched on a rotted piling,
hunched in its shabby raincoat
like a terrorist, smoking long
cigarettes of mist,
coolly staring at life,
 waiting for the final bomb to go off,
waiting for the end of history.

EARLY AUTUMN: A STILL LIFE

The cock pheasant and the fallen apple
(a transparent) share the top step
of the grey paint-chipped back-porch.
Both have been cut from their sap,
the bird from sky and cattailed ditch,
the fruit from its high branch.
On the laundry-line a bedsheet flaps
a rhythm quiet as a dying rain.
Against the side of the house
my brothers' mud-splotched boots
beside their shotguns catch
the final auburn of the sun.
There's a smatter of blood
along the snapped-tight beak
of the pheasant that's redder
than its red-brown feathers,
and a small bruise on the apple
where it struck the earth,
so that the former resembles
the moon with a single crater.
I am five and sitting on the bottom
of the porch. No one is looking for me.
It is the twilight time between supper
and my lukewarm bath. I know a few things
more than the things my eyes can see.
My brothers shot the cock with a gun
earlier that day in the potato fields.
It will decay as the transparent ripens,
one fall leeching the sap from the other.
And it will take a long time and no one
will even notice their traded skins.
and because I'm five and know some things
(and feel what I can't give a name to)
I have already sided with the apple.
I love how strange our changing happens.

READING MY SON TO SLEEP

Last night, for the first time, I went down the well
my father went down with me.
It plunged deeper than the back of the little skull
whose edge lay page-thin on the white pillow
and darker than the earth's dusk seeping in
to blot the secret passwords that I spoke.

"Hello," I tested with each downladdering breath,
the letters pattering like rain in the murk
and echoing off the cavernous stone. A blink,
a butterfly's tentative settle, and the slight
way back had briefly closed.

Another blink, and I was left
with the aftersound of uttered entrance,
my eyes guttering, arms loose as rope.

With an inward cry I could not help
I watched darkness flood the praying-book.

Andrew Steinmetz
[b. 1965]

Andrew Steinmetz is the author of *Wardlife: The Apprenticeship of a Young Writer as a Hospital Clerk* (1999) shortlisted for the Edna Staebler Award for Creative Non-Fiction as well as for the QWF First Book Award and Mavis Gallant Prize for Non-Fiction. He has two poetry collections—*Histories* (2001), shortlisted for the A.M. Klein Prize for Poetry, and *Hurt Thyself* (2005). He lives in Ottawa.

FROM "HISTORIES"

VI

brain tumour lady
known
to this hospital

followed
by one
of our cancer guys

was found by
the gates
of Price
Club

post-seizure

on
exam
nothing

too exciting

abrasions
cuts

some minor
savings

otherwise
as
I said

a brain tumour

VII

one hell
of a lucky guy

shot
in
the head

not sure
by whom

    crazy trajectory

in

        one ear
   out
the   other   cheek

bullet
had bat
sense

you got to see his films

XII

sailor
Russian

speaking
giant

Vodka
drinker

card
player

fell from
deck

cheated
death

on
exam

no skull
fracture

confused

wants a
divorce

shuffles when
he walks

out
to sea

homesick
ship

in a bottle

xv

camp
survivor

second
this month

bizarre

brought
in
by ambulance

with general deterioration

and long term memory
deficits

thank god

XVII

street person
frequent flyer

hypoxic disoriented

unreliable historian

says she's the queen
of Spain

drinker

inappropriate

ex-teacher
high-school
band leader

reminds me of someone

XVIII

end stage male

picked
up
in the park

closest
kin
unknown

AIDS related
no phone
number

previous visits well
documented

last
seen in
drag
in clinic
nine months ago

lost faith
in treatment plan

and in multidisciplinary teams—

tachycardic
hyperventilating

breathing
sounds
like a blow torch

XXI

stroke victim

this woman was
hospitalized
over
the summer
and
released
to a rehab centre
with poor motor skills

where she spent another
few weeks
before
she was put back on the streets

    brought in today
by children
who say
they
        want their
old mother
back

JARGON

posterior fossa lesion
convertible, available in red and black

delirium tremens
footballer, Belgian national

wound dehiscence
boiling kettle, humid whistle

pneumonia
hooker, Red Square and vicinity

clavicle fracture
Roman dramatist, circa 400 AD

peptic ulcer
blue chip stock

productive cough
heavy metal, band of the 80s

the malar bones
in Celtic folklore, evil twins

thoracic duct
a triple backwards flip

ganglion
client-server program, see Internet

TAHITI

You stretch out on the canvas and, well
look at us, far into this marriage
we've gone
native. A pillow behind
your ear suffices
for exotic
on our floating island,
this white sand mattress
with fitted sheets, that creaks
on four cheap, see-through plastic coasters.
Where do we come from? What are we?
Where are we going? I don't care.
Nude, you and I are modern
as can be. No futile white bird,
no injection of regret, no adjustments
are necessary here. A necklace of red teeth
marks about your shoulder, puts to shame
the pointillist masters we left ashore.
There is but one savage
side to this. The fruit which hangs

from us both, detaches
in lesser hands
than ours.

OLIGODENDROGLIOMA

Seventeen letters across.
Draw it on paper,
write it down. Caterpillar,
centipede. See, it moves

off the page, and
drops, a soft tractor
under leaf or tissue.
Now expand the tree,

find your terminology—
Neoplasm, Brain—
on a lower branch
crawling with information

like cells appear well-defined,
compact, and rounded.
Actually, avascular.
Macroscopically, a pinkish smear.

Imaging studies show, how
they grow outwards from
white matter into grey matter.
Chemosensitive, yes.

Median age at diagnosis,
40-50 years. Either
sex. Shave your hair.
In a week or so.

Depends on size,
location. Ordinarily, no.
She wanted everything I had
on Oligodendroglioma.

LATE

You were late, a few days late, which surprised
neither of us. Lying in bed on Sunday morning
propped up on powder white
double pillows, lazy as supernaturals

we talked about you getting pregnant again,
boldly, as if 'having a third'
would fully perfect us, as if, anyhow,
something, like the birth of a child,

had been sadly missed. I have always
been fond of that supine
conversation, the hours of logic rich
chit chat, the improvisations of such people

in our position, glancing up at the bedroom ceiling,
without the consolation of stars or smoke,
who yet seem enchanted
to gossip about themselves, and not others,

for the possibility of new life incites a particular
perspective, it presages some involvement
in the hypothetical, as we both
make childbirth out to be a powerful afterthought of ours.

To be sure, as per the conversation, 'There will be sacrifices,
and added expenses…diaper changing, sleepless nights,'
not to mention more sore nipples
and much less time 'for us'. Side by side with the pillows

stuffed under, we kept the channels of diplomacy
open, until, the inevitable
happened, again. Given that 'a third' could well
annihilate us, I turned to you

and you turned to me, and we
made love heroically.

John Degen
[b. 1965]

John Degen has published two books of poetry, *Animal Life in Bucharest* (2000) and *Killing Things* (2002). A first novel, *The Uninvited Guest,* will be published by Nightwood Editions in 2006.

SIBIU

the name is familiar,
and on the platform sign it is even the same colour
as the famous sausage wrapper
salam de Sibiu
the only meat for weeks and now,
just another late night railstop,
another wheel inspection,
another chance to listen to the darkness of the hammer
on steel, me stretched
across three seats
in an unconscious compartment

it's all done by sound;
I've figured that much
on this the slowest
night route through only the most impossible of places—
Transylvania; still not real even after
I've tasted their local cheese—
the wheel must ring a pure and lasting note,
to prove it hasn't weakened or cracked.
I'm trying to guess this man's height
by the number of steps he takes
between hammer blows;
taller for certain than the last town's, but still
nowhere near the three-stride man in Cluj Napoca,
old Three-Stride—I miss him

here in the dark, listening to steel
ringing
I'm looking across the world,
that curve I saw from the airplane window
to everyone there

deep in afternoon,
and instead I can see him
in what he's missing at this
same moment:
tea, half-finished on some wooden tabletop,
a radio perhaps, perhaps a game
of backgammon, suspended by the rumble
of our arrival, so he
can go and measure himself
between swings;
his sound, his ring unique—determined
as much by his own strength as
the air here, and the density
of trees and granite surrounding
this mountain-station home—
after half a life here, he would be no good anywhere
else; hearing faults in the steel tone
where there are none, simply
because there the poplars
are younger because of a fire, and the soil more acid
from the pines

there is no such thing
as *across the world*—and at this thought, he
has reached the wheel nearest me, the
hammer blow vibrating into my neck,
his breath audible

his must be overweight;
I'm sure he likes beer

futility
is wanting even to see past this
stop right now,
a tiny pasture of lives, those awake
to the night train rocking toward Bucharest,
those asleep, who don't see these invisible workers
for weeks at a time, and
are delighted when they show up
in the tavern

those things, and a line of sausages,
dry and perfect,
stretched out into a ringing blackness

UNDERGROUND

the meaning of underground has changed again
—there was the hole Pete and I dug beside
the tracks in some little town I don't remember—
as well, the reason for the hole
—who remembers these things?
why we go underground

better to forget,
especially there, in the heat of the sky
just turned afternoon-old and dried out,
weeds dead above our heads, and suddenly
some kind of everything shaking, like
neither of us
has ever understood,
the walls of our grave sliding in
on each other, playing
mine disaster to the two of us
scrambling up and out,
remembering obviously, to roll away
from the screaming iron wheels,
hardhats and shovels half-buried below us
Pete had spent two summers before this cutting
grass in the cemetery, and now
he hates holes altogether
—that and deep water; just another
kind of hole really

I'm underground much of the time now,
though they're careful to let in some sunlight here
and there to stop me screaming

it's nothing dramatic, really,
just the tunnels below the city, marble-walled

and too slippery too often, like we forget
how soft we really are;
where you'd go maybe to purchase
a silk tie on a day you've managed to
tunnel all the way downtown without one;
so unlike, in its similar aspects,
the underground nature of other places

once in London, climbing the hot cylinder
of Covent Garden when the elevator broke down;
how does a Canadian boy work
himself around the world,
under the surface, so he
finds himself coming up out of it,
on some hundred-year-old spiral in the dead capital?
only to sink again, years later, into musty Prague,
a nervous man, sick in the guts,
breathing a river smell that can't ever be washed
from the walls—
so deep in fact that you
count the temperature changes
while the escalator carries you to the surface

in Bucharest they keep the sun in
the subway when it's time to put it away
for the night,
and there you taste its lingering all day,
air like a shove
to press against when you leave the train;
in that made cave,
I think I found the wall that is farthest
into the earth, behind a toilet so old,
it must still be there, hidden around corners,
at the end of corridors
most Romanians even will never choose
to see, being wiser than me, and not
stopping for one more beer
downtown, before burrowing home

and while, here, everyone around me
knows there are only

shops and wide avenues,
polished with money, beneath the streets,
I hear the breathing of that city
worker behind me, amused and, I think,
a little unnerved that I found his private toilet,
a room about the size of a large man's casket,
in the basement of Bucharest, about as
deep as you can go and still
have water run downhill,
himself in a hard hat, breath
solid from inhaling earth

NEIGHBOURS ARE DANGEROUS

They are shooting old women
in the flower gardens, hanging
children like Christmas lights.

I recommend isolation,
hiding and not answering
when called for.

There is merit in broadening
your appetite to rotted things,
the papery bark of softer trees.

Remove anything yellow
and believe it is wonderful
to sleep in rivers.

It is the alternatives now
that comfort, the livers
of wild hares, the breath of housecats

you steal for warmth, a dirt
blanket, and the happy knowledge
there is nothing uglier
than what you are.

THE RATS OUTSIDE ME

Spines pulled in an inflexible
French curve, all haunch to keep their mouths
at the earth, licking dust,

they are scuttling eggplants, gray-brown from
rot but clean in their fashion,
in the way wet gravel is clean.

I question only the where of them,
their sudden and marvelous attendance,
their subtle rule,

like they've read their own stories, and laughed
well over them, wondering how we have
so completely missed the point of being rat.

Two of them wrestling in an alleyway
on Huron Street, a rat wheel in perpetual motion
until the wall breaks them apart, hissing,

punch drunk they face me,
certain in the direction of events to follow.

And, after visiting Michael for the last time,
I watch one cross Elizabeth Street to the hospital,
heading in to visit the disease.

CROW

Crows, you notice,
prefer to very tops of trees;
being claustrophobic, a cage
of branches at mid-trunk
would set them panicking.

Born time-wasters, they're
the TV watchers of nature,
enraptured by shiny things.
They perch beside highways,
at the very tops of trees, and
gaze liquidly at the big
river of shiny things, flowing
in two directions at once.

Proud of their own mystery,
they like to show up
just when it seems their shape
against the sky
is most symbolic of—
what?—death, intelligence
in the woods,
laughter let slip into the past.

While you walk your parents' dog
through a winter forest
of bald branches, they appear,
at the very tops of trees, and speak
of their own arrivals, disappearing
just when you settle on
what that pure
throat noise might mean.

Michael Crummey
[b. 1965]

Michael Crummey lives in St. John's, Newfoundland. He has written three books of poetry, *Arguments With Gravity, Hard Light* and *Salvage*, as well as a collection of stories. His first novel, *River Thieves*, was nominated for the Giller Prize, the Commonwealth Writer's Prize, the Amazon/Books in Canada First Novel Award, and won the Raddall Atlantic Fiction Prize and the Winterset Award. His latest book is the novel, *The Wreckage* (2005).

THE LATE MACBETH

His body divorced him slowly
like a flock of birds leaving
a wire, one set of wings at a time—
still in sight, but past retrieving.

Extremities first, his right foot
dropping asleep, forcing a limp
until the left faltered numb,
conspiring to abort every step.

Fingers and tongue deadened, as if
wrapped in a muffle of feather down—
each affliction painless and shameful,
like a ship run aground in sand.

His infant child seemed to chase him,
her development a mirror
image of his progressive loss;
her wonder, reversed, his terror.

Still, he got on with things, wrote
the last poems, read. Tried to swallow
the panic that galled his throat,
never mentioned the dream of crows.

After his voice abandoned him
his wife scissored an alphabet
and they relearned the grace of words:
letters raised like a wick, and lit.

At the end he was stripped of all
but that fire, its sad, splendid
glow. When his wife offered him
the sedative they knew would end it

he asked "How long will I sleep?"
spelled it out, letter by letter.
The fear had left them both by then.
She told him, "Until you're better."

NEWFOUNDLAND SEALING DISASTER

Sent to the ice after white coats,
rough outfit slung on coiled rope belts,
they stooped to the slaughter: gaffed pups,
slit them free of their spotless pelts.

The storm came on unexpected.
Stripped clean of bearings, the watch struck
for the waiting ship and missed it.
Hovelled in darkness two nights then,

bent blindly to the sleet's raw work,
bodies muffled close for shelter,
stepping in circles like blinkered mules.
The wind jerking like a halter.

Minds turned by the cold, lured by small
comforts their stubborn hearts rehearsed,
men walked off ice floes to the arms
of phantom children, wives; of fires

laid in imaginary hearths.
Some surrendered movement and fell,
moulting warmth flensed from their faces
as the night and bitter wind doled out

their final, pitiful wages.

'OBSERVATORY ON MOUNT PLEASANT' (1890)

Paid off a ship in St John, New Brunswick
and no work to be had until I got word
of a building going up in Mount Pleasant.
The foundation already down
when I arrived and the foreman
took me on as soon as I mentioned
being several years on the tall ships.
It was twenty stories high when we finished,
and I was sent up the pole to hook the block
and hoist the framing for each floor.
Each time up I could see more of
Lily Lake at the foot of the mountain,
the crooked arms of the apple trees
laid out in orchard rows,
and there was always a handful of nuns
saying the Rosary outside the convent below.
I waved in their direction from every storey
but they went on praying as if they hadn't seen me,
perhaps it was my safety
they were bringing to God's attention.
Stayed on until the place opened in October
and the night before I shipped out
they sat me in the chair beneath
a telescope the size of a humpback—
for the first time I saw constellations
the way a saint perceives the divine,
almost clear of darkness.
When I carted my tools down the hill
those stars came with me, a branch of
ripe fruit almost close enough to touch.

'A TRIP TO THE LABRADOR AMONG THE ESQUIMAUX' (1882)

Left home on July 3rd with Captain Abraham Herl
being my first start for the Labrador,
a pleasant breeze behind us and on the 7th
we stopped over in Indian Tickle, laying up

a night in the lee of Breen's Island;
then down as far as Hopedale among the Esquimaux
where I took a good view of their materials
passed on from the days when our Lord
Jesus Christ was preaching in the holy lands.
The people seemed strange to me as it was
my first time among them and I could not
understand their language which some claim
is descended directly from Cain
but they showed us many curious things
and I was delighted with them.
We stayed over a weekend and attended
a service in the Moravian church
where the German preacher offered prayers
in that queer hum rutted with clicks
and burps, and several among us thought
to be offended on God's behalf.
But he prayed for a good trip of fishing
for the visitors in a more familiar tongue,
our traps came up full off the Farmyard Islands,
and Captain Herl suggested God is not
so particular as some would have us believe.

ARTIFACTS

An old couple lived here before you and I.
Brother and sister, raised in this house,
forced home after years away
by a stingy pension, the death of a spouse.

They didn't get on at all in the end,
the neighbours say, led separate lives,
divided the six rooms between them,
ate separate meals at appointed times.

Stuffed in a drawer, we found sheets of paper
columned with scores, their names scrawled at the top—
they must have argued over words for years
till first the Scrabble, then the talking stopped.

A sad story told by sad artifacts
we never thought might spell out our own.
A house divided as if split by an axe.
Two people sitting to their meals alone.

Karen Solie
[b. 1966]

Karen Solie was born in Moose Jaw and raised in southwest Saskatchewan. Her first collection of poems, *Short Haul Engine* (2001), won the BC Book Prize Dorothy Livesay Award and was shortlisted for the Griffin Prize, the Gerald Lampert Memorial Award, and the ReLit Award. Her second, and most recent book, is *Modern and Normal* (2005). She lives in Toronto.

CARDIO ROOM, YOUNG WOMEN'S CHRISTIAN ASSOCIATION

You won't know me. Any resemblance
to the woman I was is purely
agricultural. That fluff. A pink annual
given to low-born intemperate acts
unbecoming a modern person. No more.
I'm tough. Nothing
could eat me. No profligate billy
with a hacking cough, or that old goat
and his yen for plagues, floods, and burning
fun places to the ground. Not you,
either. There was a time
I rolled like dough, plumped up
to be thumped down with artless yeasty
chemistry. Dumpling. Honeybun.
I sickened some. But evolved
in a flash, like the living flak
of a nuclear mistake. In space-age fabrics
I've moved more iron than a red
blood cell, climbing and climbing
the new world's dumbest tower. I'm on
to this. Alongside the rest
I sweat it out with the smug one-party
affability of a sport utility
vehicle. Deceptively little cargo space.
Even covered in mud I look great.

STURGEON

Jackfish and walleye circle like clouds as he strains
the silt floor of his pool, a lost lure in his lip,
Five of Diamonds, River Runt, Lazy Ike,
or a simple spoon, feeding
a slow disease of rust through his body's quiet armour.
Kin to caviar, he's an oily mudfish. Inedible.
Indelible. Ancient grunt of sea
in a warm prairie river, prehistory a third eye in his head.
He rests, and time passes as water and sand
through the long throat of him, in a hiss, as thoughts
of food. We take our guilts
to his valley and dump them in,
give him quicksilver to corrode his fins, weed killer,
gas oil mix, wrap him in poison arms.
Our bottom feeder,
sin-eater.

On an afternoon mean as a hook we hauled him
up to his nightmare of us and laughed
at his ugliness, soft sucker mouth opening,
closing on air that must have felt like ground glass,
left him to die with disdain
for what we could not consume.
And when he began to heave and thrash over yards of rock
to the water's edge and, unbelievably, in,
we couldn't hold him though we were teenaged
and bigger than everything. Could not contain
the old current he had for a mind, its pull,
and his body a muscle called river, called spawn.

JAVA SHOP, FORT MACLEOD

From the highway, a signal fire on the verge of prairie
so long in half light now that it is autumn.
This is a place you know to stop moving,
the tired joy of a door where you left it
and the Oldman Valley burning orange,

all your finest summers in its leaves.
It's a hinge of worlds, for you have loved poorly now
on both sides of the foothills.

Inside, frying is a kind of weather, a Florida
for flies, the doughnuts afflicted,
the coffee malicious.
Tiny friendless salads make you weep.
You've missed him by 15 years; he rested here
travelling west one summer of his life
before you. Build him out of cigarettes,
lousy tap water, what you know of his arms
and the things he looked out on. Much of it is gone.
Lean on the past and it gives. A small grace.

When it's dark, head east
past the horse killing plant. No deer for miles.
You left a line or two in the water
farther up the valley,
though someone else lives in your house.
Cross a friend's threshold and aging passes
like an unkind word between you.
Nostalgia is a prettier season. Leaves
fall on the river and a few are the colour of wine.

SICK

Thinking I am out of town,
friends steal my newspapers as I dissolve
like a lozenge in my semi-detached,
not quite myself,
and this starting to make a lot of sense. Outside,
weedy alders bow to weather, sighing,
wishing themselves hardwood
or southern Devil's Claw. Sullen crows
mimic wreckage and rust
and the neighbour's dog sobs with loneliness.
How solitary each noise in its net
of air, enough empty

between them for wind to bawl through
with its vowels end to end. Aching,
at least, is quiet.
The rest won't shut up. Bursting
through stalks of the mongrel houseplant
with awful furred leaves, flowers
like small red alarms
and the cat, drinking,
sounds like going over Niagara Falls in a barrel.
Curled beside me for hours, he shows his teeth
to what never sleeps in his head. You left
on the third straight day of rain, left me
the germ of an idea,
a little something to chew on as citizens hammer
the accidents of their lives into suburbs
and this first winter storm
tows months heavy and grey as freighter
and fog behind it.

ALERT BAY, LABOUR DAY

Rusted boats—*Stella Lynn, Pacific Lady*—
photograph well on black water,
their holds filled with rocks.
The men add one each night
and yell for storms. Happy hour
stumbles in from the dock
at noon, smelling of fish—
or fish-shaped memory,
since the fish are gone.
Tourists ask if the halibut is fresh.
The waitress has a bruise
on her cheek. Walls here
are made of luck and girls
walk into them.

John MacKenzie
[b. 1966]

John MacKenzie was born on Prince Edward Island. His first book, *Sledgehammer and Other Poems* (2002), was shortlisted for the Atlantic Poetry Prize and the Gerald Lampert Memorial Award. He lives in Charlottetown where he is on the editorial board of *blue Shift: A Journal of Poetry*.

RIDING THE ROUTE FOR NATURE AND HEALTH

Bad things are happening, and that's good.
—MICHAEL LEON

past random apple trees, around hurrying orange caterpillars
between fields of tall corn under a sky refracting
me amid this devastation beyond town
into a roar of front-end loaders, a scrattle of
steel buckets & blades pushing into shale, the crumbling

edges of shale pits lined with garbage, cut
with earthen ramps packed under notched tires of rough dump trucks
& the scarring treads of bulldozers (this one
still toppling trees, ripping earth, tearing out
stumps & roots)

blackberries ripen on the edge of this
red turns to deep purple-blue, stains
my eyes the colour of the bruised sky & rain
falls through the slanted rays of the falling sun while
the wind at my back skirls
like distant bagpipes after my ears, me fleeing

the city building itself out past & over blackberries
filling holes left by extracted trees with concrete & fiberglass
breathing formaldehyde into root systems
& rain falls through
the slated rays of the falling sun
as I sing

the drone of bike tires on gravel, my sternum buzzing
a deep hum, vibrating trees
drowning machines in sonic waves, the whole
world rattling with my passage &

the sky still is not still, the sky is
still patched with Autumn blues greys & blacks
my laughter rips cloud banks out whole &
throws them down like swatches of Night, pulls
three-mile-wide sheets of Light across the western sky

I turn back to the city, legs pumping
against the solid wall of wind it blows out,
the wind rushing from town bends the flimsy
yellow & orange of butter-and-eggs, the intricate
intermittent white of queen anne's lace, tolls orange
bell-like bunches of dog-berries, makes
whole fields of purple clover rage northward & crash
against treelines like wild alien seas &

my laughter is an array of sledgehammers
slamming fractals in september-tinted air
my howl of dismay the same,
blurring metal cracking through everything torn
everything stolen
everything expropriated

through these still green trees I see
streamlined buses plow dense air between
toppling towers & feel
cool beads of hilarious death in my armpits, a sudden
grinning growth of bone through
the flesh of my jaw.

DRINKING WITH THE NEUROSURGEON

So I cut into the head, see
my bone saw squealing and throwing sparks—
it's hard to keep that blade sharp—

smoke drifting in thin blue curls up into the light
me bending and blowing on the pencil lines
to clear the blood and bits of bone enough
to see what the hell I'm doing

I make one cut and then a couple of crosscuts
and the head opens up like a goddamn door, or a window
cut in the wall as an afterthought because
you thought you might want to see
maybe the sunset
maybe the blue herons painted into the cove at dawn
or in this case
what's going on in a guy's head

And the stuff he had jammed in there!
I'd never been that close to a blue heron before
damn thing thought my hand was a mackerel...
long scissors of a beak came clipping out of the hole—
if one of those sunsets he had stacked beside it hadn't fallen just then
thick with red clouds
and sent that bird flapping back towards dawn
I'd be smoking with my other had

Yeah, a lot of stuff in there
I'd catch the edge of something with my probe
and a raft of night would go feathering
down towards the brain stem; sometimes studded with nails
sometimes gleaming with bits of dew
and sometimes falling into a bright well at the centre

And below all this, the thing he had lodged
in Broca's Area, all his vocabulary of desire
and commitment arranged round it as spectators
was a four-and-a-half by nine Black Crown pool table
with Simonis cloth—the Pleiades hung over it as lamps
And him and god chalking their cues
smoking cigarettes and playing nineball
"Double, or nothing," he'd say after every game

I closed him up, and as far as I know,
they're still playing

NOW WE SING OUR DESCENT

When we invented distance, we decided we had fallen.
That the shock of landing had broken us like brittle rocks.

We did not ask if we had gone too far. Instead,
We invented dimension, hoping it would give meaning to distance.
Time was next, and we realized it was too late to turn back.

Points, you see, had become lines,
And lines turned into walls and damp ditches
And the frenzied leaves on trees in the wind.

There were surfaces behind surfaces,
Under surfaces, beside surfaces;
our fingers were drunk with nuances of texture.

And when we went walking, we found up-and-down in the earth,
And to-and-fro upon it. We called this direction
(Again claiming we invented it), and equated it with purpose.

And purpose was the one fruit we ate,
Planting husks as seeds in every place we passed,
Until fragments of cities and beliefs clung to our feet.

We decided our fall had impaled us on each moment
As gloriously as beetles on a collector's pins.

Now we sing our descent: a psalm of how
We have invented everything except the hoarseness of crows,

And how we breathe in the night
As the wind sends its gusts through us.

THOR, SHANGHAIED BY YAHWEH TO TEND THE WORLD, RAMBLES ABOUT MACHINERY AND HARD WORK

Boy, what do I know about machines and their clank of metal,
or raspy calluses that snag on delicate silk and fancy cotton shirts?
What do I know about things that drip oil, sweat and throw heat,
hurry Ragnarok and entropy, things which pound and pound
and turn out spare parts?

All I know is this: the work of rebuilding the world everyday—
of reconstructing
atom by molecule, cell by cell,
the repetitious Universe—is harder than it looks.
But at least it's not precise.
I get to swing my hammer, and sometimes
(as ya know) I get to crack rockfilled skulls.
Now pay attention!

Hauling on this lever here (ya see?) brings
the Sun creaking up over the eastern edge of the world—
but make sure ya press this button first. Once!
Just once! Or else the rush of gas will snuff the pilot light
and there'll be nothing but a big dark ball hanging there
until we pull down a panel of sky and one of us (likely me) crawls
across rusty rafters to re-light it…

…Hey, boy! Did ya see where I left that hammer?
Today I gotta make a stream and
a shiny trout poised half-out of water—
his body tiled against the friction of re-entry;
his fins machined, his tail articulated; two great chains gaping
his mouth open; and a symphony of steel cables playing
his constant flutter of gills.

Christian Bök

[b. 1966]

Christian Bök's first book, *Crystallography* (1994), was nominated for the Gerald Lampert Memorial Award. *Eunoia* (2002) won the Griffin Prize. He created artificial languages for two television shows: Gene Roddenberry's *Earth: Final Conflict* and Peter Benchley's *Amazon.* He currently teaches at the University of Calgary.

FROM "GEODES"

earthquakes low on the richter
scale crack machicolated cliffs:
ramparts, bulwarks, parapets,
collapsing over time into other
variations on the same barricade.

you climb across crenellations
in the form of these sentences:
the buried ruins of battlements
in a fortress sapped by miners—
a toppled panoply of turrets,
cupolas, minarets and steeples.

spiked vocables in these caves
make a phalanx for the pharynx,
their syntax a cheval-de-frise,
a stalactiform portcullis to bar
access to worlds beyond words.

explore this schismatic edifice
through drainpipes and ductwork,
crawl spaces for interconnecting
vaults of nothing but cornices,
all these chambers but clusters
of grapes on the ivy of tunnels.

storm ditches,
ankle-deep in bleached flour,
lead you astray
through catacombs as convoluted
as warrens in an anthill
or canals in the cochlea of an ear.

you step across
the chasms between the words
on these pages,
taking care not to lose footing,
yet you fall into them:
elevator shafts without cables.

a spider rappels down its silk
filament to attack a butterfly
trapped in a cobweb of amber.

landslides
drag you down a funnelled pit
through the waist
of an hourglass
into an oubliette for all sleepers.

gravel showers
bruise your body till you swoon,
the sand a fluid
solid, spilling time away
into dunes on display in tiny jars.

geology writes
a eulogy for all that it buries
by pressing words, like moths,
between pages
of a mammoth encyclopaedia.

floating guano dust transforms the reality
of these caverns into a sepia photograph.

stagger through the cave
into a dark planetarium
where, looking up, you see
looking back, a nighttime
sky full of tiny ruby stars,
the eyes of a thousand bats.

vampiric angels who scream in a chorus
castigate you for disturbing their sleep.

the standing ovations
fall from the ceiling
in leathery fragments:

a book with its binding unstitched flung
away at night from the heights of a cliff.

these caverns exhibit avant-garde
sculptures that commemorate
patient, but unknown, architects.

dolomite pagodas, built in one grain
of dust at a time, melt in the rain,
like models of mushroom clouds.

obelisks glazed with a glycerol film
of water, as if made from kiln-fired
ceramics, bake in a slow geothermal.

limestone saunas swelter in acidic
vapour, trickles of sweat furrowing
pleats into curtains of sandpaper.

each memory is eroded, not erased,
for the cavern never ceases to record
its history in the code of its crystals.

BIREFRINGENCE

See in silk-screened kimonos
blowtorch scars on metal,
wings of iridescent
insects,
the aurora borealis.

See in stained-glass windows
spotlight gels for sunlight,
broken slides of hoarfrost
crystals
magnified through polarizers.

See in gasoline rainbows
eyes plucked from peacock fans
fuelling dreams of burning
asphalt.
Words kaleidoscope together.

Houseflies
see the world through gemstones.

Todd Swift

[b. 1966]

Todd Swift's third book of poems is *Rue du Regard* (2004). His work has appeared widely in Canadian and international journals and he has worked as a screenwriter. He ran Vox Hunt, the unique Montreal poetry cabaret from 1995-1997. He has edited six anthologies, including *100 Poets Against The War* (2003). He has been living abroad since 1997.

EVENING ON PUTNEY AVENUE

When all the lawns are shutting off,
neighbours each with a porch light to close,
I stand in my driveway and smoke alone
not allowed to smoke inside my house
and look down Putney Avenue, left and right,
as I was taught to do before crossing,
but stay in my place, watching for the moon
to change, as people wait for green.
The boy and girl shoot past in a red car,
she turns her face, an instantaneous affair,
then it takes Mortlake. A family with another

girl slowly talks though the leaves,
acknowledging no part of me. I step back
into the lilacs, to let them go without
having to recognize my slight presence.
She also turns, her eyes see my new haircut,
but she goes on with her parents,
her skinny legs in black summer shorts.
She accompanies my mind to the end of the block.
Come back, come back and love me,
I almost say. Once, this was the street where
I played soccer-baseball, and kick-the-can.

I must know the ground here like no one else,
the way the caterpillars crawl along the arm.
I am middle into my third decade now, at home
to have what comes back after a breakdown.
I lost a lot here, and when I was gone.
I toss the cigarette off the curb and prepare
to go back in. My parents are in there, warm.

The spring air is chillier than you might expect.
For all the things I do not have, I have
this night, suburban and sublunar, to collect,
like a paperboy cast in stone.

WATER, RUNNING

Our marriage is water running
in a bathtub with no plug.

For a moment, I want to disagree,
then don't, impressed by the image:

your image, for what is, after all
only you and me. Or, me and not

enough of you. But then, language
doesn't always connect so truly

to somewhere else: fall over and across
another thing just so, neatly joining

worlds together, like difficult puzzles
working out suddenly, from new-angled

words and other meanings piling on—
like those many-layered fountains

you loved, at the gardens in Istanbul,
which in their motion are symbols of

an Islamic paradise in letterless
signs more pure than if written;

like cold champagne cascading
over wide glasses at a wedding.

CINÉMA DU LOOK

Looking isn't love,
but it also pays attention.

The deliberate openness
with which blinds are left

apart, curtains wide, lights on
at all hours of the day and night.

And I, who must
work for a living, bear witness

to her changes, the shifts in
scenery, the *Cinémathèque*

française of her bedroom:
black and red lingerie, braless

t-shirt hours; the choosing
of a skirt or dress.

THE INFLUENCE OF ANXIETY AT THE SEASIDE WITH TEA

She saw the beauty of the sea and could not rival it
For lack of depth, for cut and clarity. It screened
Itself like a blue movie. It was a mandolin. Flat,
And on a continuous feed. The sea was a pool

On a spool, a fluid, wet circuitry, a freakish
Cola, without sugar or fizz. The sea was in business
To sell waves to sand; to deliver cetaceans to nets;
The sea is a grey-green, moon-led elephant

Who always forgets. She sank into the Sargasso
Of herself, and touched a wreck. It yielded doubloons
And Maltese falcons and other encrusted valuables;
She scooped the ice-cream starfish and the jelly

Of the sperm whales, and the cardboard villainy
Of certain sharks. She slid like a shadow, a dagger
Of slim ease in a pressurized medium. She sang
Oxygen and filtered sunlight, and salty tunes.

She was overcome by *Harmonium*, poems flushed
With quince and tea and royal-rococo references
To the world and imagination; dove, in homage;
She wrapped herself in a peacock-daubed kimono

In silken envy. How could she not be immensely
Injured by the creations of Key Largo and San Juan?
The ocean and its sisters set out a store of baubles,
And she bought them. She was the eye and womb

Of the stanzas that melted and ran through the town
Like rough blue-white bulls storming a seawall.
This was the first performance of the storm, the horn
Section was off. The rain pulled toads from its hat.

The world was brushed with cream like a scone.
Happiness was inherited and could not be taxed.
She swam Olympic strokes, and sang circular tracks.
The sea undressed, a Parisian girl, *oh la la, mais oui.*

LOST AT AUSTERLITZ

Water On Mars, sun at Austerlitz,
Human Genome Mapped, us lost:
driving, six hours from Budapest.

Your U-turn got us up to Slavkov
after a love-battle we now regret.
In 1805, this light sliced through

dawn mist, struck lake ice, cut off
the Hapsburg army's final retreat.
N marked the general's tent above

wavelike fields, golden, bloodless.
Enough to have been here, Napoleon
announced, to his still-living men.

Austerlitz, June, 2000

Barbara Nickel
[b. 1966]

Barbara Nickel's first collection of poetry, *The Gladys Elegies*, won the 1998 Pat Lowther Memorial Award. Her work has appeared in many magazines and anthologies, most recently in *A Cappella: Mennonite Voices in Poetry* and *In Fine Form*. Her latest novel, for children, is *Hannah Waters and the Daughter of Johann Sebastian Bach* (2005).

MARION, 1935: TO MY TWIN SISTER

The Hudson River, where we used to fish
in freckled rushes damp against our skirts;
its water like a silk scarf wound a hush
around our guarded chatter, laced with hurt.
I fashioned our escapes. We slid from naps
unnoticed to the woods and narrow path;
the junipers whose crusty tears of sap
seemed like our own, the dregs of Father's wrath.
I chose a hook. You fastened it.
We clasped our hands and cast for rainbow trout.
You hauled one in—I raised the stick and hit
its judging eye, like Father's shot with soot.
We battered it a hundred times in mud;
our petticoats emblazoned with its blood.

FLIGHT

Embers smoulder under sand,
coals criss-crossed with lights I send
up with a stick, watch a city
below extinguished with each hit.

Over Montreal, my brother
prepares to land. He will ensure
a perfect descent. Hazy fire,
late sun on the St. Lawrence far

as the yard from his childhood room:
garbage burning, August, his dream
to find an opening and run
touchdowns, touchdowns past the arena,

cement yard, graveyard, town limits,
into the sky where he'd meet
an older self descending. At thirteen
he saw himself: checking routine

lists, *flap selected, one hundred above,*
the runway lines brief
as clover under his feet. *Sixty knots.*
Control locks. Down.

                    My stomach knotted
on the six-block plod to school: steeple,
roofs, bricks, hedges, crabapple
bashed on the sidewalk. I tightroped
the cracks and a leaf became a ripped

sleeve fluttering in the ditch outside town
where the girl's body was thrown, a stained
scrap the police missed. I dared
another glance down, saw the murdered

girl's grave dug by ants, the place she was picked
up in all the sidewalk's pocked
corners. My walk took years. I teetered
along that high wire way in terror

of passing trucks, of one step
off the line. Was he intercepting
footballs? Over the line at twilight
was my brother falling like the lit

tips of waves that mesmerize
years later, waves that might erase,
as they run toward me on the shore,
this city of embers? Perhaps his hair

carried fire at dusk across a field,
the screen door slammed, the bathtub filled—
I can't remember him. That summer
he must have slid his hand down the same

banister as I did, heard that squeak
of wood under moist palms, the clock's
faint heart. He brushed the hallway wall
as we had our mother's womb.

                   Wail
of a night train—the murdered girl
was in his class. He heard a gale
stirring acres above us as I
heard her. On the spring day

he climbs out of St. John's and reaches
cruising speed, I approach
a footpath in that city. He flies
to Gander and returns: one flash

for all of my steps by the river,
weight of bags, dog shit jumped over,
stone by stone the high tower revealed
at the rate of my slog up the hill.

Waves toss up their burning wings,
feathers, even harp strings to the waning
sun that seems closer than the plane
above, drone familiar as wind. I lean

back, listen to it cross the Gulf.
It drags an unsayable grief:
If he should, if he—
                  He lifts
his two-year-old son, who laughs

to be tilted so high above the rug
and his father's chin, who trusts the rigging
of his father's arms and sees no map
below, only the chest he topples

in giggles against, and begs for more.
Supper. Uniform in the mirror
checked. Schedule: Halifax to Boston,
back by midnight. His son

falls asleep, his wife is rocking
in her chair, timing each creak
to the little breath, little rise and fall.
I skip a stone and watch it fall.

CHANGE ISLANDS

So named because I've heard
people here changed
islands by season, wintered

on the South and on the hinge
of spring swung to the North
Island, exposed to the slap

of the sea, then back. No one on the path.
Past small graveyards I sleep
by sea urchin skeletons, give

no thought to the phalanx
of cloud coming on. No grief,
except my pail lacks

the partridgeberries I seek.
In Chaffey's Cove, lobster traps
of broken slats and twine slack

with age, perhaps ripped
by tide, invite my hand inside:
bedroom, kitchen, parlour

where they took bait, and died.
Except the small one who, lured
by herring, tangled in the rooms,

jerked toward a slitted heaven
and found a hatch, a moon
to slip through into a haven

of sea, flux in the gulch, in
and out, applause of water
over stones and surge, again,

again, no house, no mortar,
feast of red-berries, heave
of tide, like Plath's stunned flies

I believe in heaven, here.

THREE POEMS FOR VIOLIN

Practice

At five each day I watch sun ignite
air-dust in this corner to a swarm
of gnats the metronome's steel finger swats,
while giant flowered armchairs stalk the room.
My violin is a skinny girl.
I tap the measured belly, ribs, neck;
strings pulley me, cross-eyed, beyond the scroll.
Father shrugs his paper. Mother cooks.
My scales pinch the winter afternoon and slide
off-key, whine like children lost at fairs.
Mistake. I want to break cracker-thin wood
and see it burn, limbs turning blue in fire.
Instead I watch the dust gnats glint
and pick the hardened sore beneath my chin.

Competition

I'm next. Fright spurts through me, threading
a way pricked by stares. The bow scuttles
across the strings. Music is a bead
inside my chest—it rises to my skull,
says, *Let me out.* I only feel a shaking,
new breasts that hurt like pinpoints underneath
the ruffle that my mother sewed. Bouquets
inflame the doors on every side. I breathe
and wait for judgements final as a knot.
You lost, the pencils blurt. I want a voice
unravelling, a spiral from my throat,
a curve unfurling, loose as silken floss.
Outside, the broken step, the smell of thaw;
a crocus like a bruise in muddy snow.

Busking

We play near aging cheese and scattered rice,
among the pumpkins, gulls and smell of fish,
breezes, clatter jesting on my face,
the jostles of the crowd and passing swish
of silk unseen. Our lines of music join
the cappuccino screams, juggle above
a pile of ripe tomatoes; seeds spill down,
and juice and music mash up in a sieve;
Mozart, the people shout. I laugh as doors
open, wind snatching notes and rumpling clothes.
Our cases on the wet and sticky floor,
the clinking coins on velvet, crumpled bills.
Beside my violin, a tiny boy
is moving to the shadow of my joy.

David O'Meara

[b. 1968]

David O'Meara currently lives in Ottawa. He is the author of two collections of poetry, *Storm still* (1999) and *The Vicinity* (2003).

THE WAR AGAINST TELEVISION

I know about the time, as a child, you'd stare
beyond far-off cottages on the opposite lakeside
wondering how it would feel to die. Remember?
Do you? You were hardly serious then. We've all gone
through that stage, the bright half-terrible change
when first scanning stars, trying to grasp where distance

ends, but after a summer of thinking, that distance
carries on beyond comprehension, resistant to any stare.
To be young is a kind of trance that doesn't change.
Majesty, like terror, slips in from the side
like a wind, whose broad fluctuations seem gone
though that first stinging draught we remember.

Our thoughts make noise; we are what we remember,
are the love we've lived, are the travelled distance
our own stride made. All that seems gone
is every distracted hour spent with a vacant stare,
blankly accepting that nothing will form inside
of us, content that nothing should change.

Each year should be a gathering, not the exchange
only, of anticipation to regret. I remember
at sixteen, working gas pumps—summer job on the side
of Highway 62—I watched clouds advance in the distance
across a blackening hayfield. Pausing, I stretched to stare
at the downpour coming on, daylight gone

to a grim contusion; the heat, traffic, for a moment, gone.
A stark, clear sheet beat straight down and didn't change
direction, the wet edge of it inching onward, luring my stare.
I saw the line of rain blacken asphalt, as I remember
the squall dashing through me, then spinning into the distance
west and beyond. A long while I stood beside

that dark highway. I wanted to stay right there, outside
myself looking in, attentive to every instant I had gone
through, reliving the days with a kept distance
even as I wanted to flee, hide, attempt to change
everything I had happened to be. The doubt I remember
still disturbs, like a mote that burns the pacified stare.

Living's impossible; a full-time job trying to change
ourselves into something we love before we're gone.
We can't catch our breath. No wonder we stare.

BRICKWORK

A red brick wall, framed
in timber beams and mortar,
collects the last gold of November warmth
on this lit morning.
It hasn't rested, though idle all these years.
A brick wall is stoic toil.
Compare one to your mother.

Or one afternoon, when an old lean-to
is removed from the back of a house,
check the darker patch left there
where sunshine did not abrade, and
consider the original
unfaded hue.

That colour is older than you.
That colour is the light from the same afternoon
as your father's father's birth.

On this corner, in this alley,
in short glimpses left
between plate glass and rolled steel, brickwork
still dogs us on our hurry to the places
we'll be meeting.
Stone-faced, it gazes on the circus
of weather. While the high-wires whistle, and gusts

trapeze between corporate blocks and a bare patch
of maples, it has composed
itself in an ordered frieze of dignity.
It wants nothing but to brace a roof
or front three-quarters of a room.
It would like to stay there—
to be a kind of proof.

NOMAD

Gafsa to Tozeur, three abreast, in
the back, piled close on wheezing station-
wagon seat-springs, the hood-stripe
cutting yawned-at early light
through olive groves and rollers of desert sand.
One hour, tops. South-west,
south-west. I could feel his hand
nudge near my ribs as it grappled
inside the brown-wool scarps of his cloak.
For what? I tried to guess.
A tool. Bread? It might have been, for all I know,
a cellphone. His face was an auburn stone,
submitting no evidence of the prolonged
spelunking at his torso
as he wrangled with the driver over every dinar,
a taut fringe of frayed white cloth
pegged behind his ears, the soft linen
polishing a bald scalp that crowned the furrowed
carapace of his brow and forehead, dry
as the salt-cracked sufferance of the Chott-el-Jerid.

Then a wide shapeless sleeve
puffed and filled, slunk
lengthwise to the cuff, like the digestive
bulge of a snake's latest meal, and the nomad's
fist appeared, clutching rumpled currency. And
that hand, his right:
like leather. Like dark sandpaper.
                            I know

I stared when he opened his palm, finely white,
buffed and smooth. Half of the three fingers and the top
of his thumb were gone, forgotten
since the mishap that fused the stump of index
to middle. The hand withdrew, deep inside, then his face
beneath the hood. The rough scratch of road
stretched on, under the magnifying sun.

LETTER TO AUDEN

Well then, sir, I thought of you again just recently:
        New Year's ticked in with scant fuss,
    The so-called millennium, hyped
        To bring disaster—not quite the end of us
But certainly an indisputable wholesale mess.
        There *was* noise, drunkenness,
        Fist-fights, cab-shortages, looters—
    But nothing resembling accidents
        Caused by crashed computers.

Nothing collided at midnight but our glasses in hand, then
        We hugged, blew horns, and kissed,
    While everyone across the globe,
        If not in bed, were pissed
On vodka, lager, chardonnay, so for one night at least
        Most aggression had ceased
        And the future seemed certain and stable
(Though a good friend of mine raced round the room
        And flattened the coffee table).

I'm sure you'd like some gossip, who's out and what's come in,
        The inside scoop on movers
    And shakers, the current poetic forms,
        (If anyone writes light verse
Anymore, if some of your books are still selling…)
        That job might be overwhelming
        But the world's much the same: factions at odds
    Over money or race, and—as always—
        Incompatible gods.

Yes, you'd find our mixed-up planet feels far too familiar—
    We can hardly cry a
  Tear as we wipe each other out;
      So long as some Messiah
Can be called upon, we march united to one grandiose Nada,
    The unlimited Florida
    Of history's retirement. Religion
  Will marinate us the way *we* sauced
      The passenger pigeon

As we shell out millions on Roman candles that take one
      Quarter-hour to exhibit
  While the gene pool shrinks, the ice-caps melt,
      And forests go to shit.
We must look real fine to those Emperors of history
      Who didn't mind infamy
      If it showed a little panache.
    Sir, I like what you said: *This great
    Society is going smash.*

Not really that we've ceased to care; we *never* did.
      But back when we were wrapped
  In skins, didn't have a match to burn,
      Ate with our fingers, and crapped
In the woods without benefit of Handi-wipe,
      We could bear to have the type
      Who fly right off the handle, crack,
    And commence a reign of Holy
      Terror, but at worst attack

A few weak cousins in our tribe and steal our fire.
      Oh, we like to notice how
  Barbaric our kind could be back then,
      How fine we're sitting now,
And shake our heads at Genghis Khan, the Viking raids,
      Inquisitions, and long Crusades;
      But those secure in that quaint notion
    The worst offences are in old texts,
      Disregard commotion

Reported in the TV news and daily papers
       And pine to think that Goebbels
    Was sent here from some other planet
       With Gulf Wars and Chernobyls.
And sir, I understand, if the bio I read was yours,
       You were around for two World Wars
       And witnessed the dread atrocities
    Of Spain's troubled clash—not to mention
       The Sino-Japanese—

So it's grim to quote you the latest stats, which school-kids
       Haven't had to study yet,
    But the recent span that joins these centuries
       Could just be the bloodiest.
Our weapons, quite new, are still as highly distressful
       Though now they're more successful
       And are televised when they kill.
    Nothing's changed. We have our madness
       And our weather still.

But the recent trend that might disturb you, more than
       Committees awarding
    Olympic-medal status to Beach
       Volleyball and Snowboarding,
Is the growing flair we have for being targeted
       With stylish, well-marketed
       Must-have technological gadgets—
    (Apologies to Guinness on their
       ingenious floating widgets...)

Fax, e-mail, cellphones, the Net: you should see the stuff
       We've thunk up since you died.
    Fast-food restaurant drive-throughs
       And electric toothbrushes aside,
There is no finer delusion that we're saving time
       Than this busy pantomime
       Of screens, links, beeps and double-clicks
    As if we'll turn our twenty-four hours
       One day to twenty-six.

Now we never waste an hour on antique hobbies
    Like sitting in silence
  Or whittling wood. What's the use of
    All that awful patience
When a thousand stimuli are ours to sample
    On-line? For example:
    No one needs to bother writing verse or
  Stories anymore; one button's
    Touch will make a cursor

Wink out crack programs like makegoodpoetry dot com.
    Just key in your preference
  For mood, style, or form; pick a tone,
    (Moral outrage, for instance),
Suggest some treasured images from heartfelt theme-words—
    Flowers maybe, or birds,
    A season, or place-names near your home
  To give it local colour. Press
    Enter: You've got a poem.

Without our pesky human meddling, paperbacks will
    Soothe like Vick's Vapo-rub,
  And doubtless find their way inside
    An Oprah-type of Book Club.
Our legacy in this Newest Age, like railroads
    In the last, are bar-codes,
    Micro-chips and encoded files
  That make generic products fit
    Around our tele-lifestyles.

High-tech firms and franchise now shape the Things-to-Be—
    Really, why begrudge them?
  (Anyone in opposition
    Is clearly a curmudgeon
And thinks it quaint there's home-cooked meals, virgin woodland,
    And letters written longhand.)
    Euro-banknotes and Bill Gates
  Have duly compressed the world's breadth
    More than tectonic plates

So that pretty soon we'll share the same opinions,
    Swallow the same cuisine,
  Dress in fashions dictated by
    One glossy magazine
And pause with ironic smirks for history to pop
    Its last champagne and stop
    Unfolding altogether. Then
  We won't have to bustle about
    Trying to make things happen

Since there's plenty of old stuff just lying around.
    We've got Greek pottery,
  Roman aqueducts and temples,
    Pisa's tower (though tottery),
That Big Wall in China; Mozart opera; Be-bop, Blues;
    English sonnets, Haikus;
    Moroccan rugs and German beer,
  Cuban cigars—Ok, I'm skipping
    Over quite a lot here—

But history, more than ever, is now a snazzy show
    Put on for the tourists,
  As if no one lives here anymore
    And culture just exists
To sell, promote, consume, and generally entice
    Travellers to our merchandise.
    (And correct me here if there's some doubt,
  But wasn't the Great Wall constructed
    To keep the tourists *out?*)

Sir, enough; I must admit, since looking back over
    The past eighteen stanzas
  It seems *I've* wandered from the point.
    (There is no rhyme but Kansas.)
In this lyric's first line I had started to say
    How the last New Year's Day
    You'd been on my mind. Why? Who knows.
  It's true I'd completed, in just
    Seven months, not one but two bios

That described your duration. And lately, I'll add
    I have mostly inspected
  The crowded near-thousand pages
    That forms your *Collected.*
You've memorable lines, are unrivalled with meter
    —You knew where your feet were
    And quite happy to show it—
  In the end, sir, I'll attest, you're
    One impressive poet.

Maybe the danger of our frequent disregard
    Was what you might have meant
  About our damaged lot as humans,
    Which sent me on my tangent
Of bellyaching about the post-post-modern condition.
    If our one ambition
    Could be to close the gap between
  Our public and private faces
    Then happiness might mean

Attending, at last, to what is most commonplace:
    Unbounced cheques, our neighbours'
  Warm affection, the friendship of rooms
    With sun and hardwood floors,
(If only life could arrange itself neatly as a rhyme,
    Or the balanced way we climb
    And relax inside a hammock)
  But nothing we'll ever know is that
    Patly epigrammatic—

As if our existence were one simple rule that campers
    Practice when residents
  Of the woods: *Take nothing but photos;*
    Leave nothing but footprints.
Who can say with assurance that the wide scowl of Age
    Will temper its umbrage,
    Unwrinkle, and offer a cheek;
  That the verse you gave form to
    Will be noticed next week

Or judged far too stiff and irrelevant, and you
    An outdated denizen
  From some other century, the way
    We think now of Tennyson.
Maybe the dates we live inside are unfixed borders
    Which we got our orders
    To move across one day, no word
  That our part was even successful,
    That our values endured,

But these first days of the newest year, of taking
    Stock and inspecting the view,
  I caught myself looking backward,
    And Wystan, I spotted you.
With ashtray, drink and carpet slippers, you still seemed bent
    In keen astonishment
    On naming the plague of our neuroses,
  Suggesting those who suffer worst
    Prescribe the better doses.

Truth is, I've no good reason for writing you this letter;
    It's rife with mixed regards—
  The way we feel true warmth for friends
    While cheating them at cards.
Perhaps I need forced rhyme, or idle chit-chat *entre nous*
    To guess what Dante knew
    Justifies champagne: something about love,
  Interest, praise, and gratitude,
    Or all of the above.

WALKING AROUND

    for Dorothy Jeffreys

Each city, since I left
I've been returning to—
curbs, bus shelters, doorframes,
stoops, the descending view

from the top of steep, one-
way streets that reach down to a square
and some avuncular statue, where
the space whips up a breeze

of polluted cirrus, and slides it across
buffed granite and glass,
above the five o'clock surge of mass
transit. All of those

generic or iconic
shapes of brick and steel—
flat-tops, spires, high-rise and three-storey
walk-ups—still

flit past my mind
in its liquid cradle, transporting me
through striped awnings and intersections, vines,
graffiti and clotheslines.

I'm somewhere else now, but I keep
moving through. My head
strolls the street-life, back
in cities briefly visited—

Vancouver, Kwang-ju, Montreal,
Miyazaki, Tunis, Rome—
If any of them ever felt like home
it's because I wandered those places arguably

enough, but I can't really tell, even
in the little time that's winged by
since then,
where I wanted to get to.

And why go anywhere? Just
that we need a pace to adjust
the mind's anxious racing and slow it,
carry it toward some

hint of destination. And so
I just walked, past wrought-
iron fences, off-ramps, bistros
monuments and grocery stalls,

down traffic-lapped avenues where crowds
rushed, late for a movie below
uneven ledges that glow
in mid-summer like long, sun-burned collarbones.

And because I often walked,
lingering in each city's new, unfamiliar grid
I was compelled to articulate
a restless part of myself, half-hid

and too uncertain to crack open
easily, until somehow, one day, this sudden
uncluttered question
presented itself: *where will I find*

a place I can live and be happy?
And I took that question, like a dog, for a long
walk, looking down into its unspeaking mug,
a stubborn pug

that shadows me again, turning
back, running ahead,
waiting at the crosswalk. A surprise
if I found I was learning

anything in this self-taught frogmarch
to nowhere. I mean, what
are the chances I'll ever bulls-eye that
skittish, civilizations-old

inquiry? But isn't that the reason
why anyone
walks for long hours, to bounce
the terror of not knowing

what their life is about
off the forms that surround them?
I strolled this doubt
through side-streets home,

markets closing, my boots'
iambic shuffle echoing into alleys
and down man-holed drains
near grey stains

of rotting lettuce, the pedestrianesque
figure of someone looking
for something. *Qu'est-ce que
c'est?* Some reverie,

some undimmed thankfulness,
a peerless moment
where nothing's surrogate, just
is, I guess.

(Wanting now to clarify
that I was not alone,
though a few years gasped by
in that apprenticeship

of being apart from you—and me
still learning to love more
and better...) Even happy,
we'll half-imagine

living in another
world, dumbstruck to say
what we would put there—news,
technology and architecture

that doesn't yet exist beyond a sketch,
floorplan or pasteboard maquette.
Like ghostly ads
of extinct brands—chocolate, hats, cigarettes—

on these brick facades, the past
is not far, suggestive
of the future we're at a loss to shape.
We might find our life in any landscape,

but moreso here. Each city a turnstile
of details, questions, private moments
stirred by *a single weathered threshold*
or the touch of a single tile

or today,
this corner and a dampness in the air.
What am I looking for?
Where was I going, anyway?

Tonja Gunvaldsen Klaassen
[b. 1968]

Tonja Gunvaldsen Klaassen was born and raised on the Prairies. She has published two collections of poetry. *Clay Birds* (1996)was shortlisted for the Gerald Lampert Memorial Award and won the Saskatchewan Poetry Award. *Ör* (2003), was shortlisted for the Pat Lowther Memorial Award. Her suite of poems, "August," won a CBC Literary Award. She now lives in Halifax with her husband and two sons.

INOCULATION

Polio, scarlatina, rubella, rubeola, roseola
diphtheria, tetanus, morbilli, pertussis
fairy rings of bacteria and virus

the swarm of wings, a greeting
of cripples, rattles, the attenuated, the dead
enemies sworn in blood. I guard against

even a chance lick of honey
sweet venomous ambrosia
spores and spores of fevers dreaming

disease.
How many stings
separate you from heaven?

How many stern nurses
plunging needles of poisons into your fat little leg
while I clamour the bells?

Ten days later, I watch for spots, bumps, pox
hives of memory cells
humming white and blank on the way to your heart.

Is it enough? You have
my eyes, your father's hands
his life line, my fate…

a new umbilicus,
the mortal door
closing.

FROM "AUGUST: AN ANNIVERSARY SUITE"

1 *Paper*

Opening to
a private sky

birch bitings and burnt flutter. Our tent stretched—
smoke over the threshold when you ushered me through.

No talk—
night in the low roofs of our mouths, night

hidden in a stand of aspens, out there and between us,
newly ringed, keys in the ignition.   Idling

stardust, mosquitoes.
Koriusai, Utamaro, Ursa Major's erotic drawings,

closer now
to black scribblings, hole punchings, a confetti of yeses,

the reversed Star shining from a yielding margin of universe.
Yes, yes—

        Perseids, hominids, black-eyed susans, sleep.

III   *Leather*

A shaver
to rough-house mouth, stripping the shadow that last night

bristled.
Unshaven imaginings:

what pinks that shadow pulled
apart. Your face masked in the dark of my favourite

rose and sorrel
scarf,

brushing a cloud.
I'm nailed to the spot

wretched over
belt loops, notches.

Polished toenails, cold tiles. Like that morning in Versailles.
Light faltering through milk bottles and cobalt

bric-a-brac finds you teased me for buying,
filled with lotions and cologne.

No *cuir de Russie*, but
the deadly bouquet of horseplay where jawbone meets the ear

lost
to Zorro's razor—the sting of soap and water.

I've already lost you,
husband—to this other you—husband

buttering toast, answering the phone.

iv *Linen*

Whisking a béchamel, buttering toast.
You've got all the pots in the house out to poach

eggs florentine. *The Joy of Cooking* splayed. Sleeves
rolled, forearms flexed,

forehead creased.
Eggshells in the *bain-marie,*

bananas on the sideboard, freckled and sweet.
A little rum, a little cream.

The breakfast table dressed in the washed-out wedding gift *fleur de lis*
linen with fraying seams (skirt to my knees).

Forks set down in a flourish the way you might lay a heart
or lead with a spade at the same table after dark.

A bed of spinach and sorrel, a forethought of salt.
And afterthoughts:

where's the nutmeg, do we have nutmeg?
But I must grace the table as a guest,

trace the *fleur de lis*, the butter and tea-stain motif
—and wait.

v *Wood*

Pheromones. Something roan. Billy Bragg on the stereo.
Broom handle, collarbone. Just a lucky so-and-so.

Rough-jaw, U-haul, screwball
bully in the butter.

Woo woo woody-woody
hip-roofed, lean-to, ask you: kissle me low.

Hocus pocus, Hi-Fi, *hexen-tanz* marzipan.
Farmer's daughter, chamois cloth, honey on the butcher's block.

You-who, voo-doo, buckwheat infusion
eyebrows askew, ask you, ask you.

Nightshade, lampshade, ponytail, shoulder blade
off the shoulder, off the cuff, pawpaw in a paper bag.

Unbearable, *d'érable,* syrup in a tin can,
lights on, lights off, go on—dance your donkey dance.

Woody-woody, wuderove, dirty stove, wodwo
hunky Guthrie cookie cutters

slacky feller
          felled.

x *Tin*

Expecting tin can lanterns, a party:
cold trout on blue willow, spark of the river's tinsel.

The aluminium canoe, a tinderbox we slide ourselves into
tipsy on the river's sulk.

An anniversary gift, better than confections
or silks. Scissors won't open it. A secret

the clouds conjugate north of the weir.
Tenir. To hold. Tongues of silt.

August: the aspens open their tissues, temptations.
The river, a rival

current.   On the surface: flotsam, a million proofs.
Clutching the paddle, shove out the thoughts that nudge—

xı *Steel*

It began in July. Hives rising on your skin—welts, petals,
a worsening infection of dream-missives

under the daily calamine of reassurances. A cumulus
line, an aisle—the bleached skies—pillowslip to pillowslip in the sun, a bride

weighting each white flutter with stones.
Something is spilling in the air, the vases have tipped, the light, and

the neighbours, now, are glancing through the slatted fence,
rakes abandoned, thoughts of notches. Heads of false lupin aspersing pollen:

confetti, illicit driftings. Aspirin-dulled, I'm awake and
blinking through viridian: the filigree, the forgery,

the shining affidavit tracing the temples.
Distance, a borrowed blue

met with green blades, a mean streak of questions,
sheet metal lightning, the tumble-down affair of clouds over the garage.

> Day-knave lilies darkening, sharpening their knives—

xııı *Lace*

Letters
scribbled on the backs of things—

unopened envelopes,
torn corners, roof estimates, flyers. *Were you up in the night?*

A longhand drift
of morning's matter-of-fact kind of muddle:

butter and wax, pollen and salt,
pollen and pepper;

I dreamt of the sea and rush grass; errands, meeting schedules.
You should have wakened me—

loop holes of logic propped against the sugar bowl
or slipped sidelong between the racy pages of the novel

we've been reading aloud in bed. Notes: what you heard in the night—
wisteria on cedar. Sirens. Rain.

A change of mind, something crossed out.
x x x — desperately and always will —

Christopher Patton
[b. 1969]

Christopher Patton writes and tends his apple trees on Salt Spring Island. His sequence
"Broken Ground," from which "Red Maple" is taken, won *The Paris Review*'s 2000 Ber-
nard F. Conners Prize for Poetry. He studies at Zen Mountain Monastery in upstate New
York, where "Weed Flower Mind" is set.

RED MAPLE

Acer rubrum

Four plates of raw
iron, folded over one
    another, saw there was no
        way to hold the world.
        The world did not mind—

turning, it looked
as a child would, to itself,
    and found a life in the muck
        a mare's hooves made
        as she stamped and cried.

When the plates split,
a foal descends, and her pain
    is not everything it
        knows: the leggy
        cluster prancing

under cirrus
celebrates an awkwardness—
    honour to the universe
        the hole I came from
        sends forth to eat.

    Wobble-legs falls.
Gets up, different. Its red-green
    flower: adders' tongues, flawed
        trumpets, baby-
        squalls of flower-birds:

    the spring wind shakes
it through ten thousand forms,
    forms falling through themselves like
        a train station
        departure board's

    rain of changes.
Foal grows then, knows harness.
    Being tightens to one thing
        and another—
        and when the train comes,

    its works are done.
Lying lightly on the grey
    mud of the old carriage road,
        or pressed by boot
        soles into the mud,

    confetti, red
paper for a celebration:
    a branch coughs in the wind,
        the flowers give
        up their attachments.

THE VINE MAPLE

becomes an image
of what it fears: beneath the conifers,
        leaves arrayed in parallel sun-angling planes that flare
        gold in such deep shade or
    brandish fire-fighter reds as fires rage
in fall on open slopes; spreads through regions moist to wet, clear-
    cuts often, and lava flows; wants either courage

    or rain. Sites on fire
are later favoured by Douglas fir, from whose needles
        the gold-nubbed chanterelles poke with their undulating
        gills; beneath whose flutings
    of ridged, rough, mud-brown bark the wood, admired
by rained-on Coast Salish as fine fuel, even as it threw
    troublesome sparks, seeped a pitch that soothed wounds and tempered spears,

    salmon weirs and fire
tongs. Thin green bracts emerge from under
        scales on every cone, three-forked slips like the feet and tails
        of hiding mice who've failed
    in some small quest. (Bees, droning their beware
nearby, hoard from black cottonwoods a sticky balsamic
    anti-infectant resin, and one unlucky mouse has mired

    in the hive.) The Great
Spirit gave to the Salish redcedar
        to honour a man always helping others. Tree
        of Life with scale-like leaves
    overlapping in a woman's long plait.
The bark made clothes, the wood became their dugout canoes
    and bailers, combs, fishing floats, cradles, coffins, spirit

    whistles and berry-
drying racks. Above, below the cedar
        whose kindness is such that a stranger needing strength
        need only stand beneath
    with her back to the trunk, my landlady,
a lawyer, half-Déné, from the porch pours rainwater out
    of our old beer bottles. It is enough to see clearly.

DOE'S BONES

—A sunlit lot. Clearcut.
    Slash smoulders. Crabs of a beer-
coloured grass. A torn-up midden heap,
    its tiny lustreless bits
        of oyster shell. One lady-thin
        translucent alluvial fan

of scallop. A doe gone
        off to moss, snake-work of back,
a scatter of ribs.
           Dear bones. I hate
    that I love. What have I done?
        (A blank slate, he said. But I can't!
        I told him—this is what I want.)

No answer. A lichen
    antlers cut alder.
             I move
heavily downslope through fern and thorn
    toward a shore. An ocean
        throwing ocean up. This is it
        to give life? a plume of white spit,

bark scraps knocked up and dropped
        on shore rocks—and now a raw
red sawn face. Sea-worn log end-on. Dread
    uneven drum.
           Well. How apt.
    It has been more or less a war
    to get here. And here is so far.

FROM "WEED FLOWER MIND"

23

The seed has flown. It falls to loose dirt. Down,
gone, sown. Forgotten. In woods, no such as weeds,
and the flesh, red mud, gives
way with ease to the shovel; holes open
at my feet for red oak, dogwood, white
birch, sweet gum: loose teeth I pack in. But look what
comes up: a weed-sprout, in hand,
trembles, snail-tendril, seed testes. Bladder campion?

24

Touch-me-not? —Two bells. Rise slow. Break.
—Sitting spent. Flowing in ditch-grass, a fresh
trickle now, where coltsfoot
lions pounce, and leafy new
ladders climb of blue, wet nipples: the return
of forget-me-not. I asked her to help me, she turned
away, *I don't know how
to help you.* (I turned away—I couldn't make ...

25

I couldn't take it.) Outside the garden grew
a dragon in my grain. Held high a steel shaft.
Ached with weight. Made maw.
Drove down again. To pry dirt wide
rocked back and forth. To sledge young cedar (rag-strips
of red bark, wet flap on wood) sharp the tip,
true the aim, then broad
the arc and down hard. Posts in, raise fence. Who knew

26

he was already in and through? A panicked fire newt
darts through the weedage of my father's unused
plot: squash vines, rampant
parsley thickets, monkey weeds as children
we grew there from seeds. His wisteria blooms
a second time on the roof, modest in autumn,
he sells the house, moves down
the coast, remarries. Who knows, he may have found a future

27
to settle the past. Come gone love, come wisdom. Lost
in the holly, a beautiful weeping lady: deadly
nightshade, *solatrum*, soothing
painkiller; misreading turned her
solem atrum, black sun, eclipse: it
isn't half as poisonous as thought.
Bittersweet. The red berry
darkens and dries: doe eyes. Once more, the old mistrust,

28
quivered, nervous. . . . Her gaze lifts and passes
above human things. Soon it is dinner.
My work is to prepare.
I walk out to the garden in a light rain
(the monastery needs it, too, a dry
August) and kneel in the bed (I don't know why
I am crying) where fawn
and doe, gone now, flicked their tails and browsed grass,

29
and a web, abandoned, broken, gathers evening
between a mess of oatgrass and a fencepost:
slant stalks, turned tree, blast-place
of long-past. Stars of insect shells
and calls. They're all over. And now a verb-weed
opening: the noun-flower has gone mostly to seed:
to lose, to fail, to fall
head over heels into the earth, where a rough unfastening

30
power moves, wordless and generous, unknown.
To know it moves and lives . . . oh, enough.
Returning, early evening,
with ordinary gifts: carrots,
tomatoes, dill weed, sugar peas in a beat-
up white bucket. A step. I shift my weight
to test a flag we set
down this morning. Each stone a path. We are not our own.

Stephanie Bolster

[b. 1969]

Stephanie Bolster is the author of three collections of poetry: *White Stone: The Alice Poems* (1998), which won Governor General's Literary Award and the Gerald Lampert Award; *Two Bowls of Milk* (1999), which won the Archibald Lampman Award and was shortlisted for the Trillium Prize; and *Pavilion* (2002). She teaches in the creative writing program at Concordia University, Montreal.

SEAWOLF INSIDE ITS OWN DORSAL FIN

Seawolf Inside Its Own Dorsal Fin, Robert Davidson, 1983. Screenprint.

I sleep in the red of my rising
arc, curled tight and finned

within fin, rocked by black
water I rock. I learn this one part

of myself, each degree
of its curve, how the water

foams against warm skin.
My fin learns me, the thing

it is part of but does not
belong to. We make each other,

my fin and myself, myself
and the taut water.

When my fin breaks the sea's
skin, through shut eyes I glimpse

wave within wave, stone
within stone, I surge

through all the layers,
my own incessant crest.

HEDGE

It divides: there from here, play from duty; it tries to let us have it
both ways. Creatures inhabit it, evolving in forever-dusk until their vision

trespasses leaves and our skin. Who owns the contents?
Evidence of crimes goes undetected; gun, doll, stillborn lamb. All wet,
because the plant can't fathom growth without. On the A93

from Perth to Braemar, a hedge of beech rises ten storeys. Story has it
that such growth was permitted in memory of those who planted it,
in 1745, before they died in a rebellion. The 8th Marquess of Lansdowne

quashes that: it simply is, and worth maintaining. The queue of cars
that winds beside it looks constrained, but snug. What of our bets?

Less intrusive that arranged stones, it nevertheless requires
pruning, and so necessitates a modicum of forethought,
like a marriage. Protection against possible loss. Shut *in*. To hedge-

hop is to fly at very low altitude, which does not mean safer, given
proximity to the odd rampant branch. When threatened, the hedgehog
rolls into a ball. Hedge-sparrows: brown-backed, common.

Those whitethorn hedges of childhood. A treasure-trove of coins was
found inside a hedge—*une haie*, in France. There for several hundred years.

ON THE STEPS OF THE MET

When the first wasp would not stop flying near me I sat still
and let it stay. All thin legs and yellow, it did not find my skin
but the silvered mouth of the Pepsi can. It crawled inside

and then another joined it there. I let those two
fill themselves while I finished my greasy knish and though
how I would soon not be here and how painful

not wanting anyone. One wasp staggered out
and flew, and then the other, and in Manhattan
they were two cabs on their way in one direction. Inside,

what I had loved most: the folds of the woman's scarf
in Vermeer's portrait, their depth of shadow,
how the fabric came so close to itself without touching.

EDGE OF THE RIVER

Tamarack, shamrock,
black water with a stone in its throat. Black willow:
Very shade-intolerant. Branches brittle and breakage

frequent. Limbs under water. Black ash: *Neither as strong nor*
hard as white ash wood. Black hawk falling. Squirrel call. Teeth against
teeth against hunger. Variations of predation. What's swallowed

still warm in the throat. I don't want the names of vegetation
in my mouth, only his tongue, his different speech. Variations
of flight and flightlessness. Crows are rooks, but rooks

are sharper and still blacker. Nettles can make healing
teas. Bluebells by the river ringing someone's
gone too far.

CHEMISTRY

Instantaneous Photographs of Splashes, Arthur M. Worthington, 1908. Gelatin
silver collage.

Inept in everything except perception—and even there
subjective—I'm only partially my chemist father: I never
threatened to explode my childhood with experiments

but watched my mother release a blot of half-and-half
into the glass cup that held her coffee and a hurricane
ensued before her spoon dipped in to smooth things out.

When photographed with utmost care—the care of my father,
demonstrating for his students, gave to filling his pipette
and counting tears of danger as they mixed with mildness—

a drop of water falling forty centimetres
into a bowl of shallow milk will make a rising
circle, widening until a phallus strains upwards

from the centre, milk and water bound.
With its tip congealed into a sphere, the column falls back,
the globe drops in and the milk is a little more

watery. This quick gift's gone unglimpsed as I wash dishes—
my hands dank in gloves—and muse on some dumb
wall of brick. Across the continent my father watches

another sitcom while my mother waits for my next call.
Each time she reaches the ringing first: my words travel four
thousand kilometres to the saucer of her ear.

By the time I speak to him I've achieved that even
surface, coveted aftermath of his childhood combinations:
after the bang and froth is that silence we both live beneath,

small water fallen into so much milk.

Adam Sol

[b. 1969]

Adam Sol is the author of two books of poetry, most recently *Crowd of Sounds*, which won the Trillium Award for Poetry in 2004. He teaches in the Laurentian@Georgian University program. Originally from Connecticut, he lives in Toronto with his wife and two sons.

LIFE, MCKENZIE

This is the envelope, my gap-toothed friend.
A week before your wedding, you were with Hudson, thumbing your players
    into place,
and suddenly the chaotic music, the headwreck.
The screen goes ebullient blank: you've been sacked. You can't get through it.

Northward glares the gaping airport, escape, the seedy excursion.
Another winsome undergrad to spill your brilliance over.
And Monday? What will happen Monday?
Will there be a Monday?

Don't do it. You are tight-lipped as a Kirts ravioli,
but I know about you.
I was with you on the roof blowing smoke at the telephone wires.
I was in the gutter picking up pins.
I held your hand on Terry's knee. Your excuses are stupid,
but it's not reason enough to put yourself to sleep.
Even with the news, your fiancée's
been tinting the windows for you, as she promised.

Listen to me.
Let the limousines yawn in the morning.
Let the dumb doves dive into windows,
and your Maura murals frown down from the walls.
Let Dick clang out his sorry songs of stone and mercurochrome.
What do they know?

You've got sweet elephant ears to look forward to.
And the fanfare, the ridiculous radicchio,
the in-laws and crazed caterers gathering on the Columbus horizon like a

swarm of wasps—
Isn't it a glorious, hysterical music?
Don't kill yourself, you asshole.
Let them make for you a new exasperation.

WISHING YOU BETTER

So strange to find you here now,
after our disasters. The snide past provides us
its occasional kick in the teeth.
The whole walk back to your hotel
I've been tracing the scar on my arm.

And here you are, face softened
for every finer shades of expression.
Your hair has gone brittle since I last
held it in my fingers. You're separated,
and your mother's bottle finally broke her.

Remember the picture at the carnival?
Your face hard as an old lime,
and the sign behind you, daring us to enter?
I dared you to kiss me. I dared you to tell
your husband who you really loved.

It's true I like to think I was right all along,
not just about Michael, so gentle
after he was angry, but about every
stolen phone call, every secret kiss,
every murmur on the soccer field.

Sarah, whichever of my foolish words
still churns inside you,
that is the one I treasure. Even now,
despite the lobby's clank and drone,
when you remove your overcoat,

home wafts from your sweater,
the smell of burning charcoal. I must tell you
that all my hopes from those days
are bees battering windows.
I want to wish you better.

CONCILATORY LETTER TO MORGAN

Enclosed is the crushed ice I have promised you.

Last night a few of us jolted the mirrors loose at the Mineshaft,
our teeth glowing in the blue light like deepwater fish.
Shirley was there, your smell in her hair and an obvious lie.
She said you were here and gone.

I know you keep doing this: buzz into town, biplane,
staying with her quiet like you're hiding from the fuzz,
then just when the detectives break down the door,
poof! Dust on the stereo, dust in the tea.
Your motives lucid as a cartoon thought balloon.

But it's me. Don't you remember our promises at the concrete court?
Your mustard artichokes, our hestiant tongues?
Remember the broken tooth, the towering tuxedo, coconut milk boiling
sweetly in a rusty wok?
Where is the other half of the dollar Morgan?
50,000 hubcaps and see if I wasn't right all along.

Oh, trying to say what I feel
is like sculpting with live spiders.

Morgan, forgive me. If this letter reeks of old anger,
if the paper is chintzy and the ink all splotched,
imagine me here on the roof of the library,
fabricated history of the known world shelved beneath my thighs.
Isn't there some message in this for us?
Can't you picture us in handstand,
slowly pushing it all back into the earth where it belongs?

MAN WHO SLEPT BETWEEN BLOWS OF A HAMMER

Was there an immanence, or was it just blank blank blank,
the way white vans might pass through a window's reflection,
sounding out like a brush on a drum? The flick

and flash, and you're going to have to accustom yourself to my absence,
as to a broken watch.
It was late, there were rocks in the road,

and I was hiding in the dark dank of the city near the dormitories.
I was in awe of the street cleaners and their terrific appetites.
I was aware of the loneliness of lamps. Then began the mystery,

complete with homemade hats and clever demands.
I was alone, and then grandly accompanied. The young master said,
I don't want your goddamned library card.

It was a festival of denials: there was the No,
and the Nono, and the Please no.

Let's say I never enter heaven.
Let's say my estimable qualities have worn thin as paint.
I could have forgiven if I'd known.

And yet between brutal rhythmic truths
there was plenty of time to remake my remarks.
So what if it was dense with sad-faced boys and their tired epithets?

Once, I slept next to an infant prince
and could sense his fear and confusion,
so I invented songs for him in running dreams.

That is to say, I was sorry to be so old.
That is to say, I snored myself awake.
Now, as a runnel of rain figures through my hair and down my cheek,

and the sense that something has happened passes,
I sing half-syllables through my sleeves.
Another of my failed languages.

PSALM OF SCRANTON

And a woman there served me eggs.
Over hard. Oil

crackling on the decimated white. No
shoes no shirt and yet
                              she served me. Yea,

Grace still struggles on this earth,
            in her grey apron.
                                        Woman of vigour!
Woman of lonely hills! Cracked
cuticles and a slipped disk will not be the sum
                        of your inheritance! Even now,

lined along the noose of highways that surround this city,
                        mile markers are counting out our longings,
            tallying our deeds and misdeeds,

and for the righteous there will be a long rest in Bermuda,
a new couch, another son. I declare it
                              who am the voice of justice.
I have scoured out my house with chalk.
                                        Dear woman,
            remove your hair net and your tarnished trinkets.
Slough off your loss and chewing gum.

            Tomorrow I turn my feet to that great
city by the waters, but tonight I may yet bathe and sleep.

Ken Babstock

[b. 1970]

Ken Babstock was born in Newfoundland and grew up in the Ottawa Valley. His poems have appeared in several Canadian journals and anthologies, and won gold at the 1997 National Magazine Awards. He won the Milton Acorn People's Poetry Prize and the Atlantic Poetry Prize for his collection *Mean* (1999). *Days into Flatspin* (2001) was shortlisted for the Winterset Award, and the K.M. Hunter Award. He lives in Toronto.

CARRYING SOMEONE ELSE'S INFANT PAST A COW IN A FIELD NEAR MARMORA, ONT.

Summer gnats colonized her molasses black eyes, her flicking,
conical ears. She moaned, a badly tuned
tuba, and tassels of ick dripped
from her black-

on-pink nostrils like strings of weed sap. Waking from a rhythmic
nap in my arm, you wobbled your head upright
and stared at the great hanging skin-
bag, teats, dry-docked

hull of her ribs, anvil head, and the chocolate calm in her eyes
that gazed back as I carried you closer, wading
through goldenrod, mulleins, thistle
all artfully bent

clear of your soft exposed feet. Ants worried the punky
tops of knotted fence posts, and caution flags
of gossamer and milkweed fluff
marked each rust-twist

of barb, but that was all that divided you and her. I felt briefly
happy to be prop, peripheral in this exchange,
this unfolding bundle of knowing that
was you in

an overgrown ditch where the air swelled, shaking itself dry
in the sumac. What was I shown that I haven't retained?
What peered back long before the cracked
bell of its name

came sounding off a tongue's hammer and fenced it forever? Know
that it happened, though—you were a drooling lump
of living in the verdant riddle. That heifer
remembers

nothing of you. Let chicory, later in life, be bothersome blue
asterisks footnoting one empty, unrecoverable
hour of your early and
strange.

FINISHING

Every mitre only as clean as the chop saw
it's cut on. Any gouge, puncture, or flaw

in baseboard or casing is quickly forgiven
by almighty Spackle; your putty knife turns uneven

joints into smoothline, turns nickle-sized hammer dents
back into the wood's true profile—
                            at the owner's expense.

Thin wainscotting strips are worthless poker hands
you keep throwing back to watch land

at attention, soldier-straight, from the bathroom door
right down the corridor's

parade route. That easy. That fast. And if the framing's well built—
no vicious lean, tilt,

or bad wow—the aesthetics should be clear, even simple,
like topping a self-portrait in oils with an eye-pleasing dimple

that doesn't exist in real life.
How else to render a bland, formless grief

into something at least sellable? The mere appearance of beauty's
not beauty, but it's reliable.

Just finish. Get paid.
At night, alone, you'll redeem or undo what your hands have made.

TRACTOR

Like mill wheels through a dark current, its herringbone
treads paddled through clumped earth and stone,

tossing pressed clots of brown dirt off their
upswing to fall, then, and remingle, aerated.

The small hinged cap atop a burping exhaust pipe
flapped in slow panic like the mother killdeer who'd taken a clip

from the tiller blade's edge for playing the martyr:
watched her furrowed nest of three eggs ploughed under

yet kept up her act while the flared cobra hoods
of the hammered rear-fenders cast shadows over sunned clods.

The valentine of the bucket seat perched on spring-coil: a metal palm-
leaf saddle burnished to a beach stone's gleam

that said a scooped-out I love you to any-sized ass.
A grumbling muscle, the grey bowels would hiss

and steam tendrils of mist if a sun shower passed over,
otherwise content, compressed in a throaty, subsurface worksong or

hymn that rattled its tin and heated the field's own dizzying heat.
I seemed to live on the thing when not in the bunkhouse, flat out,

dreaming spindly, front-axle dreams of the earth's intractable
turning under bloated, gear-cog tires that stood still

as they spun. We learned to be emptied, to become pure
function that summer. Dragged, reversing into row after row, acre

upon acre, until distance accordioned, time folded,
moments, hours became interchangeable dead

space our labour languished inside of. Drawing
figure eights with the gleaming hoes we hunched over, avoiding

green seedlings that appeared every other second or so
like metronomic ticks pacing our breathing, becoming a flow

we sat and worked in and ignored, spitting. Our necks gathered sun,
tightened, itched. Not four people pulled on the implement but one,

one, one, and one. Cowed into silence by the Go-Down-Moses,
near-nirvana breadth and bent grind of each day. An aching gnosis

punctuated by deerfly bites or an arm's numbed buzz when
a hoe rang the deep bell of a dislodgeable stone. We had fun,

alone together, dredging up privately what it was like to be elsewhere:
a moored midlake raft, drugged in a rec room, or almost untenable under

upright acres of mirrored glass, in a seed row of streetlight.

THE 7-ELEVEN FORMERLY KNOWN AS RX

Back in the day, I was proud of my vast palette
of candies; those for a penny over the front
counter, for kids and grannies, and the more
potent display locked in the back cabinet,

only ever given away if you'd come with a note
declaring you blocked, arthritic, headachy
or just couldn't say what was wrong for the frog
in your throat. Now, I sell mouthfuls of salt

to the stoned. It was snug in here, I was kept
stocked and swept by a family of five from Lisbon.
Now I'm grudgingly manned by tattooed kids
in green tunics helping themselves to the porn. And

the light in me's a perpetual migraine, I'm a super-
nova on a quiet corner, beacon to that fleet
of 4Runners and Acuras disgorging their thunder
of hip hop and jungle. I haven't slept since 1983.

To make space for the flavoured coffee station and
an ATM, they knocked out my east wall, expanded
onto the ribbon of lawn—not at all what that Aussie
meant when he defined "sprawl." I used to dream

in flamenco played on a push-button tape desk, or
the gurgle of talk radio on a Saturday, but I'm
lobotomized now, a drooler, listening to the Freon
drone from the dairy and drinks cooler. Gone

the licorice whips, manila envelopes, shampoo,
shaving kits; I'm all Scratch'n Win, *Vanity Fair*,
shellacked fruit, and the crinkling bladders of months-old
chips. I squat in my numbness and stare, recording

each night's parade of freaks on hidden surveillance
film. I'm hyperaware. I've begun to loathe
the intervals between guns when I have to convince
myself I'm still here. Oh, Maria, shelving hockey

cards while muttering lines by Pessoa; Papa's spirals
of suds greasing the glassfront; the boy out back
whacking tennis balls off my brick hip as the day
falls away. We stayed in the black but that

wasn't enough, nor was attaching Rx to the family name.
Atlanta home office faxes directives re: New Promo,
end aisle-ing my insides. They demand perfect rhyme: "I"
ground down, cauterized, shelved in the back of "franchise."

PALINDROMIC

"A patrimony all our own: the hours when we have done nothing. . . It is they
that form us, that individualize us, that make us *dissimilar*."
—E.M. CIORAN

Christmas alone, by choice, with a tin
        of sardines and bonnie 'Prince' billy
sharpening the blade of the cold on
        the whetstone of his voice. A melee

on the morning of the first of the year
        over who should pay what to who
for the nothing we got the night before.
        There'd been *lots* of it, but it amounted to

loss, I guess is what I mean, given the pain
        and embarrassing, hours-long absences
of someone with someone else whose name
        should stay out of this. Fences

went up around friendships. The exacto blade
        in the thermometer kept snapping
off segments till there was nothing save numbered
        hash-marks seen through a static

of frost. I went for a walk in a parka I bought.
        Zipped up; the city as a fuzzy-edged
dream sequence afloat to indicate thought
        in the head of a smiling protagonist. Cadge

a light from a passerby and now your head's
        the lantern from the 28th Canto
shedding light on hell. "Oh me!" you'd said,
        and no laughter, canned or

otherwise, leavened a life that felt filmic.
        Sometime in March, the plaster over
the tub got pregnant, or Anish Kapoor was snuck
        in to redecorate. Its water burst near

April Fool's and spring arrived stillborn, I was
        reading something that hasn't stayed
with me, when the soldiers arrived with shovels.
        It was Mendelssohn screaming at Stoppard,

I think, or Stoppard screaming back, in the letters
        section of the NYRB, about Housman,
was it? As penned by Stoppard?—whatever,
        I remember an exchange of epithets and now's

a little after the fact seeing as the play itself
        never came. One night in May, a barkeep thought
I looked tired and slipped me a pill: I got soft
        in the neck, large in the thumbs, and a spot

of crimson light sang *Agnes Dei* from the foreground
        of my vision's left field. Wall calendars
were argyle socks; all those X's in rows wrapped around
        June under colour shots of designer blenders.

It was like a training regimen to ensure I'd place last
        in the race to accomplish, accrue, attain,
or think straight for a day and a half. I didn't dust.
        Meeting resistance—a door opens onto more rain—

I'd fall back and regroup, reuse the same ringed tea cup
        and liberate a pack of Dunhill from the long ice age
of the freezer. Watched others watch their Weimaraner pups
        grow to full glamour in the park. Massaged

the kinks of appointments from the hurt muscle of months,
        dredged each nightbottom for spare hours
to stare at. Just a therapist and me and a lot of not much
        to work through, more like locating doors

I might walk through if I'd get up and walk. Hypodermic,
        or fifty candies, or warm bath and a pine box:
repeated it all to myself, but self laughed, knew it was weak
        and would linger. Self trips self then mocks

the starfish of limbs washed up in the gravel, another X-
　　　　brace to hold square a day. I read a novel wherein
many were worse off, so read it again, while flecks
　　　　of grey ash mixed with eczematous snow in

the deep gorge between each page. To open it now's
　　　　like opening a text from the Middle Ages, but
you can't, it's glued shut with dead skin cells and sweat. Sows
　　　　at the Ex in August nonplussed with the crowds at

the gate. Too much lost, in ten minutes, at Crown and Anchor,
　　　　and my house keys freed from a pocket while
upside down in those ergonomic gibbets hung from the Zipper.
　　　　So head down for the night on the deep pile

carpet of clipped-lawn embankment that skirts the expressway.
　　　　Stuff fell in the fall. No one took pictures.
Or painted the scene on wood panel in oil, of the day
　　　　none of my friends and I decided not to go halves

on a driving trip through some of Vermont. I read Frost
　　　　and stayed where I was. Thanksgiving
I thanked someone for the chance to play generous host
　　　　to myself as guest at the bar where, having

been dosed earlier that year, we went back for more.
　　　　By November I was an art installation
begging the question are empty days at the core
　　　　of the question of begging the question.

Borrowed money so's not to be anywhere near Christmas,
　　　　while the snow whitened what no longer
wanted to be looked at. I know now I was missed.
　　　　Then was a different story. I think we're all stronger

George Murray

[b. 1971]

George Murray's books of poetry include *The Hunter* (2003) and *The Cottage Builder's Letter* (2001). His poems have appeared across North America, Australia, and Europe. His first play for children, *The Swan Chronicles*, was produced in Manhattan by Loco-motion Dance Theatre in 2003. He is the editor of Bookninja.com.

CAGE

A period of least resistance is upon us. Quickly,
finish everything! Only nothing
may be left undone. Do you now find it

impossible to look strangers in the eye
without speculating where
the surgeon's pen might mark their forehead

with the crosshairs of future incisions?
In an infinite number of books
written by one monkey at one typewriter

where only one key still works, it states that
someday some intrepid explorer
will follow the overhead ducts to their source,

and the darkness that sweeps the edges
of our understanding
will be mapped. The wall around

this garden is a metaphysical one,
an insurmountable idea
that keeps us out and heaven in. Assuming

our bodies will be left where they fall,
which do you bet
will eat us first, the birds or the worms?

Will the worms eat us and in turn
be eaten by birds? Will we climb
the food chain from the inside? Will we rise

as though a gorge, as though a hand reaching up
from the depths of the lion's throat?
Are these questions pointless, or are they

points without question? Hell-on-earth
has been in the planning since
shortly after Heaven-on-earth was abandoned.

Maybe all this worry can be cured,
perhaps we are suffering
without need, maybe the answers we wish

would find us already have, are resting
on the backs of our tongues,
waiting for a cool drink of water. There is

a difference between a prison and a cage,
though such subtleties are lost
on some. We are now tied together, friend,

in modes more unfortunate than blood.

PIKE

Enjoy these light-headed moments
because eventually your
eyes will feel as heavy as stones.

Each half-year is only a nickel
of the decade:
would that we were richer still, or more miserly.

We are sailing these unknown seas
in a medicine bottle;
we are steering with a slender pestle.

Look out there on the street: our children
run amok, playing ball
with the helmets of our soldiers,

pouring water and goldfish
into the airtight bowls
favoured by our astronauts.

The city's buildings are thick incense sticks
against the cobalt sky
and the wind is blowing the scent

of their burning across the countryside.
The only way to digest this
is to mimic the birds and swallow

enough broken stones to help.
Is the pike all this news
comes down a pointed pole

on which rests the head of a rebel leader,
or just another kind of fish?
Begin, O cosmic weavers, to spin your loom

and make for us toques and flannel!
The weathermen say
it's going to be a hell of a winter

and there are still so many repairs
to reckon with.
The bellies of our men are barely covered.

Try to look on the mystery of life
as a playing card might:
it is natural to be shuffled and dealt.

We may still be resting and playing today
but tomorrow is Monday,
and on Monday everyone has to work.

Only at the maddest party is the talk
of retribution
and only at a funeral does no one speak.

If the old texts are right and nothing
but a column
of smoke holds up the heavens,

then we must all work together
to keep the fires burning
so Paradise might never fall to earth

and we might never be crushed
under bliss.

THE LAST OF THE SINNERS WAITS
ON A ROCK FOR NOAH

I stood with the calm of a hunting stork,
the patience of a scarecrow: arms outstretched
for balance, one foot drowned to the ankle
in the floodwaters, the other tucked
inside a knee, one sole gripping my leg,
the other palming like a fist at highest peak.

I lost count at forty days, but still know this—
by twenty the water had chased us up here,
by thirty the heads of my people had sunk below
the rain, by forty memory deserted me
to the awareness I was now all body: bones
and skin waterlogged and dried into this pose.

Around me at times birds flew: sparrow,
split-tailed swallow, nightingale and thrush,
each winging on its last breath
then spinning down into the sea—
never one with a moment's thought given to
saving itself on an arm where blood still flowed.

Sometime recently, I couldn't say when,
a strong but, later I learned, unfaithful crow
came gliding just above the hushed surface—

its cry petulant, as though tired of carrying
the sky: those ailerons, suited to soaring,
camouflaging it like a thief against the Black Sea.

And in its flight, so curiously near, I caught
sight of a dark eye as it closed the distance
to pluck and eat from my hair a twig and leaf,
another determined refugee of the water,
perhaps an only remaining relative,
and in that gleaming oculus I was revealed—

salt flats like a teary desert of dry riverbeds
stretching back from my eyes, cracked
white tide rills running like fossilized evidence
of earthly trauma across my desiccated lips,
a bleached crown of black hair withered
and hardened, standing from my head.

And, as I started in fright at the face
of a stranger, the fickle crow flew off unfed,
its wings disappearing over the horizon,
and I was alone again, for a time, until
a seemingly tame rock dove swept in, lighting
on the taut and burnt muscles of an arm—

its slim, peaked body heaving with just
enough breath to keep alive the twitching
of its head, and it stayed a moment
preening and warbling, rummaging for food
among the jetsam of my beard: only
relief, good intentions, and hunger in its eyes.

But in its fearless fetching of leaf and branch,
the balance I had for so many days struck
between me, the mountain, and the sea
was broken: and slowly, with a creak in
the bones like a keel in a storm,
                                  I began to tip.

In the apology of its stare, also reflecting
both myself and the blue-on-blue horizon,
another scene played before it too fled—
widening eyes, a scorched head tilting away,
the skyline listing to an angle viewed
most often by the awakening and the dead.

DESPITE THE HUNGER AND DELICIOUS TASTE

Despite the hunger and delicious taste of it,
knowledge frightens me—
I don't *want* to know how lightning works,
or gravity, or the speech-dance of bees.
Cuneiform markings on clay tablets should,
in my opinion, have stayed unreadable—
there would still be wonder, no disappointment
in the boredom between farmers.
I want to live without an awareness
that day and night are simultaneous,
without the ability to reach the white beaches
of Greece on a day's notice,
without the surety that thoughts are *not*
created and housed in my heart.
I want to believe that a cold spread of fear
that feel like déjà vu *is* déjà vu,
that when cats stare and hiss at nothing
they are actually confronting something,
that the red and purple spots left floating after
staring into a light are visions.
Is there no recourse for the simple soul
who won't let himself think in allegory—
the impregnation of women by the sun,
the healing properties of musical instruments,
that the sea was once stirred to procreate
by the consumption of severed testicles?
What I'd give to exist
in a state of perpetual ignorance
of things like the distance between stars,
perhaps *hundreds* of miles above—

or to live thinking the moon has a first name
and children, that they fall in the rain
to be raised by her lover, the sea—
that sometimes when she touches the hills
in the distance someone is crushed—
or that a companion sits there,
some ancient shepherd or dirty satyr
waiting to greet her, to help ease her
creaking bones down into a wide bed of earth.

AN EGYPTIAN SOLDIER ON THE RED SEA SWIMS
AWAY FROM MOSES

Even before the swells began to crash back in
I had a bad feeling about the situation, but under orders,
persisted as any good soldier would: pressed on

regardless of the high walls of black water groaning
and straining as though against the side of an invisible
but poorly constructed dike. So far ahead

we could never have caught them anyway, the excited
roar of the Jews, scrambling out of the trench
of sea, tipped off some engineers' instinct

in my mind and I began to divest myself of metal—
first my sword, then my shield, then bronze pauldrons
and the ringing helm of solid copper on my head,

even the gold trappings about my ears and waist
falling surreptitiously from the back of the chariot
and down to the ocean floor where they may,

for all I know, still rest to this day among the skeletons
and fish: rotting to a coral green in the salt of that angry
and insulted tide. While the callings

my people have embraced range from fishwife
to concubine, potter to soldier, farmer to Pharoah—
every soul raised in the Delta, Egyptian or Jew,

knows the particulars of flooding: it starts with
starry signs that pock the pupil of sky, a foetid thickness
of air, a deep humming of insects,

the numeric significance of water growing as it trickles
through the dampening night. And, yes, while
at every phase of my denuding I mourned the loss

of my family's fortune, honour, and luck—
as the bound sea collapsed, its halves of water
rushing together like a majestic clap of hand or

siblings long apart, I was given a vision and embraced
my new position under the sun: that of prognosticator,
diviner, augur of water to cleanse the land—

the only Egyptian naked enough before the fist
of the Jewish god, the only one unidentifiable
in the roiling waves, the only one enough disguised

as human to be left floating, alive, head bare
under the burning Eye of Re—
tattooed arms free to strike out in any direction for land.

Anita Lahey

[b. 1972]

Anita Lahey grew up in Burlington, Ontario and lives in Ottawa. Her poems have appeared in the *Malahat Review*, the *Antigonish Review*, *Prairie Fire*, *This Magazine*, and in buses in Ottawa as part of the Transpoetry competition. She won the 2004 Great Blue Heron Poetry Contest and the 2003 Ralph Gustafson Prize for Best Poem. She is also the editor of *Arc: Canada's National Poetry Magazine*.

FROM "CAPE BRETON RELATIVE"

CHAPTER II

In Which You Are Welcomed By Black Flies, Twenty-eight Brands of Mosquito, and Children Who Jump Recklessly From Bridges

And water, cold and deep as prehistoric
joy. A Tim Horton's every hundred feet. Your whistling
uncle who calls you Shorty and Dora and Dummy. And the man

with the dog at the Mira Ferry Irving: doling
lollipops, selling gas. Main-à-dieu frogs spit their wet
hellos on your car. The house clumps into view.

Daisies, alders, three stumpy pines. Strawberries
sugar the air. Lace webs windows, trinkets creep
down walls—Nan's varnished Marys, sacred plastic

heart on a bitty wooden plaque—too polite to ask
why you drove all this way, where it is you're trying
to get. Stand atop the bank. Remember a black dog, Grampy's

limp, Nan's wrinkly Os of surprise. Those frogs in the pond
nearly drowned you, Dummy, when you were three. Hard
bites ring your neck. Your uncle in the fish plant cracking

legs off crab, ramming their brittle heads, hollowed
orange dwellings about his feet. In winter he'll carve
his meticulous faith: fire trucks, dolphins, swords. What'll it be,

for you? Kids on bridges gust into place, plastered
in short wet suits. You never meant to join their careless
leaping. Swim through the kitchen splashing old

prints onto walls. Your uncle whistles down at the new
cushion floor. Wring out a seat, two cups. Empty his
pail of jokes. Your shoulder in the door, eyes on the chair

where she ought to be sweetening her tea.

CHAPTER V

In Which You Are Told, Once and for All About Fishermen

Greedy lot. Always after complainin'.
Gossipers, oh my dear, if you heard them.
And tender—stay right at home when it's rainin'.
Three hundred grand: Imagine such a sum
for a month of lowering, hoisting. Them pining
for more. Couldn't smile either, sea might thumb
their arses. Never pleased, no joys.
Buncha sooks with fibreglass toys.

Greedy lot, they are. Always after bellowin'
the price of this, government that. Rough weather?
In the old days lobstermen drowned and kept rowing.
Now it's waterproof suits and GPS, feather
pillows, motors what shine. Whispers glowing
onscreen, a white cold pulse—together
they make the ocean talk: Rocks here. Sand there.
A rich man's traps come prepared.

You reckon they're windblown, muted
by the sea? Your grandfather was a superstitious
fart with Palm Sunday crosses in his bow who hated
to float, drank till three, till four, till the most vicious
rowing got him nowhere. His pilfered traps. Polluted
nights in his watery, try-try heart, cleaning dishes
no one was meant to catch. Times he fell gentle, kind as sin.
Whiskey, salt and guilt, it's them, what mar your kin.

CHAPTER XIII

In Which You Attempt To Jig Mackerel, Then to Cut Them Up
in a Process Known as "Cleaning"

Your job: to wipe out a school without
mangling a thumb on baubles that crook and snake
into fish-mouths, skin, whatever lets them in. When in doubt
keep lowering your prongs. These fish aren't afraid
of the dark. They'll tug when they want to come out.
They rise in threes, panting through eyeballs, opaque.
Your father once told you fish weren't cursed with nerves:
"What a creature doesn't feel, it deserves."

Once a fish is on a hook, it might refuse
to let go. Adopting the pose of the faithful
it hangs by one lip, deflecting light. You yank & lose
hold—your flapping mouth. This facial
reduction before the kill. Mackerel don't sing the blues.
They bleed and pelt the thighs of the boat, its palatial
gut. How ordinary, quick, this staining of the pail,
this weighing of bodies, scalping of scales.

Your uncle hacks through all but one before you summon
the nerve to try it yourself. The blade extends
from your hand; it hears a taunting: please, come in.
One cut, back of the gills. Turn the knife. Now. Rend
flesh from bone, ease into a state of filet, fresh lemon
sharpness numbing your tongue. The thrown carcass intends
to lie tragically on a wave, sending a skeletal moan
into the sea that gave it up. Your dripping hands; a seagull drone.

CHAPTER XV

In Which You Wander The Island, Pondering Geography

With him you belong
any old place: faraway cliff-top
blue in his eyes, grassy hollows
warmed into his chest. You climb

daily into that crevice
below his jaw, survey the jagged,
sculpted world. It matters not
what you see, you see it round-eyed,

blessed. Prepare, even now. This nook
will fill in: avalanche, dust, some squatter
who follows you scrambling into love
one tired old night. Without his muscular

laughter, thighs and plains, list
your criteria for home:
berries underfoot or a bird-sized
pocket in which to furl, high

above teeming streets? Will you tramp
through swampy yards or claw
your way into clouds, from one wobbling
sphere to another? Will you at last lose

him, or recover yourself? It comes down
to liquid crossings, glass in dappled
sheets. Salt clumping pores, rivers circling
ankles. White gashes

in the sky, through which only you will fit.

THE DRIP-DRY METHOD

An airy kiss, our fabrics come
alive. Face cloths wring

dances from laden rope. Your
grey-haired jeans yee-ha
over green tomatoes. We hunker

indoors, wondering how to begin
our own jig—when, for God's sake,
here will be enough. Tie up

the hollyhocks, prostrate, breaking
their backs. Pick the peppers, fold the clothes.
Weeds writhe beneath the morning

glory, overgrown and slithering
through the back door. Can't we spare
a wooden peg to fasten our promise

to that line? Please. It is you
I have chosen. Keep me

hinged, assure me of this patched rug
we've laid down, which fades daily
in ways I don't understand. What we do

for love. I would gladly be wrung, hung—
bash myself against walls

of humid air. We need an honest
soaking, then the pegs, the windy harvest
dance—you and I wrestling with all that

ripens and blows between our seams.

TRAVEL PHOTOS

I am trucker, I am
the son-of-a-bitch you thank,
ought to, every day, you:

gnawing gristle, zipping jeans, sucking
back that whiskey sizzle, gold
plating your throat. My motto: You got it,

some baggy-eyed trucker brought it: leaky
watermelon, booze, tubes of goop. I,
trucker, don't be thinking

fucker, it rhymes, so what. My turf: Potholes,
the sky-hole, this metal tent (plastic
interior) crouched over rubber planets hurtling—whooeee

—through two-lane nights. Peeling off
one mile at a time. I. Driver with cramped
legs, yanking my horn for the school bus—me

grinning, soaking into leather, breathing
out the back. You think it's fun, the Trans-Canada
slog through New Nowhere? Crumbling

tar, rotting shoulders, looming from every
curve: the chance to careen, to skid. You & your
pulsing dash, fifty-inch setback axle, goddamn

giant potatoes in your path, nickels up north
and Easter eggs wobbling over plains, down
some prickle-pine valley past a road-kill

skunk. I dream with eyes propped, edges
closing in, double-yellow warnings
racing all the way to God. I am hauled

from behind the wheel by the world's largest
fly rod; tip toy cows, big immobile fuckers
with Kodak smiles, their paint-chipped flanks

crashing into traffic, falling east now.
Send the kids postcards from Stickney,
from Pokiok, Sackville, Petitcodiac: any place

with a name worth a stamp, any place I've pitched
my steel tent, anywhere I've stopped to piss, eat
scrambled grease, with ketchup, click

the shutter. Tonight. A woman
in wildcat fur, camel heels, mauve
dusk stroking my orange-brandy

cab. Never wanted her, just
the brash pink of her
on my cooling cab—hints of meadow-valley

nirvanas. I am chauffeur, harbor Buddhist
leanings: One coffee, one picture per
stop. Me, trucker, motor humming, breathing in time

to her glassy photo rocking back and
forth. My boredom, her thighs.
Take the wildcat woman to Cabano,

maybe Jemseg. Cross to Mars Hill, Maine,
somewhere. Free her from
the mirror, window down, wind

rejoicing. Nothing wrong with torn-up
mauve and a narrow road, load scattered in sun,
off a bridge, rinsing pine-needle hills.

Suzanne Buffam
[b. 1972]

Suzanne Buffam's new poetry collection is *Past Imperfect* (2005). Her work has appeared
in various journals in the United States and Canada and has been anthologized in
Language Matters and *Breathing Fire: Canada's New Poets*. She won the 1998 Canadian
Literary Award for poetry and currently lives in Chicago.

THE STARFISH

A wave reached up to tug my hem.
Because of you I let it pull me in.
And then I turned from where you stood
delighting in my own delight at yours
in my soaked skirt, and swam towards
the middle of the lake. Between my strokes,
erratic, slack, small buffetings
that gave the day, your laughter
from the shore, their shape. Your skipped

voice lit across the waves and gave me
something vanishing to aim for, something solid
to outreach. Did I want you to lose sight of me?
Just long enough for me to learn
how being lost would feel? I felt your watching
for my face, my wave, for any solid part
of what I'd led you to believe. I leaned
back in the lake and let it take me, almost,
under. Above my waist, fanned out around me
in the waves, my skirt rose up and made of me
a shape I couldn't take on shore or keep.

LIFE WITH FOLDED UMBRELLA

Neither rain nor shine for days
and days and everywhere the grey
grains linger on the still-

green fidgetings of things not yet
reclaimed. All summer we sat
in its generous shade, and watched

the plot we'd planted come
into its own slow going.
We didn't think

to thank it for its role, so deftly
and discreetly played out on the bare
stage of the deck. Now the wide

white canvas canopy
is folded on its pole. I sit
behind the windows and consider

how it fits into the simple triptych
of their frames: set off
a little to the left, and taller than

the staggered aspens in the background,
and beyond, along the ridge
of cordgrass and blue asters

on the slip of island that divides
the glassy saltmarsh from the tides,
the shaggy shelvings of the pines

—now ponderous and drab, now
springing swiftly into business
with a sudden lift in wind—

it nearly fills the centre pane.
It makes a simple shape
against the grains, now furrowed

like the folds of snow-draped
fields, where what you see
is not so much the story

going forward, as the space
the story clears
for what comes next.

SWEET BASIL

To make them last, I planted them in sunlight
in a half-filled drinking glass.
This way, according to a friend, they'll stay
what we call *good*
for days. Which means, I guess, stay green—and
    maybe even

grow a bit
before the smallest, topmost leaves
give in, at last, to letting go (of what? go where? Go *bad*
    we say
when we don't know ... the body going off
somewhere we can't

yet follow, not yet
gone, and us, still not quite ready to have
done with it, no longer able to make
use ...). And yes, it seems
this *is* the way: late afternoon, day two, and still

these stiff twin tongues
unfurl from every seam, as if the broken
body's news has yet to reach them
from below. How can't
they know? Or do they simply

disagree? I keep a photo of myself, at twelve, just then
beginning to grow proud—my body
among cousins in the bathtub, facing straight
into the future. The water cuts us
at the waist. Regardless

of its government, these slender
tendrils keep on drinking in
a kind of after-half-life in this glass,
where light above, and light below
meet halfway up the stem.

THE ONSET

Farewell to insects, farewell
to the numerous finches,
to wandering coatless
under the palm-sized
leaves of the maple.

Turn up your collar, sharpen
your intellect, prepare
again for hunger.
If only the body
could make up its mind.

If only the river
flowed one way—
but there goes a bottle,
caught on the chop
of a wave pushing north

back into current
while the depths plough south
towards candour.
In winter the river
will lock. Too late, too late

the wind in the branches
will chant, but today—
bright aberration, brief check
in the chain leading up to
decision—the wind

is lifting the fallen leaves back to the trees.

Sue Sinclair
[b. 1972]

Sue Sinclair has published three books of poetry. *Mortal Arguments* was one of the *Globe & Mail*'s Top 100 books for 2003. *The Drunken Lovely Bird* (2004) was shortlisted for the Pat Lowther Memorial Award and won the United States' 2005 Independent Publisher's Poetry Award. She grew up in Newfoundland and currently lives in Toronto.

SATURDAY AFTERNOON

The somnolence of shoes
in shop windows; even the light
doesn't reach them, bounces off
and is escorted away before it can cause
embarrassment. There's no need
for a scene, a calm and plain refusal
is essential. Cool
and composed, they maintain themselves
in a dimly-lit interior, only half

thinking, giving merely the impression
of thought. Don't, they say, don't,
like all things behind glass. They look
over your head, purposeful, averted
gazes, as though seeing a brilliant
and hazy future you can't achieve
but might, if only they looked at you
that way. But you are fallible, you have loved
too much. There is nothing to be done
about this; you are too much like the light.

RED PEPPER

Forming in globular
convolutions, as though growth
were a disease, a patient
evolution toward even greater
deformity. It emerges
from under the leaves thick
and warped as melted plastic,
its whole body apologetic:
the sun is hot.

Put your hand on it. The size
of your heart. Which may look
like this, abashed perhaps,
growing in ways you never
predicted.

It is almost painful
to touch, but you can't help
yourself. It's so familiar.
The dents. The twisted symmetry.
You can see how hard it has tried.

GREEN PEPPER

Glossy as a photograph, the bent
circumference catching
the light on its rim. Like a car's
dented fender, the owner desperate
to assess the damage, unable
to say, like the sun, *it can't*
be helped.

Conspicuous and irregular
all its life, born
with its eyes shut tight,
as though there really were a collision
it was trying to avoid. But it hasn't
happened yet—there is only
the impact of light: it has never

been in love, never drifted apart,
never fantasized about another
fragrant vegetable, never
been flattered, never been denied,
never wanted more than it has.
A life governed by absence:

the gleam of white
on its hollow body.

COLLAR BONES

Why do they make us think
of birds, the spreading of wings?

Only the mind is more in love
with flight. Desire

rises, hinges at the throat:
here is where we glimpse

one another, in the aerodynamics
of bones that skim the neckline, glide

from shoulder to shoulder, two halves
of a single bone healed

separately. Through us
they wish for a lost

amplitude, hint at a symmetry
that might have been.

THE PITCHER

Unafraid of the dangers
of perspective, of distance,
round as a fruit, sure
of its proportions,
it confides in us its secret:
an inch tall, an inch around,
dainty lip and handle
ready to pour.

You want to hold it in your hand
because it fits, and makes you believe
in a place as small and certain
as that, like the way we remember
childhood
              through a keyhole:
our tiny mother,
tiny father, the tiny bed
in which we slept. Did we dream?
We did not. The sun rose
again and again, digging up the day.
Endlessly we began. Our cheeks were rosy.
We cried tiny tears.

The pitcher shines, the persuasive
curve of its body leads you
into recollection. So small
there's no room for doubt.
But what doubt did you have? Some things
you never quite forgot, and some
you always believed were true.

Pino Coluccio
[b. 1973]

Pino Coluccio's first collection of poems is *First Comes Love* (2005). He lives in
Toronto.

DIMENSIONS

TV's made you plump.
White hair
and polyester frump

say to write you off.
And so I shut the door
against your cough.

What I wouldn't give
to travel to
the way you used to live,

to see you in a dress
and kerchief, a barefoot
little shepherdess

or leaning on a hoe,
ballsier but like
a Bouguereau.

You cough and shatter that.
And cough again,
refusing to be flat,

insisting on dimensions
that your past, no matter
that extensions

of it reach to even
now—the clumsy way
you hold a pen—

can't contain. I bring
a glass of water to a living,
dying thing.

TIME PIECE

"Tick," it said (again), the clock.
When he listened to it talk,
seconds had the sound of feet
tapping down a darkened street.
What he scribbled, when it scanned,
seemed to have a second hand,
and like the seconds, seemed to pace
the empty circle of time's face.
When he made it rhyme, his song,
like a cuckoo's muffled gong,
saw another hour slip
the trembling present's nervous grip.
He watched a couple in capris
trim their blue boat's sail and breeze
across the sunned-on choppy lake.
He watched a barber's scissors take
a little off the top, and hair
collect around his plump red chair.
Awake, he dreamt of them, the barber,
the blue sloop huffing towards the harbour.
And tried to keep, in what he wrote—
each word composed, each word remote,
each word a tooth in turning gears—
the time reliably for years.

MY IMAGINARY WIFE

This is my imaginary wife.
It's lonely without someone in your life
to talk to after work about your day
and share your weekends with, or special dinners.
But real wives marry only winners
who net more than double my gross pay.

And so I made one up. I bring her flowers,
our Scrabble matches last for hours and hours—
thank God I found somebody I could marry,
gorgeous, if, it's true, imaginary.
The highway of our love is paved in years.
And when I want her to, she disappears.

GETTING IN

It wasn't bugs buzzing but the lights,
which few of us had seen before. The Queen
was on the wall behind the desk. Nights
of bad roads had come to this: men

in line for miles, guessing how it stands.
Reap three fields of wheat and weed the peppers—
we sweated seven shirts. And for our papers?
Hands was all they said. Show us your hands.

We caught on quick. They wanted men for work.
Our hands—we held them out—were hard as bark.
We eyed each other nervously, and then?
Hands was all they said. We all got in.

STANDARDS

The bony babes in Gap who lazily
stroll with Starbucks cups at U of T,
Photoshopped or bio-engineered,
see me dreamy-eyed and think I'm weird.

And then, with bosky dos and shoes from Browns,
the tall and toothsome daughters wearing frowns
who sit in Yorkville sipping Chardonnays
squirmily avert my swimming gaze.

But me, no matter how desperate I get,
my standards will never descend
to hairy-legged fatties or anyone else
who'd settle for me, and pretend.

Asa Boxer
[b. 1973]

Asa Boxer is a Montreal poet and critic who won the 2005 CBC Literary Award for a suite of poems entitled "The Workshop". He is also the winner of McGill University's Mona Adilman Prize for Poetry.

FROM "THE WORKSHOP"

Grease and Rust

Every tool is the anointed king of its work:
even as it waits and fades into the general mess,
even if it sinks to the status of a handle
poking from a box behind the curtain

beneath the counter, a wire coiled
round the grip, its head near drowned
in a pool of screws... A coat of oil
repels corruption while the handle waits.

The vise is seasoned black with grease.
Black grease is cleanest in the shop
where rust is the enemy; clean means
strongholds of metal free of rust.

Everything blessed with oil, like the hair
of heroes and saints, prophets and messiahs.
Grease fills the surface-scratch that'll never heal,
settles deep into the score against all agents of rust.

Each tool is patient and confident it is meant
for the job it was designed to do best; it will wait
if it is used for only a moment in a rock's life
or for a thousand years in the tribal life, it will wait.

The workman has observed this waiting,
this slouched hanging from the board,
like the one square hanging in the ready
with a level to get it all straight

the way the other levels laid aside wait
with bubbles of air, like held breaths that can tell
when all is aligned and gravity agrees
that the work is plumb with the heart of the world.

Some say the patience of the workman
is the virtue of his shop, but, truly, the virtue
is motion. Rest is not how things get done.
Rest is how rust creeps into the world.

The Apron

A clean apron is a sign of illness.
Like a fresh-bristled broom,
a sharp pencil, an instrument
kept in tune, a stainfree apron

is suspect and should not be allowed
to leave the room unabused.
The workman's prized apron hangs alone
on a spike in a vertical beam

next to a clutch of aprons
that serve the craft
with varied cloths
for different moods of labour.

The favoured apron
is of leather enwrought
with cracked, caked, baked-on grime,
and eighty years of elbow grease.

It retains a paunchy curve or two
from one old man, who worked well enough
to keep it clean and pliable and non-flammable,
an armour against oil squirts and acid spills.

It rebuffed the meteoric showers tindered
by the friction of the circular saw
grinding through sheets of flashing; remained unaware
and undaunted by the glare of an occasional

slow comet of light shooting through the dim air.
The apron hasn't time enough to speculate
the hazards posed by the random arc
of a brief, minuscule spark.

The carbide teeth shrieked through wood,
the whirr and thump of the jackhammer drill
flicked shivers and sharp slivers at the chest.
The apron deflected them all with a tisk,

a sizzle, a kiss of smoke.
The apron carries scars enough
to keep a tribe of ears in wonder stories,
enough indeed for an odyssey:

at least one whole chapter devoted
to how the slumbering blowtorch roared
and spun to give the seasoned apron
that black-eyed burn and why.

Another chapter on the oblong patch
that covers the spot that fizzled away
when acid spilled its clawing biting frenzy
of bubbles over glove and apron,

invisible but for the foam at the mouth,
like some rabid spirit let loose in the shop,
what serendipitous sign spilled out that day,
and what it hissed.

Chapter upon chapter of soiling,
burn, and battle-scar
spanning generations of shop
in a sea of work in progress

for the home above the workshop,
the home the workshop serves,
maintains, and adorns with labour
and a labourer's rusty cicatrices,
            and a labourer's oily stains.

HOW TO LIE

Keep it simple, tidy,
take a noncommittal stance.
Most of all be flip
and keep it uncontrived.

Contrivedness is avoided
by steering clear of rhyme
and any sense of rhythmical order,
but have it memorised

by subtler work-a-day schemes,
the way you keep your PIN,
the access code to your e-mail,
the combination to your lock.

Pitch your lie on a chunk or two
of the bedrock of figure and fact
and remember that the greatest lies
are delivered with a smile.

A good liar knows that
it's a bad rap to take too often.
A good liar lets you win a time or two,
and every few or so he hustles you.

A liar is a gregarious creature,
he makes many friends and quick:
talks of their enemies with enmity;
talks of their friends amicably. Frequently agrees.

In company of enemies,
act the spy on the friends you told
you'd spy for until the camps
of right and wrong are scrambled.

Surely, this is the liar's boon:
to find at last a lunar gravity,
a mind that won't pursue
effects to causes, nor rig up pasts

to chain to the present moment,
because the diligent liar
knows his lying well enough
to know himself in truth.

THE LOBSTER

Sunk behind its dingy window
in a supermarket aquarium,
the lobster turns a muzzy eye
on the great *élan* of air.

Exposed to every scrutiny; it waits,
claws bound, an antenna snapped.

Not a crawl-space, nor a shadow.
Still as stone; invisible, it hopes.

It hopes a lobster's coral hopes;
it thinks a lobster's murky thoughts.
But its brains cannot conceive the sea
outside the lobster-shell. Desire, thus,

keeps slim to fit the narrow life within.
You will never hear the baffled lobster cry,
"What crime could be so great it moved the sea
to single-out a bloated shrimp like *me*?"

It's a muffled clatter, this life that smudges by:
rattling cartloads of death perambulate past;
smutchy children nose and thump the glass;
vague eyes and teeth wink pearl hints

of what's to come. This wispy world
suffused with light; a lobster's carnival-
afterlife. Where each impression colours and brews
through nerve, and muscle, and sinew.

Where a thorny heat keeps life fired
to a reddening shriek. And God,
God boils it through.

Matt Robinson
[b. 1974]

Matt Robinson's *A Ruckus of Awkward Stacking* (2000), was shortlisted for both the Gerald
Lampert Memorial and ReLit Poetry Awards. He is also a recipient of the New Brunswick
Foundation for the Arts Emerging Artist of the Year Prize. His newest collec-tion is *no
cage contains a stare that well* (2005). He lives in Fredericton, N.B.

PARKING LOT PASTORAL

gasoline swirls. beautiful
like bruises, leaked
diesel, and un-

leaded lakes irrigate
this asphalt. reclaim it.

an irony like birthday cake:
sweet, layered; too
decadent to

be healthy; ornamental. the
chemistry of the memory

of an animal revenging
ideas of
branches, roots, leaves.

FROM THE OCEAN, INLAND

halifax: the afternoon is hot and passengers
gather, a condensation by the departure gate windows.

bags scrape against the tile floor. as the time
approaches, a tide-like order develops. redevelops.

later, in motion, the window is a charcoal or pencil
sketch, smudged; all newsprint concrete and power

pole t's: repetitive and unsteady—
a grade one printing exercise. somewhere

before bathurst we are a drive-by
theatre; we are a traveling circus, mid-way.

an old man, a buick, a mother, two kids: soda pop sticky
with summer, the people stare and wave themselves away.

after coffee, the drummondville morning
is workmanlike; a grass stain on faded denim.

on approach, montreal is a spilt pallet
of cardboard boxes, bleaching in the sun.

SPRING

the streets tonite are
crystalline; white, and

this cold: harder and
more violent than

second-day-of-spring
march should be. mom is

making funeral
arrangements (but not

to plan ahead). i've
come to realize

people die weather
or not; whether or

not it's rain, sun, or
snow. they go. they go.

NOTES TOWARD AN APARTMENT STORY

                              it could begin, this sketch
of our basement building, with how

we—in *medias res*, my father and i—emerge. day's-end
ghosted with sprinklings

of plaster, scaling the back stairs' green-carpeted well;
my allergic dust-cough hacking out

the backdoor's failing, its dusk-screened evening light, like
a confused dog's announcement

of morning.   or, with the decision—
we'll say it took place

at the dining room table (the bills, scattered shingles of mail, all
shovelled aside and coffee cup-pyloned)

—with the graph paper pact
to build the thing, to frame that space, at all.　　　　or maybe

with no words, as such: simply the felt penned diagrams—
the rasp shuffle of paper; a father's

near silent geometry?　　or,
perhaps, all things considered, it *should* begin after the fact.

start with the pine shelf, all
six feet by three feet by ten inches, varnished and still there,

these four years since i've moved from the province, my brother's
snapshots now tacked to its sides.　　　　but

here's a thought: to begin—an appendix: a catalogue
of excisions, the things we left others

to do: like the plumbing and wiring—the real guts of the chore,
knowing full well that was not

our forte. knowing too well that most things we do,
whether we wish them or not,

become in the end
a mere list of deferrals, a counting of spaces. like left-over linoleum:

the spilt-shuffled tile puzzle of what's
been, been left, been left out: to stand, or to sit in a place.

Michael deBeyer

[b. 1975]

Michael deBeyer is the author of *Rural Night Catalogue* (2002), which was shortlisted for the Gerald Lampert Memorial Award. His poetry has been published in numerous journals. Originally from Ayr, Ontario, he now lives in Fredericton, N.B.

BEGINNING OF THE SEASON

A new fountain in town
sends river water into the sky,
the mouths of it quartering

a bed sheet, then braiding it back,
reborn in white ropes. Dovetailed
the ecstatic light of it, and,

if slow enough, reassembles
itself, the repetitive arc to it,
like dance or song returns

to its own falling, through.
Milky shadows newly bolstered
by something younger, below.

The fountain is articulated spinelessness,
an image for you to fit into
your long boat's long lazy chairs.

The town, I say, is open for you,
your teeth, your hair, the way your finger
draws small circles in the air, just so.

SATURDAY VENTURES

The way the butcher's daughter
scrapes the sweat from the meat

is an art. Noon in the market. Fresh
brushed teeth. The stink of cheeses.

Here, in the crux of the L,
I'm waiting for you. My own bag

a bag of potato blues.
And hearing your voice there,

from the squash wagons, buried deep
within the fleshy meat of the fruit.

IMAGINING THE BLACK BEAR INTO THE PARKING LOT

I don't know that it would be fair to think of it,
to pool the black bear this way, to pull it out,

the way it may have circled, steam culled from the body
into the morning air, its gentlest behaviour.

Matted hair above the ruff, a reddish winter coat
going to seed; hair cut against the forest's

bluntest tools; tooth in nail, berry-seeded jelly.
Each limb needle-pointed with dew, bearing inspection.

Belly up for the sun to filter out the night damp.
Stomach taut. The embedded, richly earthy musk.

That it left last autumn's colour with a temporary
impression; a paw print deep enough to put a fist in.

THE BODY OCTOBER

October is the transition zone moving over
the valley corridor. The roadway,
lit by trees as they shed their skin, is still.

Factory air leans for it cannot leave the ground:
strange herald to the marriage of orange and grey.
October winds in the cool light, lifting the clouds

from the shelf, showing no rain, or rain defined
as a crystal lattice, observable in the sound of it
on October nights. This is the beginning of the year

in palindrome, a hinge in the present opening
all of us to a list of years, taking from then to now
and translating it perfectly. Like placing a ruler

against everything, the measure in the hands
of the silent draftsman. Its sky drawn in
as granite flecked with a month of migration.

HOME: THE WEST WALL

There is a space in the landscape
that recalls a home, a home swallowed

by the earth's weight. Four walls are left
that stand for the rest. They hold

no paintings, or are paintings themselves;
the vision of artists who swore

up and down them. Their vision in the paint
as it peels off the walls, loosening its wings

like an archaeopteryx, falling. And in falling,
there, angels' release, an imprint of time.

Constructing walls to break them, to inhale
the sedimentary plaster cuff, tearing the lath

which seems the final means of support, yet
through the west scaffold: an apple tree in bloom.

Joe Denham
(b. 1975)

Joe Denham was raised in Sechelt, on British Columbia's Sunshine Coast. He has worked a variety of jobs ranging from health-food store clerk to prawn fisherman. *Flux* (2003) is his first poetry collection. He lives on Lasqueti Island, B.C.

BREAKFAST

Stiff as a crustacean's carapace
we cram into rain gear and stretch
on gloves to the auxiliary's muffled yodel
and the gargle of percolating coffee
A quick cup and smoke on deck
with some *Nice to see your smashed-*
asshole face this mornin', then toque
and flashlight on, and climb down
into the forty-below-Celsius hold.
Bent into the boat's cramped belly
cold air clasps our lungs in a metallic
vice—crystallized to ice upon inhale,
melts to mist with each exhale—as we
load totes down through the hole's
narrow mouth, feed it the frozen flesh
we caught and killed last night.

SCOTCHMAN SALVAGE

Don't slip. The bark's been skinned off
these cedars by the grapple-yarder pull
and tug-haul down the Strait: they're slick
as *umbilicaria* lichen after downpour; one mis-
step and the space between logs
will suck me under
and seal. What is it about risking life
to salvage stray gear
that enlivens? Stab the pike pole
into softwood. Inch near. At the front
crook an arm over the tow cable and sink

down onto submerged logs, water
vortexing my waist. One look back
to the boat idling at the edge of
the boom, then thrust the pole-hook
to snag the balloon's frayed line. Spike it.

GUTTING

Peel back the squirming tentacles
and slice the beak out like the stem
of a pumpkin. As I flip its head inside-
out, I can't help thinking *sentience*
of a four-year-old child, can escape
from a screwed-down mason jar, emotions
are displayed through shifting
skin colour. The dead, still-groping body
in my hands is dark, its sepia fluid
soaking into my sweater and gloves.
I bring the glinting blade down and
cut the blue-grey guts away, catch
my reflection in the steel-shaft
mirror: guilt-wracked, gut-sick
for two buck a pound, fish feed,
tako sushi on Robson Street.

MENDING

Black mesh torn by the rock shelf's clinging
resistance, its gnarled-tooth gnawing, this trap's
become a sieve all but octopus, Dungeness
and dogfish slip through. Between
strings I take the mending needle
spooled with green twine, stitch
the gaps the way my skipper sealed
the gash in his own palm
when a hook embedded in the line
hauled through his hand and ripped it open.

Everything out here is sharp-edged,
broken. Half our time working with holes
we've no time to mend. I take
each spare moment to tie frayed ends:
reef for tension, knot the twine,
and cinch down tight.

SPLICING

Three skeins of fresh line
unwound at each end into three
crooked fingers. Burn the tips
to wax nubs, intertwine. Dusk
sifting down through Bowen Island
cedars. Gulls perched silent on each
dock-cleat. Creosote. Cog grease. I fid-pry
the tight poly-spiral open and slip
a waxed end through, my stiff hands
moving to the auxiliary's hum underfoot,
the slow *slish* of slack water. Inside
the wheelhouse the skipper's cooking
chicken, other deckhands playing rummy,
smoking pot. The day's settling like till-silt
but I've got one last job to do: link
these skeins into one strong line we can use.

Shane Neilson

[b. 1975]

Shane Neilson's poems are taken from *The Beaten-Down Elegies* and *Seized*. His poems were nominated for a National Magazine Award in 2004. Trained as an MD at Dartmouth, he practises family medicine. He was born in New Brunswick.

LOVE IN PRACTICE

And love as blight or the kind of drought
that kills all green, leaving no work
but to weep and level the scorched stalks
with mortgaged machinery; the weather-beaten
crops that couldn't stand pestilence, frost,
or love turned on itself. As soil erodes
and fronds arrest their growth, the season's lost
and fault is no one's. What's left are debts
that must be borne until another year. I've tried
to touch that man who'd throttle a neck
as he did a cracked drive shaft, his grip belied
by how much he felt each failure, a black
and hardened ruin. Love as negative, in reverse,
but still in terms of violence: a kind of verse.

OPEN HEAD INJURY

Out on the balcony, our domestics raged
open air, the marital stamps and yells public.
Spectators gathered on the sidewalk, wondering
What's the fight about? Hatred's throttled
urge clenched my fists; I stalked to the stairwell.
Now memory blurs; did you seize my arm,
whisper *Don't go* too low to hear? I'm unsure.

I remember a sensation of push; off-balance,
I crashed through the wooden railing. Just two
seconds of freefall before my concrete splash,
blood compressed to high pitch in the ears:
din increased until I lay flat, flinching in seizure's

horizontals. My throat gurgled and choked,
ballistic arms beat to electrocuted songs,
and vision was a spattered easel of stars.
A grimace spread across my face, tremors built
to furious swats and kicks. Open head injury:
wet, I leaked out from a hole.

Above, I saw a small, unrecoverable beauty
that overwhelmed the waking world—
your face a small blot, the sound of steps
rushing down the stairs.

IN THE MRI MACHINE

The sounds of battle: a scrape,
a crunch, the clang of swords
on shields and roar of aircraft
engines. The close quarters
of a cylinder: embalmed in a missile,
I'm shot into the clutch of armies—

The particulates of matter
and one man on a plastic slab,
lying so still that a black bear,
ambling through the hospital,
would nudge him with its nose
and leave him for dead—

As the MRI works, I pray it can't
detect failures. On cue the machine
catches, slows to the rhythmic thrum
of a hammer striking a coffin.
It knows the brain's a tangled knot
of blighted thought, a gnarled whorl
of the soul's dark root. Then it moves
to the lush pastures of the body,
a harvest of grains and tubers
in the long magnetic season.

BEDSIDE DELIRIUM: FAMILY VISIT

for my father

Dreaming of origins: watching the house
built at age ten, lumber in heaps and men
idle until my father commands them
to erect a crossbeam. *Make it level, edge in.*
A simple bungalow, frame open to elements.
The blueprints pure suburb: in this prefab
neighbourhood, our house is made to fit.

After a week's work the roof's up.
I'm underneath, sweeping sawdust
and broken nail-tops from the concrete
foundation. Men walk above, steel-toes
tromping as shingle's laid until a crossbeam
yawns and cracks at its ends, then buckles
and breaks. My world splinters.

On the hospital bed a weakness spreads.
Am I ten again? No—my daughter plays
with the mechanical bed levers. *What happened?*
Dreams are bid: my punctured brain writhes,
another seizure descends. I hear *skull fracture*
whispered as medical heads blot my sky,
try to rouse me.
                    I wake to Dad's face
drawn tight in an ancient posture: that old look
of dread I haven't seen since I was a kid,
buried under lumber. In a flailed construction
I fix on his eyes, place a level upon the world.

Permissions

Mark Abley
"A Wooden Alphabet" and "Down" from *Glasburyon* and "White on White" and "Edgewise" from the forthcoming *The Silver Palace Restaurant* (McGill-Queen's University Press) are used by permission of the author.

Gil Adamson
"Message," "The Apprentice," "Black Wing," "Unpleasant Coincidence," and "Rest" from *Ashland* are used by permission of ECW Press.

Ken Babstock
"Finishing" from *Mean* and "Carrying Someone Else's Infant Past a Cow in a Field near Marmora, Ont.," "Tractor," and "The 7-Eleven Formerly Known as Rx" from *Days into Flatspin* is used by permission of House of Anansi. "Palindromic" is used by permission of the author.

John Barton
"Body Bag," and "Sky News" from *Hypothesis* are used by permission of House of Anansi.

Walid Bitar
" Sports," "Pasha," "The Fourth Person," "The Island Porcile," and "Open Sesame" from *Bastardi Puri* are used by permission of The Porcupine's Quill.

Christian Bök
"Birefringence" and excerpts from "Geodes" from *Crystallography* are used by permission of Coach House Books.

Stephanie Bolster
"Seawolf Inside its Own Dorsal Fin," "Edge of the River," "On the Steps of the Met," and "Chemistry" from *Two Bowls of Milk*, and "Hedge" from *Pavilion* is used by permission of McClelland & Stewart.

Tim Bowling
"The Last Sockeye" from *Low Water Slack;* "Love Poem, My Back to the Fraser," "Great Blue Heron," and "Early Autumn: A Still Life" from *Dying Scarlet;* and "Reading My Son to Sleep" from *Darkness and Silence* are used by permission of Nightwood Editions.

Asa Boxer
"How to Lie," "The Lobster," and an excerpt from "The Workshop" are used by permission of the author.

Diana Brebner
"From Eleven Paintings by Mary Pratt," "The Blue Light of the Neutron Pool," "Port,"

and "The Pictures of My Heart" from *The Ishtar Gate* are used by permission of McGill-Queen's University Press.

Julie Bruck
"The Woman Downstairs Used to be Beautiful," "Timing Your Run," and "Who We Are Now" from *The Woman Downstairs*, and "Cafeteria," and "Sex Next Door" from *The End of Travel* are used by permission of Brick Books.

Suzanne Buffam
"The Starfish," "Life With Folded Umbrella," "Sweet Basil," and "The Onset" from *Past Imperfect* is used by permission of House of Anansi.

George Elliott Clarke
"Look Homeward, Exile," "King Bee Blues," and "Monologue For Selah Bringing Spring to Whylah Falls" from *Whylah Falls*, and "Blue Elegies: I. v" from *Blue*, are used by permission of Raincoast Books.

Pino Coluccio
"Dimensions," "Time Piece," "My Imaginary Wife," "Getting In," and "Standards" from *First Comes Love* are used by permission of Mansfield Press.

Kevin Connolly
"Porcelain Jesus," from *Happyland* is used by permission of ECW Press. "History Channel," "Down to Earth," "Rise and Shine," and "Repossession" from *Drift*, are used by permission of House of Anansi.

Geoffrey Cook
"Moving In," "Lorne, Nova Scotia," "Fisherman's Song," "The Seals at Green Rock," and "Watermarks" from *Postscript* used by permission of Signal Editions, Véhicule Press.

Michael Crummey
"The Late Macbeth," and "Artifacts" from *Salvage* are used by permission of McClelland & Stewart and "Newfoundland Sealing Disaster," "Observatory on Mount Pleasant (1890)" and "A Trip to Labrador among the Esquimaux (1882)" from *Hard Light* are used by permission of Brick Books.

Michael deBeyer
"Beginning the Season," "Saturday Ventures," "Imagining the Black Bear into the Parking Lot," "The Body October," and "Home: The West Wall" from *Rural Night Catalogue* is used by permission of Gaspereau Press.

John Degen
"Sibiu" and "Underground" from *Animal Life in Budapest* and "Neighbours are Dangerous," "The Rats Outside Me" and "Crow" from *Killing Things* are used by permission of Pedlar Press.

Joe Denham
"Breakfast," "Scotchman Salvage," "Gutting," "Mending," and "Splicing" from *Flux* are used by permission of Nightwood Editions.

Jeffery Donaldson
"Rented Space," "Bearings," and "Spending Part of the Winter" from *Once Out of Nature* are used by permission of McClelland & Stewart. "Wind" and "Above the River" from *Waterglass* are used by permission of McGill-Queen's University Press.

Susan Gillis
"Eagle Bridge" from *Swimming Among the Ruins* is used by permission of Signature Editions. "Backyard Light," "Summer Holiday," and "Sleep Walking" from *Volta* are used by permission of Signature Editions.

Richard Greene
"Whaler" and "Crossing the Straits" from *Crossing the Straits* (St. Thomas Poetry Series) and "Window," and "At the College" are used by permission of the author.

Carla Hartsfield
"On Moving to a Different Country," "A Night," "If Clouds Wore Bouffant Hairdos," "Reagor Springs, Texas" and "Selvages" from *The Invisible Moon* are used by permission of Signal Editions, Véhicule Press.

Steven Heighton
"High Jump" from *Stalin's Carnival* is used by permission of the author. *"Address Book,"* "Constellations," "Blackjack," and "The Machine Gunner," from *The Address Book* are used by permission of House of Anansi.

Iain Higgins
"65/66," "67/68," "70/71," "72/73," and "73/74" are used by permission of the author.

Tonja Gunvaldsen Klaassen
"Inoculation" from *Ör* is used by permission of Brick Books. Excerpts from "August: An Anniversary Suite" is used by permission of the author and will be published by Gaspereau Press in their Devil'sWhim Chapbook Series (#14).

Anita Lahey
"The Drip-dry Method," "Travel Photos," and excerpts from "Cape Breton Relative," are used by permission of the author.

Noah Leznoff
"Sleeping In the Grass," "An Odd Invisibility, This," "Pushing in the Grocery Line," "Blue Jets," and Cooperman's Fish: Habitat" from *Outside Magic* (Insomniac Press) are used by permission of the author.

Laura Lush
"Witness," "Deciphering the Sea," "Sumo Wrestlers," "Choices," "The Crossing Guard," and "The Accident," from *Hometown* are used by permission of Signal Editions, Véhicule Press.

John MacKenzie
"Now We Sing Our Descent," and "Thor, Shanghaied by Yahweh to Tend the World..." from *Shaken by Physics* and "Riding the Route for Nature and Health" and "Drinking

with the Neurosurgeon" from *Sledgehammer* are used by permission of Raincoast Books.

David Manicom
"Anchor Post" from *Sense of Season* (Porcepic Books) is used by permission of the author. "Love Alight" from *Theology of Swallows*, and "The Burning Eaves," "September Gale with High Theory," and "Reading Anglo-Saxon When Spring Comes Early" from *The Burning Eaves* are used by permission of Oolichan Books.

David McGimpsey
"KoKo," "The Trip," and "Edna Loses The Store" from *Lardcake* is used by permission of ECW Press.

Eric Miller
"Song of the Vulgar Starling" from *Song of the Vulgar Starling* is used by permission of Broken Jaw Press. "The Question," "September in Uplands Park," and "History of Petals" from *In the Scaffolding* is used with the permission of Gooselane Editions.

George Murray
"The Last of the Sinners Waits on a Rock for Noah," "Despite the Hunger and Delicious Taste," and "An Egyptian Soldier on the Red Sea Swims Away from Moses" from *The Cottage Builder's Letter*, and "Cage" and "Pike" from *The Hunter* are used by permission of McClelland & Stewart.

Shane Neilson
"Love in Practice" is used by permission of Frog Hollow Press. "Open Head Injury," "In the MRI Machine," and "Bedside Delirium: Family Visit" are used by permission of the author.

Barbara Nickel
"Marion, 1935: To My Twin Sister" and "Three Poems for Violin" from *The Gladys Elegies* used by permission of Coteau Books. "Flight" and "Change Islands" used by permission of the author.

David O'Meara
"The War Against Television" from *Storm Still* is used by permission of McGill-Queen's University Press. "Brickwork," "Nomad," "Letter to Auden," and "Walking Around" from *The Vicinity* are used by permission of Brick Books.

Elise Partridge
"Plague," "A Valediction," "The Book of Steve," "Odysseys," and "Ruin" from *Fielder's Choice* are used by permission of Signal Editions, Véhicule Press. "Buying the Farm" is used by permission of the author.

Christopher Patton
"Red Maple," "The Vine Maple," "Doe's Bones" and an excerpt from "Weed Flower Mind" are used by permission of the author.

Matt Robinson
"Parking Lot Pastoral," "From the Ocean, Inland," and "Spring" from *A Ruckus of Awkward Stacking* are used by permission of Insomniac Press. "Notes Toward an Apartment Story" from *How We Play It* is used by permission of ECW Press.

Richard Sanger
"Travels With My Aunt," "Raccoon," "Late in The West," and "Madonna of the New World" from *Shadow Cabinet* and "Wish" from *Calling Home*, are used by permission of Signal Editions, Véhicule Press.

Anne Simpson
"Light Falls Through You" and "Seven Paintings by Brueghel" from *Loop* are used by permission of McClelland & Stewart.

Sue Sinclair
"Saturday Afternoon," "Red Pepper," "Green Pepper," "Collar Bones," and "The Pitcher" from *Secrets of Weather & Hope* are used by permission of Brick Books.

Mark Sinnett
"Study of Two Figures (Lovers), 1846," "On the Impossibility of Seeing You," "September One," and "Coast" from *Some Late Adventures of the Feelings* used by permission of ECW Press.

Adam Sol
"Life, McKenzie" from *Jonah's Promise* (MidList Press) is used by permission of the author. "Wishing You Better," "Letter to the Cincinnati Billiard Boys," "Man who Slept Between Blows of a Hammer," and "Psalm of Scranton" from *Crowd of Sounds* are used by permission of House of Anansi.

Karen Solie
"Sturgeon," "Java Shop, Fort MacLeod," "Sick," and "Alert Bay, Labour Day" from *Short Haul Engine* used by permission of Brick Books. "Cardio Room, Young Women's Christian Association" from *Modern and Normal* is used by permission of Brick Books.

Andrew Steinmetz
Excerpt from "Histories," and "Jargon" from *Histories* used by permission of Signal Editions, Véhicule Press. 'Tahiti," "Oligodendroglioma," and "Late" used by permission of the author.

Todd Swift
"Evening on Putney Avenue" from *Budavox*; "Water Running" and "Lost at Austelitz" from *Café Alibi*; and "Cinema Du Look" and "The Influence of Anxiety at the Seaside with Tea" from *Rue du Regard* are used by permission of DC Books.

Bruce Taylor
"Social Studies" and "What the Magdalen Islands are Like" from *Cold Rubber Feet* (Cormorant Press) are used by permission of the author. "Doodle," "The Slough," and "Lovely" from *Facts* are used by permission of Signal Editions, Véhicule Press.

Patrick Warner
"Gumshoe," "Mormon," "The Bacon Company of Ireland," "Hike," and "Watching the Ocean" from *There, there* are used by permission of Signal Editions, Véhicule Press.

Author Index